Inland Shift

Inland Shift

RACE, SPACE, AND CAPITAL IN
SOUTHERN CALIFORNIA

Juan D. De Lara

UNIVERSITY OF CALIFORNIA PRESS

University of California Press, one of the most distinguished university presses in the United States, enriches lives around the world by advancing scholarship in the humanities, social sciences, and natural sciences. Its activities are supported by the UC Press Foundation and by philanthropic contributions from individuals and institutions. For more information, visit www.ucpress.edu.

University of California Press
Oakland, California

Library of Congress Cataloging-in-Publication Data

Names: Lara, Juan D. De, author.
Title: Inland shift : race, space, and capital in Southern California / Juan D. De Lara.
Description: Oakland, California : University of California Press, [2018] | Includes bibliographical references and index. |
Identifiers: LCCN 2017048921 (print) | LCCN 2017051617 (ebook) | ISBN 9780520964181 (ebook) | ISBN 9780520289581 (cloth : alk. paper) | ISBN 9780520297395 (pbk. : alk. paper)
Subjects: LCSH: Inland Empire (Calif.)—Economic conditions. | Labor movement—California—Inland Empire. | Race discrimination—California—Inland Empire. | Regional economics—California—Inland Empire. | Inland Empire (Calif.)—Politics and government. | Inland Empire (Calif.)—Race relations.
Classification: LCC HC107.C22 (ebook) | LCC HC107.C22 L37 2018 (print) | DDC 330.9794/9—dc23
LC record available at https://lccn.loc.gov/2017048921

27 26 25 24 23 22 21 20 19 18
10 9 8 7 6 5 4 3 2 1

For my children, Ixchel, Emiliano, and Niko
Para mi madre, Esperanza
And in loving memory of my father, José "Chepe" De Lara

CONTENTS

ILLUSTRATIONS

MAP

FIGURES

TABLES

ACKNOWLEDGMENTS

The idea for this book took root during my undergraduate days at Pitzer College in Claremont, California. Claremont exposed me to professors and students who believed that another world was possible and that we could organize our way to it. This was a wild and wonderful thing, especially for a first-generation college kid who grew up in California's poor rural agricultural towns. I was lucky to take a class with Mike Davis during those early years. He was nice enough to take an interest in me; invite me out for a drink; and listen patiently while I stumbled through ideas about urban space, race, and globalization. My book begins with the dismantling of the Kaiser steel mill in Fontana, California, which is where Mike left off in *City of Quartz*. It is a testament to the impression he made on me. Thanks, Mike, for encouraging me to write about where I came from. José Calderón and Lourdes Arguelles taught me what it meant to be a scholar activist. Nigel Boyle got me through college by encouraging me to think critically about labor and class and by showing me incredible kindness. Thank you, Nigel, for everything: the dinners, the beers, and the various travels through foreign lands.

I wrote the first words of this book during my time as a graduate student at UC Berkeley. It was a magical place that gave me the luxury of reading day and night. I chose Berkeley because I wanted to study with Ruth Wilson Gilmore. She was in the Bay Area for only a brief period before leaving for Los Angeles and then New York, but her intellectual spirit is woven deeply into this book. Special thanks go to my adviser, Richard Walker. What can I say about DW? He's the best. You got me through, DW, and for that I will always be grateful. David Montejano and José David Saldívar were also on my committee. Both read my work, gave me feedback, and pushed me to think about big questions and concrete details.

My intellectual travels brought me back to Southern California and to life as a Chicano professor at USC. By far the best thing about being at USC as a young scholar was the incredible people in the Department of American Studies and Ethnicity. Thank you to all my wonderful colleagues, who gave me space and time to run the tenure clock rat race. Several of my ASE colleagues deserve special mention. Laura Pulido is a fierce ally, an intellectual trailblazer, and a professional godsend. She brought me tacos when I broke my foot and showed me how to survive in an academic universe in which few Chicanx critical geographers exist. I have learned a tremendous amount from my friend and colleague Manuel Pastor. He has also opened many doors for me. Macarena Gomez-Barris served as my interim chair, a mentor, and a friend. She got things done and made academia a more humane experience for me. Viet Thanh Ngyuen also served as a one-year interim chair. He did so during one of the most trying periods of my life. Thanks, Viet, for bringing institutional support when I needed it. Nayan Shah has shepherded my dossier through various milestones. He has been consistently generous and kind. Jody Agius Vallejo provided professional mentorship and a patient ear when I most needed it. To Veronica Terriquez, we miss you but I'm happy that you are happy. I also need to thank the ASE staff—Soñia Rodriguez, Kitty Lai, and Jujuana Lakes Preston—without whom our department would not function.

Several people, programs, and institutions provided financial and technical support for this project. The Institute for the Study of Social Issues (ISSI) at UC Berkeley awarded me a graduate fellowship that was invaluable during the early years of this project. Even more rewarding were the relationships that I built with other fellows and staff members at ISSI. I received a Mellon postdoctoral fellowship from the Center for the Study of Immigrant Integration at USC, which allowed me to move the dissertation into the manuscript phase. Thanks to the amazing Rhonda Moore and the rest of the staff for supporting me during my time at CSSI and PERE. Niels Hooper and Bradley Depew at University of California Press kept this project on track even when it seemed to be going off the rails. I thank you both. Finally, a special shout-out to Peter Cooper Mancall and the office of the dean of USC Dornsife College for providing financial and institutional support for various parts of this project.

This book would not have been possible without the work, struggles, and hope of the countless workers, organizers, and scholars who provided the stories for my manuscript. Some of you will undoubtedly recognize your voices in these pages. I hope my work did you justice. Several other scholars made this manuscript better by either reading parts of it or helping me think through some of the ideas. To Edna Bonacich, thank you for teaching me about logistics and the ports. You are a tremendous model for the kind of engaged public intellectual that I strive to be. Ellen Reese and Jason Struna were patient and gave me an opportunity to coauthor an important article about warehouse workers. Eric Sheppard, Don Mitchell, Chris Benner, and Ange-Marie Hancock all participated in a book workshop that turned this manuscript into a much better book. Cheers to you all.

To my wonderful friends, thanks for your patience and for making me feel human during what sometimes felt like complete madness. Life as a junior academic and a father has made me an absentee friend. I appreciate those of you who stuck around. Carolina Bank Muñoz has been a *camarada*, in every sense of the word, for decades. Thanks for bringing Emilio and Ted into our lives. Stacey Murphy and Filip Stabrowski shared many meals, drinks, and conversations along the way about absolutely pressing and deliciously petty topics. I miss you both but look forward to our too-infrequent encounters. Johntell Washington, Sylvia Nam, and Carmen Rojas were also part of our dangerous POC PhD crew.

Finally, I want to thank the family that I was born into and the family that I have made. My mother, Esperanza Ibarra De Lara, and my father, José Torres De Lara, met when they were teenagers at a farm labor camp in Arizona. Both were undocumented, neither ever went to school, and together they made a life for themselves and their seven children: Maria, Rosa, Alfredo, Miguel, Jose Jr., me, and Gregorio. We grew up harvesting the agricultural crops and living in the dilapidated housing that too often define the past and present lives of migrant farmworkers. I carry them with me, and they have carried me when I needed them. I am also grateful for my brother Raul; we have so much to catch up on. Gracias, familia. *Saludos* too to all the De Lara clan in Coachella and to the Ibarras in Lamont. Abrazos to all my primas and primos in Somerton, Arizona.

I've had to make my own family away from Coachella. It seems like wherever I go, Manny Mercado is always nearby. He's been like a brother since I was fourteen years old. Ixchel, Emiliano, and Niko are the most beautiful creatures I've ever known. They are my moon, my movement, and my hope. This book has taken many hours away from my time with them, but they constantly surprise me with their love and resilience. Thanks to my coparent, Veronica Carrizales; it wasn't easy, but we managed to balance demanding work schedules and child rearing.

My most profound thanks go to my life partner, Wendy Cheng. I would be lost without her love, patience, and guidance. Thank you for listening to me talk endlessly about this project and for reading different parts of the manuscript. I am blessed to have you in my life. I love you.

Introduction

HUMAN DESIRE FOR PROFIT AND CONSUMPTION is a powerful material force. For us to buy the things that we want—such as a new pair of jeans or the latest electronic gadget—public and private entrepreneurs, as the agents of capital, have to construct the social relations and spatial landscapes that enable consumer yearnings to become material realities.[1] For example, the ability to buy a simple pair of jeans requires an elaborate physical and social infrastructure, including far-flung environmental resources and extended labor systems.[2] Consequently our consumption of goods is never an isolated, individual choice, because it depends on expansive commodity chains and the spaces that make them possible.[3] The choices we make are thus always embedded in extensive multiscalar relationships that string together elaborate networks of actors, places, and things. This book uses Southern California's logistics economy and the rise of commodity imports to examine how political leaders and social movement activists remapped the region's geographies of race and class between 1980 and 2010.

My research into Southern California's goods movement or logistics regime began with a series of questions about the relationship among globalization, race, and class. I was particularly interested in linking urban political economy with critical studies of race and culture. Cedric Robinson's work on racial capitalism made this intellectually necessary. One of Robinson's insights in *Black Marxism* was that the scientific rationalism underpinning capitalist production yielded a deadlier and persistent racialism. I build on Robinson's scholarship by arguing that logistics represents a major rearticulation of modern capitalism and space that must be understood within the historical context of place and race making.

The relationship between racial capitalism and logistics can be traced back to the fifteenth century, when the encounter between European merchant capitalism and the Americas generated new Latinx[4] American identities that were rooted in the confrontation between indigenous ways of life and the imperial project of coloniality that ensnared Black and indigenous bodies into the global circuits of profit accumulation and slavery. European capitalism was built on the extraction and circulation of commodities such as sugar and silver in the colonial period that required distinct racial and spatial arrangements. This relationship continued after national independence, when liberalism and the settler colonial nation-state provided the main engines that drove industrial capitalism and a new period of racialization in Las Americas during the nineteenth century. In the chapters that follow I expand on this spatial-historical reading of race, capital, and commodities to show how post-1980s Southern California was transformed by new modes of global capitalist production and distribution that intersected with the racial terrain of demographic change.

What does it mean to think about racial capitalism through the lens of a place like inland Southern California? To answer this question requires examining spaces of racial identity that are often hidden or overlooked. For example, Riverside and San Bernardino Counties have one of the largest Latinx and immigrant populations in the country, yet they are all but absent in the field of Chicanx and Latinx studies. Simply put, I wanted to learn what the Inland Empire could teach us about race, space, and power that East LA could not. Inland Southern California, also known as the Inland Empire or the Riverside-San Bernardino metropolitan area, is particularly important because it represents the terrain of racial formation for an emerging Latinx population, many of whom moved into Los Angeles's (LA's) urban hinterland to find jobs and purchase new homes in the region's booming housing market. The region illustrates how race is embedded in particular territories through the dynamic exchanges between macroeconomic processes and the spatial legacies of local specificity.

These scales are used as platforms for the three key themes that frame the book: the reterritorialization of race, the relationship between shifting flows of capital and regional spaces, and the various topographies of power that shape particular landscapes. More specifically, I examine how workers, capitalists, state agents, and social movement organizers deployed various cognitive and material mappings to link differentiated but intersecting spatial scales—the warehouse, the diesel-poisoned body, the foreclosed home, the racialized state apparatus—into a contested political space. The book begins with an analysis of how growing consumer demand, innovative retail business practices, and the infrastructure required to support global commodity chains all combined to reconfigure Southern California's landscape. My argument in part one is simple: to understand global cities we need to account for how the extended commodity chains of neoliberal economic restructuring created new social and spatial relationships among consumers, workers, and regions. Local actors and institutions were especially important to this process because they attempted to strengthen their positions within the global commodity network by investing in extensive regional infrastructure and intensive distribution systems. They hoped such investments in logistics infrastructure would attract a highly mobile and flexible twenty-first-century capitalism.

While logistics provided a road map for capital and the state to transform Southern California, part two of the book examines how it also created pockets of resistance among labor, community, and environmental groups, which argued that global commodity distribution exposed already marginalized communities to even more vulnerabilities. How people gave meaning to and mobilized to contest dominant development mappings is at the crux of part three. The final two sections also challenge the erasure of low-wage immigrant workers from the dominant logistics narrative. They show how temporary warehouse workers were important dissident voices who claimed that logistics sacrificed them as unfortunate but necessary pieces of a regional economy built on infrastructure development and the global goods industry. What justified this sacrifice, and how were warehouse workers so devalued that they could be tossed aside for the sake of the region's economic growth?[5] Each chapter explores these questions by unpacking how the specificity of place, ideological representations about race, and productive economic activities combined to shape and redefine the region.

Finally, let me provide a brief explanation of my methodological approach. One of the main challenges for me was to figure out how to move from the specificity of a warehouse in Mira Loma, to regional policy, to global networks of capital. To examine these relationships I use a multiscalar reading of inland Southern California that includes a top-down policy focus and a bottom-up understanding of how people organized to contest normative regional narratives that fixed specific racial and class hierarchies in place. I use specific geographical snapshots of Riverside and San Bernardino counties to examine some of the key forces that have shaped the region. When assembled, these snapshots produce a composite image of the various actors and processes that shape everyday life in the region. While it might be easy to dismiss what happens in a relatively unknown place as too specific and not generally applicable to the complexities of global capital and race, it is incredibly important to figure out how the specificity of these things work on the ground. General "concepts have to be applied to," as Stuart Hall explained, "specific historical social formations, to particular societies at specific stages in the development of capitalism." This is a Gramscian approach that requires the theorist "to move from the level of 'mode of production' to a lower, more concrete, level of application."[6] Scholars have spent countless hours thinking and pages writing about how what happens at the microlevel can be applied to a broader level.[7] Instead of rehashing well-documented debates about the relationship between or importance of global and local processes, I take my cue from Gilmore: "It is my interest here to reconcile the micro with the macro by showing how the drama of crisis on the ground is neither wholly determined by nor remotely autonomous from the larger crisis."[8]

Fontana and inland Southern California therefore are more than a simple case study; they provide a way to examine how a particular iteration of modern capitalism was shaped by and helped to transform a specific place. More recent scholarship has left the global versus local debate behind and has instead embraced the idea of a mutually constitutive process. Rather than arguing about whether the global has the power to transform and annihilate local spaces, I seek to understand how these two scales are mutually constitutive of each other. Instead of looking at how capital uses local specificity to its advantage, I also examine how local specificity produces a complex and highly differentiated capitalism. This more dialectical approach enables us to see how, according to Helga Leitner and Byron Miller, "local and transnational processes and practices are producing (materially and discursively) the very fabric of the global."[9]

The more than one hundred interviews I conducted with workers, policy makers, and regular community members provide the concrete data to jump back and forth between the specificities of everyday life in the Inland Empire and the larger global processes at work. Much of the material for this book also comes from more than five years of participant observation in various community, labor, and environmental justice issues related to inland Southern California.

One book cannot capture everything and everyone that makes up Southern California. What follows is a very specific view of the region that does not attempt to bear the impossible burden of trying to capture all that the region represents as J. Harrison said, "there is no complete portrait of a region."[10] This book is instead a particular sketch that illustrates how state actors and social movement activists deployed discursive tactics and material force to shape inland Southern California's landscape.

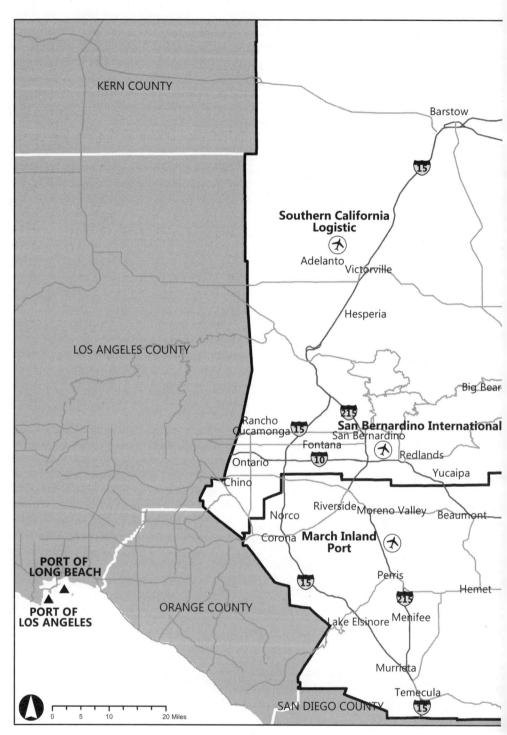

MAP 1. Inland Southern California. Map by Jennifer Tran.

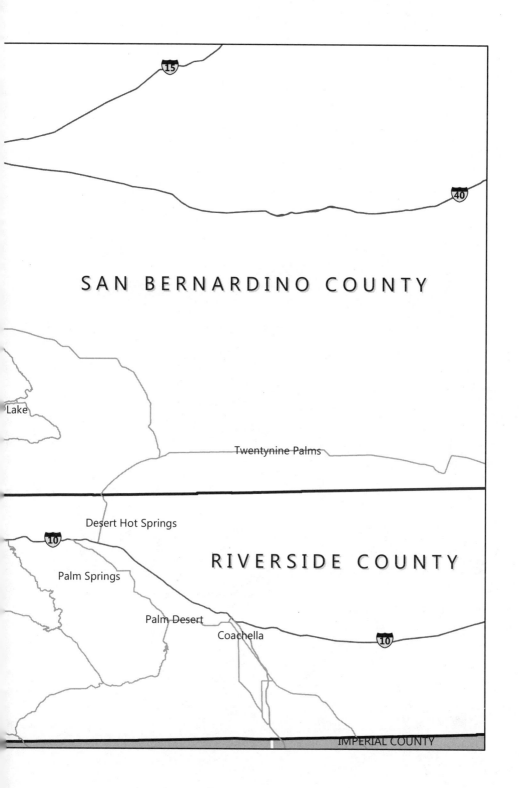

SAN BERNARDINO COUNTY

Lake

Twentynine Palms

RIVERSIDE COUNTY

Desert Hot Springs

Palm Springs

Palm Desert

Coachella

IMPERIAL COUNTY

SCENE I

———

A Space for Logistics

IN THE FALL OF 1993 approximately 300 Chinese workers arrived in Fontana, California. They were there to dismantle part of the thirteen-hundred-acre Kaiser steel mill, an iconic industrial landscape that helped build America's Pacific Fleet during World War II and provided material for the West's postwar economic expansion (see figure 1). Workers spent nearly a year marking, cutting, and organizing the mill's pieces into an elaborate disassembly system.[1] As one worker used a torch to cut off pieces of the old blast furnace, another would number and label them in Chinese.

Supervisors maintained a grueling, around-the-clock shift schedule and provided a ready supply of labor by housing workers in a nearby fenced-off compound. Workers woke up every day, waited their turn to be bused into the mill, spent the day doing hard labor, and boarded the bus back to camp (see figure 2).[2] Buses were sometimes met by protestors; they complained that the dismantling jobs should have been offered to locals. Joe Perez, head of the local building trades unions, told an assembled group of protesters, "These jobs don't belong to those (Chinese) guys, they belong to us."[3] Some of the picketers claimed to have built and worked in the mill; they wanted to be the ones who tore it down. The protesters were relics of an earlier era. The mill's construction and eventual dismantling were emblematic of the social and economic transition that took place during the shift from postwar Fordist manufacturing to post-1970s neoliberalism. Kaiser's devalued buildings and downsized people were the industrial and human residue left behind by the deep changes that transformed everyday lives across the globe.

FIGURE 1. Smoke rises from eight open hearth furnaces at the Kaiser steel mill in Fontana, CA, 1952. Photo by Conrad Mercurio, Los Angeles Examiner Photograph Collection, University of Southern California Libraries Special Collections.

FIGURE 2. Chinese dismantling crew being bused to their camp at the end of the day shift, Kaiser steel mill, Fontana, CA, December 1993. Courtesy Allan Sekula Studio.

ONE

Space, Power, and Method

HOW HAS RACIAL AND SPATIAL difference shaped the character of twenty-first-century capitalism? As Cedric Robinson has argued, "the character of capitalism can only be understood in the social and historical context of its appearance."[1] Inland Southern California and the logistics industry are important sites through which to explore how modern capitalism has been shaped by its dialectical entanglement with race and space. This requires, as Escobar notes, "setting place-based and regional processes into conversation with the ever-changing dynamics of capital and culture at many levels."[2] Warehouse work and the contentious spatial politics of inland Southern California's logistics landscape provide the multiscalar data to examine how the shifting ground of money and people intersected with local histories to reterritorialize race and capitalism at the turn of the twenty-first century. Southern California, especially it's often-ignored inland spaces, provides an excellent platform to examine how capitalism has been territorialized and enshrined as a racial project. The result of this fusing of race, space, and capital is what I call the territorialization of race. I begin this chapter by examining how regions are produced as discursive and material spaces through political performances that are grounded in the specificities of race, class, and power.

CRAFTING REGIONS AS DISCURSIVE AND
MATERIAL SPACES

Southern California became a haven for the logistics industry because regional leaders made a strategic choice to champion port-based development; they created policy pathways for logistics by supporting transportation infrastructure projects and by propagating a prologistics ideology. State agencies also stimulated logistics development by incubating a regional land market that used zoning restrictions and building codes to encourage port, rail, and warehouse expansion. Local actors and regional planning authorities played an increasingly important role after the 1980s when neoliberal reforms created incentives for municipalities to compete with one another over potential public and private investment. Southern California's logistics development regime emerged from this global economic and neoliberal political milieu; the regime included local political leaders, the port authorities for both Los Angeles and Long Beach, and private sector leaders with close ties to logistics-based development.

Even if local actors tried to stimulate logistics investment, scholars disagree about whether local choices have had much effect on global capital. Urban theorists developed two main analytical frameworks to study the interaction between local actors and global economic processes.[3] Each differs in its assumptions about whether the local or global plays a greater role in shaping space.[4] One approach privileges the different ways that localities organize themselves to capture and shape development pathways by linking local institutional capacities to new economic scales.[5] Here, different localities exercise agency by influencing how global processes unfold in particular places. A second approach assigns greater importance to the internal dynamics of global commodity chains and focuses on how regional actors can respond by inserting themselves into these systems. Under this approach the dynamic forces of global capital are given more of the power to shape development paths.

Local actors across the United States responded to global restructuring by mounting vigorous campaigns to lure new investment, even as scholars doubted that they could harness and control capital's shifting tides. The most successful efforts imposed what Neil Brenner has described as a "certain cohesiveness if not a logical coherence of territorial organization."[6] Part of this cohesiveness was produced through regional spatial narratives that rationalized particular development paths. For instance, the idea that inland Southern California could and should be a global distribution hub required boosters to produce a regional cognitive map, what Lefebvre describes as a "representation of space," to lend coherence to the logistics effort.[7] Cognitive maps are vital parts of the material landscape, illustrating how spaces are produced through a combination of social and physical processes.[8] These mental maps are cultural frameworks that help humans shape and give meaning to different landscapes. I use cognitive mapping analysis to protect against overly determined structural arguments, which pay less attention to the processes of subjective racial and class formation.[9] Narratives introduce affect and feeling into deciphering how, as Judith Butler and Athena Athanasiou note, "we do not simply move ourselves, but are ourselves moved by what is outside us."[10] Yet we should also take care not to get stuck in the cognitive and discursive analysis of spatial representations and ideologies, because material spaces still matter.[11]

My analysis of inland Southern California bridges some of the gaps between cultural studies and political economy by examining what Don Mitchell referred to as the "relationship between material form and ideological representation."[12] I take different material spaces, such as warehouses and industrial suburbs, to disentangle the relationship among culture, cognitive mappings, and the social relations of particular economic processes.[13] Regional discursive mappings provide insight that illuminates how actors shape the terrain of spatial politics. Such mappings developed into political projects because their champions used them to inscribe the social and physical infrastructure of logistics onto the material landscape of Southern California. Such prologistics narratives became spatial ontologies because they defined the conditions of regional possibility. I argue that we need to disrupt such ontologies by generating new conceptual frameworks that unmask the violence of uneven development by making explicit connections between the spatial logic of global capital and the local articulations of race. Such an approach provides a better picture of how capital, the state, and cultural notions of difference combined to produce Southern California as a distinct place within a much broader global spatial order.

Regions provide a way to examine how space is produced, maintained, and contested through both discursive and material processes.[14] Urban scholars have paid close attention to regions, especially in the aftermath of post-1970s globalization. Regions are one of the key spatial scales that urban scholars and geographers have used to understand the "new territorial structures and imaginaries" that were produced during the shift to globalization.[15] Some of this scholarship was influenced by regulationist theory and argued that the urban scale was undergoing a restructuring process that included a rescaling of state institutions into supra- and subnational forms of governance.[16]

The contested everyday production of regions is critical because they are much more than state-sanctioned territorial units. They also function as spatial ideologies that rely on specific social, political, and economic assumptions. These ideological foundations are necessary because regions "are not 'out there' waiting to be discovered, they are our (and others') constructions."[17] To create regions, as Julie-Anne Boudreau asserts, "actors deploy spatial imaginaries and practices in their efforts to achieve their political objectives, incrementally producing coherent political spaces."[18] Regions are therefore "constructed entities, ways of organizing people and place" through political and cultural narratives that link economic forces to everyday spaces.[19] The discursive and material production of regions provides an opportunity to examine how space is imagined, produced, and contested. This combination of ideology, normative discourse, and power is what makes regions such a useful geographic scale through which to interrogate the production of space and race.[20]

TERRITORIALITY AND RACE

When Shougang workers from China took their blowtorches to the old Fontana mill in 1993, they were dismantling part of a blue-collar manufacturing economy that built up many post–World War II U.S. cities. In Southern California military spending drove the region's incredible post-1940s growth and produced industrial suburbs in Southeast Los Angeles and the San Fernando Valley.[21] The region's expansion continued during the Cold War years of the 1960s and 1970s, when defense spending lured new industries and workers into the region.[22] The postwar manufacturing boom had enabled an earlier generation to pursue something called the American Dream. In fact, what it meant to be middle class in Southern California was intricately linked to the production of blue-collar industrial suburbs in cities like Cudahy, Southgate, and Maywood. These suburbs were home to major manufacturing companies, many of which benefited from defense industry government contracts. They were also almost exclusively white and were kept that way by restrictive racial covenants that prevented the sale of homes to nonwhite residents.[23] Deindustrialization, including the Kaiser mill's dismantling, foretold the end of the Keynesian spatial order that made the United States and California into a global economic powerhouse.

Something that often gets lost in discussions of regional development is the role that spatial fixing or the place-boundedness of capitalism has played in the production of racialized geographies. The paradox of wanting to erase racially marked bodies while needing their labor has ultimately been resolved through a variety of spatial solutions.[24] Work camps and barrios are just two examples of how differentiated space has been deployed to contain and control racialized bodies while at the same time making their labor available for capital. This was certainly the case when Southern California's war economy needed the labor of Black and Brown bodies but used the racist techniques of segregated homeownership and unequal wage markets to keep them in their place.[25]

Southern California's industrial suburbs were thus enshrined—as a normative idea of what constituted a good life—by a Keynesian spatial regime that was built on racial and class difference. Even though race and space are deeply entangled, the two are often treated as parallel rather than mutually constituted processes. For example, studies that address race often treat space as a container for specific social relationships. Much of the literature on Chicanx and Latinx identity is infused with spatial tropes in which cultural practice is tied to specific spatial scales like the border, the barrio, the home, and the body.[26] Some Chicana and Chicano studies scholars have argued that the spatial processes of barrio formation—as a political project of containment—resulted in the production of counterhegemonic cultural practice.[27] This shift toward space and culture was deeply influenced by feminist theories of standpoint epistemology and intersectionality.[28] Likewise, scholars who study mobility—migration, white flight, diasporas—must all grapple with space as a critical element of their work (even if the focus on mobility suggests that space and place are limiting).[29] More recent studies on race have focused on multicultural neighborhoods as spaces of conviviality and exchange.[30] These spaces, which were deeply influenced by the enactment and dissolution of racially segregated housing practices, have emerged as places where Asian, Latinx, and Black residents are learning to craft polycultural identities and practices that are not centered in white normative experiences.[31] All of this scholarship has provided critical insight into the racial state and the spatial techniques deployed by the architects of racialization.

The intersections between race and space can be traced back to European colonialism, when the imperial spatial logics of capitalist expansion intimately linked a new global order to a morality that dictated the erasure and subjugation of racialized others. Capitalism and imperialism have formed a deadly partnership in which universal assumptions about progress and modernity were tied to white supremacy and manifest destiny, including in the American West. In fact, "modern political-economic architectures" as Paula Chakravartty and Denise Ferreira Da Silva argue, "have been accompanied by a moral text, in which the principles of universality and historicity also sustain the writing of the 'others of Europe' (both a colonial and racial other) as entities facing certain and necessary (self-inflicted) obliteration."[32] This deadly moral text is critical for the survival and territorial expansion of global capital. It "asphyxiates" what Henri Lefebvre described as the "historical conditions that gave rise to it, its own (internal) differences, and any such differences that show signs of developing, in order to impose an abstract homogeneity."[33] Such normative economies are incredibly powerful because they not only define monetary exchanges; they also demarcate those who inhabit a life that is worth living from those who do not. The result has been that global capitalist space has condemned devalued bodies and the spaces they produce to a life of precarity and premature death.[34]

Much of the early work on globalization tried to figure out the relationship between highly mobile circuits of capital and the embedded specificities of local places. It made sense to ask what the deeper connections between political economy and space were if we wanted to move beyond the notion that spaces and places were more than just containers for larger (read as more determinative) social processes. If, as geographers and urban planners argued, space still mattered, then it was important to demonstrate how and why.[35] As scholars tried to decipher the multiplicity of actors and forces involved in producing something called globalization, a tension emerged between those who focused on the power of global capital to transform local space and those who argued that the local still mattered and that place-based difference was key to the production of a globalized society.[36]

Difference is in fact essential to the creation and capitalization of new markets; it allows investors to determine where they should and should not invest.[37] This is where universal and abstract models of capitalism fall short. While an abstract model may provide important insights into the relationship between social structures and space, it cannot substitute for a more concrete analysis of how various forces and actors, including gender and race, combine to produce locally specific spatial orders.[38] What's needed is a type of critical inquiry into space that recognizes macroeconomic forces while not glossing over the specificities of places and people. The key is to understand how these specificities are interconnected into a sometimes diffused web of social relations, which means that to understand the logic of global capital, we have to engage with the local specificities of space. This is an important methodological point about the importance of understanding specificity as the embodiment or experience of social processes.[39]

Indeed, only by looking at what Katherine Mitchell termed "the specific configurations of differing economic systems within their own geographical and historical contexts" will we grasp the intricate and contingent nature of global capitalism.[40] The idea that capital has a critical "logic which works in and through specificity" rather than a universal abstract mode provides a theoretical bridge that enables us to traverse the sometimes wide gap between political economy and locally embedded cultural notions of difference and articulation.[41] Social movements provide one way to examine how locally embedded actors confront the alienating tendencies of universal abstract space; they are, as Tilly describes, "historically specific clusters of political performances."[42] Movements are defined by how networks of individuals create and perform collective identities while giving meaning to their actions. These performances and meanings establish a relational position from which to make claims against entrenched forms of power. Parts 2 and 3 of this book show how social movements in Southern California challenged the moral text of development by providing alternative spatial imaginaries that were rooted in the dialectical exchange between abstract space and local specificity.

My discussion of social movement spatial strategies highlights why a multiscalar, local-global framework is critical to groups who try to challenge universalist development ideologies. Ignoring the local-global dialectic can obscure relationships of power, because as Akhil Gupta and James Ferguson note, "the presumption that spaces are autonomous has enabled the power of topography to conceal successfully the topography of power."[43] To expose the sometimes hidden relationships of power that produce specific spaces, this project begins "with the premise that spaces have always been hierarchically interconnected, instead of naturally disconnected."[44] Lefebvre was right in arguing that "the survival of capitalism has depended on this distinctive production and occupation of a fragmented, homogenized, and hierarchically structured space."[45] Local difference, racial and class difference in particular, has been critical to the survival and evolution of capitalist space. This continues to be the case as modern network infrastructures are "being organized to exploit differences between places within ever-more sophisticated spatial divisions of labor."[46] It is therefore important to examine how these sometimes obscure connections can help decipher how difference is produced and sustained. Logistics, I argue, is one example of how the spatial divisions of labor that are vital to the survival of capitalism are fixed in place through a complex interaction among race, capital, and power.

LOGISTICS AS THE REGIONAL SPATIAL FIX

Two cases in particular—the industrial inner-ring suburbs of Southeast Los Angeles and the exurban outer-ring region of the Inland Empire—provide distinct but overlapping glimpses into how different actors responded to the spatial ruptures that transformed Southern California after the 1980s. Both cases show how racial and spatial difference were central to post-Fordist redevelopment strategies.

Regional policy makers used Southeast Los Angeles as a warning to the rest of Southern California because it embodied the social and economic dislocation that wreaked havoc on blue-collar industrial suburbs between the late 1970s and 2000s.[47] Blue-collar suburbs that were abandoned by capital and by a shrinking social safety net became what Mike Davis called the discarded "junkyards of the American Dream."[48] According to local political leaders the solution was to rally behind the region's ports as a potential cure for Southern California's manufacturing malaise. The logic was simple: if the shuttered manufacturing plants of Southeast Los Angeles represented the region's Fordist past, then the ports and inland warehouses in places like Fontana provided a glimpse of its future.

Such disruptions are a normal part of capitalism, because it operates under a constant tension between needing to be fixed in particular places and having to fend off falling rates of profit that stem from decaying machinery and outmoded business models. "To solve this contradiction," as Richard Walker notes, "capital must be liberated from its shackles to move elsewhere or destroyed (devalued) to raise the rate of profit and make room for new investments."[49] Creative destruction is thus woven into the fabric of capitalist development and provides a solution to the devaluation of fixed capital by reconfiguring spatial-temporal relationships to create new investment options.[50] Kaiser's mill and the Chinese workers who dismantled it embody this spatial fix.[51]

One result is that new spaces are constantly entangled and swept up into the capitalist system of accumulation as investors seek outlets for growth. The Chinese company Shougang's purchase of the Kaiser steel mill in Fontana in 1992 was a spatial fix because it was part of a more comprehensive effort to make China into a major industrial manufacturing power. Redundant Western industrial facilities offered a solution to Shougang's leaders, who desperately wanted to expand Chinese steel manufacturing but lacked enough capital and time to build their own equipment. Chinese government officials prodded manufacturers to increase capacity when they set a national goal to produce one hundred million tons of steel by the year 2000.[52] Company executives responded by purchasing sixteen secondhand facilities from the United States and other industrialized countries throughout the 1980s and 1990s.[53] By the end of this period Shougang's traveling band of workers had

FIGURE 3. Workers load 75-ton ladles from the Kaiser steel mill onto the *Atlantic Queen* for shipment to China, Los Angeles Harbor, July 1994. Courtesy Allan Sekula Studio.

become experts at dismantling the old industrial spaces of Western economies and reassembling their remains into giant, Frankensteinian steel plants.

Kaiser's rusting carcass was prime fodder for industrial scavenging because part of it was relatively new. Corporate officials had invested $278 million to build a state-of-the-art No. 2 Basic Oxygen Process and Caster plant in 1978.[54] Yet even such massive investment in new facilities did not prevent the mill's collapse; executives blamed tougher environmental regulations and increased international competition as major reasons for ceasing operations. Kaiser provides many lessons; one of them is that abandoned spaces are not completely left behind. Abandoned spaces and people sometimes learn to renegotiate their relationships with different circuits of capital.[55] For inland Southern California this renegotiation began when workers loaded the mill's disassembled parts onto the *Atlantic Queen* (see figure 3). The ship, which left the port of Los Angeles in July 1994, transported the old blast furnace and cauldrons that Kaiser workers once used to pour molten steel (see figure 4) in Fontana to an area just outside of Beijing. Shougang officials planned to reassemble, modify, and attach the old mill to an existing steel plant. In its

FIGURE 4. Kaiser steel worker oversees pouring of hot metal pig iron from a blast furnace by means of a 75-ton ladle, Fontana, CA, May 1, 1952. Photo by Conrad Mercurio, Los Angeles Examiner Photograph Collection, University of Southern California Libraries Special Collections.

new incarnation the Kaiser mill became part of a hodgepodge superfactory that helped usher China into a modern manufacturing era. Initiatives like this made East Asia and the Pacific into economic powerhouses and drove manufacturing employment to grow from thirty-one million jobs in 1970 to ninety-seven million by 2010.[56] These new industrial regions quickly established connections with U.S. consumer markets. Rapid industrialization enabled East Asian manufacturing exports to increase from $269 billion in 1997 to nearly $1.5 trillion in 2007.[57] At the same time, the port complex that had bid the mill farewell became a major gateway for imported Chinese goods. The mill, its disassembled parts, and the factories that it helped to create formed a new circuit that connected China's manufacturing heartland to the inland warehouses of Southern California.

REMAPPING THE DREAM

Southern California's manufacturing decline took place concurrently with the numerical ascendance of the region's Latinx and Asian American populations.[58] Devalued former industrial spaces, which once provided middle-class lifestyles for white Angelenos, offered first- and second-generation residents an opportunity to buy or rent more affordable housing. The landscape changed drastically when "white people left, black people tip-toed in, and Latinos, including immigrants, moved in en mass[e]," as Manuel Pastor described it.[59] By the end of the twentieth century, expanding Latinx and Asian populations had transformed Nuestra Señora de Los Angeles into an experiment in the future of American democracy at exactly the same moment that new circuits of capital were reorganizing regional space.[60] Maywood's transformation was particularly dramatic. The small southeastern city measures less than one square mile and has a population under thirty thousand. Its population went from nearly two-thirds white in 1970 to 97 percent Latinx by 2010. Nearly half of Maywood's new residents were foreign-born immigrants.[61] South LA's new residents encountered a discarded industrial landscape; it was full of deadly artifacts left behind by an amalgam of postwar capital, blue-collar white labor, and a desiccated Keynesian state.

Neoliberal state policies were complicit with the abandonment of LA's industrial suburbs.[62] The wave of neoliberal reform that reshaped U.S. government policies favored capitalist growth but did little to protect workers from the insecurities attached to fluctuating markets.[63] For example, Ronald Reagan's throttling of the Professional Air Traffic Controllers Organization (PATCO) signaled an end of the postwar Keynesian accord that had enabled large portions of the U.S. working class to enjoy the perks of blue-collar unionism and middle-class suburban lives.[64] The replacement of Keynesianism with monetarist policies during the early 1980s led to rising interest rates that jolted the financial markets. Such economic and political reforms caused a debt crisis and paved the way for structural adjustment policies that dismantled Keynesian social safety nets.[65] Neoliberal reformers also successfully deregulated parts of the transportation, telecommunications, and financial sectors. Deregulation created pathways for capital investment to flood into new markets. Combined, structural adjustment and deregulation policies decimated the old industrial spaces that had once provided middle-class livelihoods to blue-collar—mostly white—manufacturing workers.[66]

The burden of restoring once idyllic suburban spaces was particularly daunting, because many of the Keynesian institutions that had made blue-collar middle-class lifestyles possible had been gutted during the ascendance of neoliberal politics.[67] These communities, "spiraling in downward directions," were burdened with what Albert Camarillo described as "diminished tax bases, weakened institutional infrastructures, mounting crime rates, and violence." The result was a "suburban decline" that was a "corollary to the 'urban crisis' in the older, industrial cities of the Northeast."[68] The combination of white flight and capital mobility created pockets of hypervulnerability for Black and Latinx urban residents, a process that urban scholars have attempted to grapple with through, for example, research on spatial mismatch theory.[69] More cynical readings of this process will draw a correlation between economic decline and growing immigrant populations. Similarly, culture of poverty theories that blame Latinxs and African Americans for economic inequalities tend to ignore how capital, the state, and cultural notions of difference shape the processes of racial formation in the United States.[70]

Collective abandonment of these spaces did not signal a complete absence of the state and of capital. These devalued spaces also served as "planned concentrations or sinks—of hazardous materials and destructive practices" that increased what Ruth W. Gilmore termed "group-differentiated vulnerabilities to premature death."[71] Such was the case in Southeast LA, where deindustrialization turned old suburbs into toxic landscapes, especially during the retrenchment of Southern California's military-industrial complex. Toxic residues lingered in abandoned factories and poisoned new residents long after the old production lines had disappeared.[72]

Felipe Aguirre served as a Maywood city council member and mayor between 2005 and 2013. He implicated a postwar alliance between capital and the state in his argument that the suburban communities that once provided spaces of hope for white families posed a deadly threat to the region's growing immigrant populations. Aguirre explained during an extended interview that "there were a lot of good union paying jobs here when Maywood's population was mostly Anglo." Maywood and other Southeast LA neighborhoods were the quintessential representation of postwar suburban life. But this changed when, as Aguirre described, "a lot of these companies started closing in the late 70s early 80s, a lot of those people started to take off. Then Latino immigrants came in and had to clean up all the previous society's mess."[73]

What he referred to as "the previous society's mess" was the specific spatial order produced by an expanding postwar industrial regime, held in place by racialized labor markets and segregated housing. City boosters, led by the LA Chamber of Commerce, cultivated Southeast Los Angeles as an investment opportunity by luring manufacturing companies with marketing literature from the 1920s that promised an "abundant supply of skilled and unskilled white labor," including "no Negroes and very few Mexican and Chinese."[74] While official narratives tried to erase Black, Mexican, and Asian workers from the landscape, those groups nonetheless played a key role in building postwar Los Angeles; they also played a role in reclaiming abandoned industrial spaces. Deindustrialization and white flight meant that new residents had to clean up the environmental waste that was left behind by companies like Bethlehem Steel, National Glass, Anchor Hocking, and the Pemaco superfund site. "We were cleaning a lot of these sites that were part of the previous society's prosperity," Aguirre said. "But we were cleaning it with our bodies. They did not leave these places in a very good state."[75]

Immigrants weren't the only ones who moved into devalued industrial suburbs. These spaces became prime real estate for new industries, including the global logistics sector. Former industrial suburbs became new conduits for global goods as the industrial suburban corridor was transformed into a distribution pipeline for the ports of Los Angeles and Long Beach; old union jobs gave way to new Walmart jobs. Many of these former industrial communities played host to or were located near railways and train stations that serviced the ports. The transformation was, as described in the next chapter, part of a regional effort to transform Los Angeles and its metropolitan hinterland into the country's largest logistics gateway for transpacific goods. The symbolic spatial irony of global restructuring was captured by Aguirre: "All these companies that exist here in Vernon [a neighboring city] are now basically warehouses and packaging companies where they package up whatever China sends over and they break it down into smaller units and they sell them. You might say it's 99 cent heaven. All the warehouses for the 99 Cent stores are located right here in this strip."[76]

Before moving on to the next chapter, it's important to connect all of the elements discussed so far—space, power, and method—into a coherent narrative. First, spatial ideologies are critical in the chapters that follow because they represent a central playing field in how the region was produced as a logistics landscape. Second, these spatial ideologies extend beyond the realm of discourse because they constitute a spatial method that does not separate the material from the ideological. For instance, the notion of the American Dream is a useful analytical framework because it involves both the cognitive and material forces central to the production of space. Something called the American Dream represents both the ideological construction of a normative spatial order and the material spaces that are required to make this idea an embodied and lived space. Instead of separating the ideological production of a logistics development discourse from the material construction of a regional transportation infrastructure, it is far more intriguing to examine how ideas—such as those espoused in dominant development discourses— are transformed into a material force that is exercised by and through power.[77]

TWO

Global Goods and the Infrastructure of Desire

CONSUMERS OFTEN ENTER INTO ECONOMIC exchanges without being fully aware of the social and ecological systems required to produce the bevy of things that we consume.[1] In fact, modern commodity chains are often so complex and geographically dispersed that it is difficult for consumers to comprehend the vast spatial and social relationships that make everyday consumption possible. Consumers may also be blinded by ideological and disciplinary frameworks that prevent them from seeing the deeper human connections that bind complex systems together. For example, economic models that try to explain the proliferation of goods in contemporary society often use a consumer choice lens that takes for granted the extensive social relations needed to produce and distribute commodities.[2] Such rational choice models place too much emphasis on microeconomic market decisions when trying to explain basic social phenomena.[3] The result is a rather large gap between the microeconomics of individual choice and the social relations needed to produce robust market systems. A commodity chain approach can help fill some of this gap by connecting individual consumer choice to a theory of political economy that uses logistics to explain how modern retail innovations have reshaped urban space.

It is very easy to get stuck on the physical location of the San Pedro Bay and to see the ports as a collection of terminals, cranes, and intermodal railyards. Nonetheless, the San Pedro Bay ports are part of a larger network that connects Southern California to places like the Central Valley, the Inland Empire, Chicago, China, and beyond. They constitute an extended circuit of capital that requires thinking through the relationships of power necessary to produce them. This more robust reading of logistics reveals how the fulfillment of individual consumer desire is built on an elaborate system of urban infrastructure.

Logistics performs several methodological tasks for this project.[4] First, it helps unpack the black box of globalization to reveal what John Urry has called "islands of order within a sea of disorder."[5] These "islands of order" are important because their production as fixed spaces demonstrates how actors exercise power to manage the complexity of globalization by reordering space and time. In the case of global commodity chains, I argue that logisticians used scientific rationalism and new technologies to create an abstract and ordered vision of space that enabled them to expand the territorial possibilities for capital investment.[6] In fact, the logistician's gaze provided a global spatial imaginary for capital investment by producing an abstract vison of the universe that linked places in new ways.

Second, logistics shows how the scientific management of bodies, space, and time produced new labor regimes, which facilitated a more complex and extended system of global production, distribution, and consumption. For example, the ability of logisticians to implement information technologies and efficient just-in-time (JIT) management systems enabled them to stitch together dispersed sets of local nodes into elaborate global production and distribution networks. One result was that logisticians could create efficient spatial systems that linked Chinese factory workers to Southern California warehouse workers and American consumers by ensnaring disparate places into new spatial relationships.

Finally, logistics connects the politics of regional development that shaped Southern California to the much more expansive spatial networks needed by global capital to transform itself in the twenty-first century. The logistics revolution created new opportunities for local actors to contest how they connected to or disconnected from the transportation and information infrastructures that undergird contemporary global commodity chains.[7] Accordingly, local politics and regional planning became the conduit through which private and public actors extended the infrastructure for global goods.

Logistics is particularly useful as an analytical lens because it reveals how state actors mobilized space for capitalist development and provides a different view of the systems, processes, and spaces that make up globalization.[8] This reading of logistics as spatial method uses science, capitalism, culture, and political economy to reveal "how spatial restructuring hides consequences from us."[9] The deployment of such a method illustrates how transformations in the capitalist mode of production were tied to changes in mass consumption, the welfare state, and organized labor. Logistics enables us to discern some of the powerful forces that were unleashed when major retailers like Walmart and Amazon propelled capitalism into a new age of global expansion after the 1980s. It provides a spatial representation, a type of geographical window that reveals how space, capital, and race were transformed during a key period of global restructuring. The lessons learned from this study apply to many regions across the United States that tried to capitalize on commodity distribution economies by investing heavily in port-related infrastructure. Other metropolitan regions, such as Seattle-Tacoma, Savannah, and Newark, all pursued regional logistics development plans during the same period.[10]

SPACES OF CONSUMPTION

Scholars have used commodities as a unit of analysis for a very long time, including such luminaries as Adam Smith.[11] Likewise, Karl Marx developed an entire methodological approach by demonstrating how British capitalists erected a social system based on wage labor and profit-yielding objects.[12] He meticulously revealed the complex ways that industrial products were embedded in distinct relationships of power. Focusing on the social relations of an economic process allowed him to explore how different actors could maintain or alter these relationships. Marx pointed out that even if empires and social systems were built on the sometimes obscure rules of accumulation, capitalism's inner logics, when coupled with the human desire for profit, acted as a powerful material force.[13] The nexus among individual desire, social competition, and the internal logics of capitalist expansion has proved to be one of the system's most dynamic drivers. Together, these forces provide the impetus for individuals to introduce the new technological, labor, or managerial innovations that have propelled capitalism forward. Marx's contributions were critical to the commodity chain approach because his work stressed the importance of power and society in the consumption process. Yet too many of his disciples became stuck in the nineteenth-century widget factory that Marx used as his unit of analysis. The goal here is to find links and to see production, consumption, and distribution as part of the same circuit that makes up contemporary capitalism.

Logistics infrastructure, which includes the roads and railways that deliver goods from factories to the consumer, is the glue that holds global and regional distribution networks together; it is the circulatory system of global capitalism. Thousands of diesel trucks and locomotives use these logistics arteries to deliver goods from foreign production sites to regional and national markets; they are part of an extensive overland distribution system that allows West Coast ports to compete with all-ocean delivery routes to East Coast markets. These conduits enable us to consummate the circulation of capital.[14] This more comprehensive system, which includes the spaces needed to make and deliver the goods that drive global economies and fulfill individual yearnings, is what I call the "infrastructure of desire."

Urban scholars have mostly ignored logistics and global commodity circuits.[15] While it is true that scholars have written extensively about the revolutionary impact that the shipping container had on commodity distribution, the relationship between logistics and urbanization has been understudied.[16] Economic geographers and transportation scholars, for example, conducted important research on the extensive nature of global production networks.[17] Yet transportation studies tend to leave out the social relations of extended commodity chains. Studies that have examined freight movement mostly focused on ports, gateways, and transportation efficiency, rather than on the broader social relations of metropolitan development.[18] The focus was instead on network efficiencies and on the micro-geographies of place. Likewise, social science scholars have investigated globalization by studying reconfigured labor markets, industry change, and emerging development regions, but these investigations have also left out the role that commodity circulation has played in shaping urban space.[19]

Distribution has largely been ignored because scholars believed that new technologies and transportation systems had reduced the significance of space as a factor in the global flow of goods and capital.[20] According to this logic, greater mobility had effectively annihilated the limits of space and distribution in modern global commodity chains.[21] Therefore, scholars of American cities embraced the globalization turn by shifting their attention from modernist industrial manufacturing to the postmodern decline of U.S.-based production, new labor markets, and the rise of the symbolic economy as major factors in post-1970s urban development.[22] Studies that examined the intersection of mobility, space, and time tended to focus on the circulation of information, money, and people rather than on the movement of goods.[23] Capital flows, information technologies, and cultural innovations became the defining markers of global cities. London and New York, for example, were studied as financial control centers for an expanding global economic network.[24]

Logistics was also widely disregarded by scholars who study culture and consumption. Most of the literature that tries to explain the rise of American consumption assumes that consumer desire and individual choice drive the cultural products industry.[25] The focus often centers on how consumers make choices about what to buy. One common argument in these accounts is that merchants can use cultural signifiers like taste and status to shape consumer purchasing decisions.[26] The underlying assumption is that companies can manipulate desire through advertising and marketing techniques. "Desire" is the right word, because advertisers have often appealed to basic human drives—sex, food, the sense of belonging—to stimulate buying behavior.[27] While consumer-centric accounts can provide useful insights into market transactions, they tend to exclude other parts of the commodity chain, such as production and distribution. Consumer models leave out the deep connections among commodity chains, social networks, and products. The following two examples illustrate this point.

First, greater access to finance capital expanded consumption in the post-1980s period. Increased consumption wasn't simply a consequence of the relentless desire for more stuff. Much of this yearning was underwritten and made possible by ballooning credit card debt and mortgage-backed revolving lines of credit. Access to more credit enabled consumer debt to explode from $5.6 billion in 1980 to more than $1 trillion by the end of 2007 (see figure 5).[28] A typical American consumer could use a credit card or a second mortgage to increase their consumption even if wages declined or remained stagnant. Advertising is the second example of how consumer-centered accounts can obfuscate other forces at play. Ad agencies became more important in the consumption process only after producers developed the logistical infrastructure that allowed them to brand and distribute mass-produced goods.[29]

Finance capital and advertising both illustrate why it is necessary to break with models that explain consumption through a consumer choice lens. These rational choice models can naturalize major changes in capitalist modes of accumulation while ignoring the social contexts in which individuals operate. To understand how consumption is linked to regional space, we must embed it in a "larger web of social relations."[30] Such an approach helps to reveal the actors and nodes at each stage of the circulation process. A commodity chain framework can strip away any antisocial illusion that places too much emphasis on isolated individual choice. Commodity chains, as Ken Conca, Thomas Princen, and Michael Maniates argue, show how "consumption decisions are

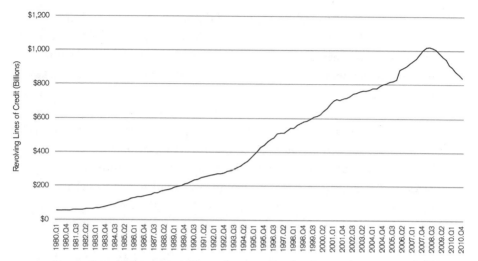

FIGURE 5. Growth of consumer debt in the United States, 1980–2010. Author analysis of data from the United States Federal Reserve.

heavily influenced, shaped, and constrained by an entire string of linked choices being made, and power being exercised, as commodities are created, distributed, used, and disposed of."[31] It is time to move beyond the transactional spaces of consumption—stores and online shopping, for example—to explore how this infrastructure of desire—in particular the logistics of commodity distribution—has shaped metropolitan space. The goal here is to examine how ports and warehouses have expanded the geographical possibilities of contemporary capitalism.

To determine why and how logistics became a prominent part of Southern California's landscape, we need to place its growth within the wider global economic context of post-Fordist restructuring, especially because regional leaders pushed logistics as an antidote to deindustrialization. North America lost approximately six million manufacturing jobs between 1970 and 2010.[32] Riverside, San Bernardino, Orange, and Los Angeles Counties lost more than five hundred thousand jobs between 1990 and 2010, a decline of 46 percent. Flexible production systems like JIT rendered older push-based manufacturing spaces obsolete. Once-mighty factories slowly withered away as capital sought newer facilities and cheaper labor in emerging industrial economies.

China in particular became a major investment target because it offered access to large pools of relatively cheap labor. In addition, heavy state invest-

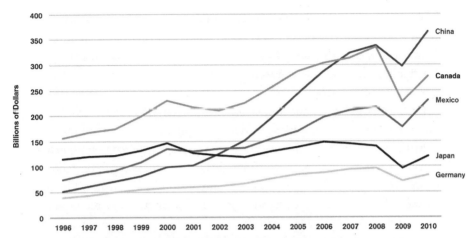

FIGURE 6. Value of commodities imported into the United States, by country, 1996–2010. Author analysis of data from the U.S. Department of Commerce and the U.S. International Trade Commission, tariff and trade data 1996–2010.

ment in economic infrastructure meant that companies could set up shop and reach tremendous economies of scale in a relatively short period of time. Foreign direct investment into China increased from $57 million in 1980 to $114.7 billion in 2010.[33] The infusion of investment and state-backed capital enabled Chinese producers to quickly overtake both Mexico and Canada as the biggest importer of goods into the United States. By 2008 Chinese goods represented 16.1 percent of all U.S. imports, up from 6.5 percent in 1996 (see figure 6).[34]

China's incredible rise as a center of production, when combined with U.S. consumption capacity, created new opportunities for Southern California's ports to establish themselves as vital transpacific gateways. Private investors and regional boosters championed the idea that Chinese imports provided a solution to the region's sagging job base, especially among blue-collar workers. A report commissioned by the Southern California Association of Governments (SCAG) argued that logistics was the "only route that the region has available to helping those workers achieve growing standards of living while simultaneously correcting the recent deep slide in Southern California's relative prosperity vis-à-vis other major parts of the country."[35] The SCAG economists and planners believed that the region's declining manufacturing sector could be replaced by global logistics. Their rationale seemed to make sense. If regions in the United States were losing manufacturing jobs as a result of economic restructuring, some could gain them back on the other end of the commodity chain by building extensive distribution networks that connected imported products with the insatiable appetite of the American heartland.

Of course capital did not completely abandon cities in the United States after the late 1970s. Cities like Los Angeles capitalized on macroeconomic shifts by transforming themselves into transpacific trade gateways. Such a transition was possible because although U.S. production of commodity goods declined after the 1980s, American consumption did not. On the contrary, U.S. consumer demand—combined with the shorter product cycles and readily available credit discussed above—drove imported commodity shipments to record heights at the same time that U.S. production declined. Values of imported commodities jumped from $790 billion in 1996 to $2.1 trillion in 2008.

Los Angeles and Long Beach adopted the global logistics development strategy and pushed ahead of other ports by implementing regional policies that expanded their capacity to absorb a larger portion of Asian imports. Local policy makers, led by the port authorities of Long Beach and Los Angeles, leveraged tremendous amounts of public resources to invest in infrastructure that allowed them to expand their throughput capacity. Billions of dollars were spent on infrastructure to modernize the ports for the global distribution market.[36] For example, net investment in both ports topped $493,732,400 in 2006.[37] Port authorities budgeted more than $2.5 billion in capital investments for the 2010 fiscal year. This did not include private and public spending on rail and transportation infrastructure both near and away from the ports.

Local officials had reason to be happy with the results. Global economic restructuring and local infrastructure spending enabled the region's share of imported goods to reach record levels. Export and import container volume grew from 9.5 million twenty-foot equivalent units (TEUs) in 1999 to 13.1 million by 2004,[38] an increase of 38.2 percent.[39] Imported container volume reached its peak at 8.1 million TEUs in 2006 and 2007 (see figure 7). While many pointed to 2008 as a year of major port decline, container volume remained relatively high. Port activity grew at such record rates during the 2000s that even a decline of 9 percent between 2007 and 2008 did not wipe out historically high volumes. By 2010 imports were on their way back up and reached 7.1 million TEUs.

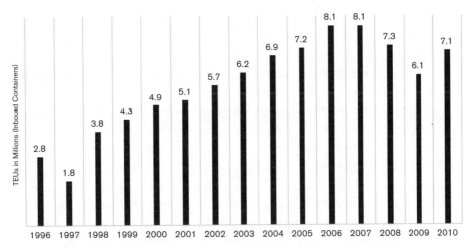

FIGURE 7. Port growth by container volume. Author's analysis of data from Port of Los Angeles and Port of Long Beach.

JUST-IN-TIME URBANIZATION

The proliferation of consumer goods was induced by one of the most dramatic changes in modern production and distribution that occurred during the 1980s, when Japanese automobile manufacturers introduced JIT production systems. Toyota was a leader of JIT managerial techniques and provides an example of how JIT increased production efficiencies by focusing on market demand. The JIT approach allowed small work teams to produce cars and parts as they were needed in the marketplace. This market-driven process was supposed to reduce costs associated with holding excessive inventories in both supplies and finished goods.[40] For example, parts were only produced after production teams received an order from Toyota's assembly crews. Toyota's JIT system was successful because it used emerging information technologies to build closer links between consumer demand and dispersed production networks. Of course this type of pull system—in which products are made in response to market demand—had existed long before JIT was invented as a concept.[41] Yet what made Toyota's JIT system so powerful was that it led to widespread adoption of market-driven manufacturing.

Companies adopted JIT's market-driven principles by integrating consumer desire into commodity design and procurement. Old top-down models, in which firms designed new products and pushed them out to market, gave way to more data-savvy manufacturing techniques, in which consumer demand shaped production and distribution.[42] Dell Computers is a quintessential example of how this worked. The company mixed JIT part sourcing with direct market demand and revolutionized business-to-consumer relations. Under Dell's system, consumers logged on to the company's website, configured their desired computers, and placed their orders.[43] That simple act of clicking a button put an entire social and economic system in motion. The company famously claimed that it used JIT part sourcing to reduce stock from thirty-five days in 1995 to six days by 1999.[44] Other companies used JIT to incorporate market information into product design. An example is the Sony Walkman. Sony engineers developed a design process that incorporated consumer behavior and desire into possible iterations of the audio device. The intention was to make products that were more responsive to market dynamics by producing exactly what consumers wanted.[45] Sony's demand-driven approach was reflective of a "cultural circuit" in which the "products both reflect and transform consumers' behavior."[46] Cultural circuits enable consumer demand to influence what is made, how it is designed, and when it is delivered.

Market-driven production provided new opportunities for retailers to increase their leverage as intermediaries between consumers and manufacturers. Companies such as Walmart and Target developed new business strategies that gave them greater power in the JIT corporate world because they built their business models around real-time market information. Walmart revolutionized retail by creating a vast information system that made it the world's largest purchaser of commodities.[47] Access to market data gave retailers tremendous purchasing power, which they used to influence what was made and by whom. The most successful retailers used their new influence to transform shopping behavior by merging more efficient supply chains with cutting-edge sales strategies.[48] They increased sales by monitoring and cultivating market demand, a practice that also transformed modern logistics. One way they increased sales was by blending style and status with low-cost goods to make discretionary shopping available to a larger audience.

How new retail strategies affected logistics workers is described later in the book. Here I want to conclude by examining how companies used cultural circuits and retail strategies to increase the flow of consumer goods. For example, retail companies increased sales by shortening the time that products spent between design and delivery dates, thus increasing overall inventory turnover. Retailers also increased turnover rates by developing business models that focused on goods with shorter product cycles. All of this was made possible by JIT supply chain techniques and by logistics innovations that enabled smaller time-to-market distribution windows. As a consequence, consumers were lured into buying the latest thing by companies that constantly updated their product lines. Old ideas of seasonal buying were discarded because the constant flow of new merchandise made shopping a year-round experience. These new tactics propelled the circulation of capital by flooding the market with a constant stream of desirable products.

Low-cost goods took on new cultural meaning by enabling customers to reposition themselves within a community of style that retailers transformed by changing the shopping experience. Retailers have routinely used space and style to change the practices and meanings of shopping. Major department stores, for example, were created as spaces in which shoppers could experience the wonders of modern commodities inside a fabricated and controlled environment. The mall, according to Michelle Lowe and Neil Wrigley, was designed as an "essential site for communication and interaction, a place for 'hanging out', for 'tribalism', where adolescent subcultures are formed and where key lifetime experiences take place."[49] Shopping places set the spatial context for transactions that linked cultural and economic spheres.[50] They gave shape and meaning to otherwise mundane economic transactions by imbuing the act of shopping with particular lifestyle experiences. Culture and aesthetics have been key retail strategies precisely because they can establish lifestyle practices that effectively link individual identity to particular commodity types and social status. For example, certain products are marked as aspirational purchases: the value of buying the thing extends beyond function and need. Such commodities function as cultural symbols that convey status.[51]

We must consider the connection between individual desire and social status more deeply, especially because it is such an important part of understanding the rhythms of contemporary commodity flows. Even if capital structures what people can and cannot buy, high-velocity retailing has provided merchants with the ability to embed style and class status into mass consumption practices. H&M's multinational brand of fast fashion, for example, which encouraged up-to-date style at low prices, required customers to buy more and to shop more often to maintain their social status. Cultural motifs—the latest fabric or scarf—created an alternative style economy that let individuals escape the limits of economic capital by converting less expensive items into status-rendering goods. Low-cost goods that mimicked upper-middle-class commodity economies created new ways for people to participate in, even if they could not achieve, similar economic status. This disjuncture brings us back to debt and finance capital, which when combined with a greater array of cheap goods, enabled more shopping. As producers adopted market-driven business models—in which goods were produced and shipped whenever and wherever people wanted them—they also developed more efficient distribution systems and flexible labor supplies. The same technologies that sped up the circulation of capital and commodities also introduced new time and space demands into the labor process. Globalization, in the words of Andrew Herod, meant "greater pressure from employers and governments for workers to become more 'flexible', both in terms of skills and, more importantly, in terms of work organization, so that corporations may respond quickly to the vagaries of the market."[52] Such acceleration in the circulation of capital was a clear example of how globalization transformed the temporal experience of the economy for retailers, consumers, and workers. As retailers made more goods available to the masses, they also increased the amount of space needed to produce, distribute, and sell their goods.

I return to this theme elsewhere, but before moving on to logistics in more detail, I want to review my argument so far. I began this chapter by discussing the role that desire has played in expanding consumption. I then illustrated how consumer desire became a powerful material force in the post-1980s period, when individuals were able to leverage credit to purchase larger quantities of goods. However, as much as consumer desire is an important actor in this story, it was producers and retailers who created the material spaces and physical infrastructure that allowed commodity consumption to play such a prominent role in contemporary economies. Finally, while retailers developed new sales strategies and business relationships to assume greater control in the commodities game, it was their distribution systems that had a profound effect on metropolitan regions. The next chapter examines how high-velocity retailing and global commodity chains reconfigured logistics space.

THREE

The Spatial Politics of Southern California's Logistics Regime

THIS CHAPTER EXPLAINS HOW CIVIC leaders capitalized on two key political and economic phenomena to make Southern California into the largest distribution gateway in the United States. I first examine how the global economic restructuring that began in the 1970s produced a crisis discourse among policy makers, who argued for strategic interventions to lessen the financial shocks tied to industrial job losses. I then review how the same global economic changes that triggered capital flight away from Los Angeles and other cities in the United States provided economic opportunities for local private and public leaders to invest in transpacific trade corridors. This mix between the discourse of crisis and the material geographies of a shifting global capitalism set the stage for a new spatial politics that culminated in a regional development regime centered on logistics. By recognizing these intersections—between the local and the global, the discursive and the material—we can glean a better understanding of how metropolitan space was produced through the contentious politics of logistics development.

Regions are particularly important as a scale of analysis because they help us grasp how local actors have used statecraft to renegotiate their territorial relationship with global capitalism. Several scholars have made this point, including members of the new regionalism school, who argued that globalization increased the importance of city-regions and provided useful insight into the "new territorial structures and imaginaries" that were produced during the globalization shift.[1] While city-regions have been widely studied, Jonas and Ward argue that this body of work has downplayed "how new territorial forms are constructed politically and reproduced through everyday acts and struggles around consumption and social reproduction."[2] My analysis of logistics addresses this gap in the literature because it brings the politics of regional development into conversation with the social and material infra-structures of modern consumption. More specifically, I use the geographic concept of landscape to analyze how regions are necessarily produced as both ideological constructs and material structures. Don Mitchell defines land-scape as "the conscious construction of a perspective, a way of seeing the region that, in concert with policies, laws, and institutions, physically makes the land, produces the landscape materially, and sustains it ideologically."[3] Landscape is therefore a spatial ideology that bridges discursive and material space, similar to what Lefebvre calls "representations of space."[4] These repre-sentations rationalize the production of particular material spaces. Spatial ideologies are powerful tools because they set the parameters for the produc-tion of space by invoking everyday language to produce a commonsense or normative understanding of dominant spatial practices.

Spatial ideologies were particularly important to logistics development because before the elaborate system of roads and rail lines that connect inland warehouses to the San Pedro Bay ports could be built, planners and investors had to first imagine and design the region as an intricate hub for global goods. These cognitive and discursive mappings supplied the ideologi-cal foundations for the region's goods movement industry. The simple notion that Southern California could and should become a global logistics hub provided a powerful ideological and moral shield for regional leaders. Prologistics policies involved an ideological devotion that committed the region and its residents to a specific development path. I use a spatial politics framework to investigate how such ideological commitments were produced, performed, perceived, and contested through cultural and economic lenses/forces.

REGIONS IN THE AGE OF GLOBALIZATION

One of the strategies that Southern California's political leaders used in the aftermath of global economic restructuring and manufacturing job losses included trying to lure investment away from other cities. In fact, interurban competition redefined regional politics and was especially fierce after the 1970s, when industrial cities had to fill the buildings and empty lots aban-doned by deindustrialization. Increased regional competition affected urban political economy in four key ways. First, regions competed to improve their position in the international division of labor. Second, they tried to convert themselves into major centers of consumption. Third, regions tried to gain an advantage over control and command functions (financial services and business management). Fourth, regions engaged in more tenacious competition for governmental redistribution of resources.[5] Southern California's political leadership used each of these strategies to position the region for economic growth during the globalization era.

City and regional planners responded to increased competition by devising elaborate strategies to lure finance capital into decaying urban centers. They recruited various sectors, including modern convention centers, lavish lifestyle shopping experiences, refined cultural spaces, and mega sports stadiums.[6] In Southern California local political leaders and regional planners used the changing economic landscape as an opportunity to mobilize the region for multiple development paths, including downtown revitalization, Hollywood entertainment, and port-based logistics. Although it is easy to see how money and power combined to produce the tall buildings and sports facilities of contemporary downtown Los Angeles and the financial complexes of Orange County, it is less obvious to discern the power and money embedded in the massive rail, port, and highway infrastructure projects that combine Southern California's sprawling regional metropolis into a coherent, if somewhat unwieldy, whole.

Nevertheless, the connections between global commodity flows and local development regimes are there if we peel back enough layers to reveal how the region expanded between 1980 and 2010. One factor that will become more evident is how policy makers orchestrated the transfer of private and public resources into the regional goods movement economy as they scrambled to make Southern California into a major shipping gateway for transpacific goods. This transfer of resources and political support for logistics development marked a new type of spatial politics in Southern California. A regional political framework was especially important because port boosters had to convince the 188 independent cities and six counties that make up the Southern California region, not all of which had an obvious relationship with logistics, that they should cooperate on transportation infrastructure projects. The act of convincing disparate entities and constituencies that logistics was the solution to the region's manufacturing crisis of the 1990s and 2000s illustrates how the ideological and material politics of space were central to logistics development.[7] Crisis and its antithesis—logistics—were deployed as a political tool by California governor Arnold Schwarzenegger's special adviser for economic affairs, David Crane, who argued that the "country is dramatically under-infrastructured" as a rationalization for public support of infrastructure spending.[8] When Crane said "infrastructure" he meant logistics and transportation. Key members of the logistics industry and regional economic boosters made similar arguments. Jack Kyser, former chief economist of the Los Angeles Economic Development Corporation (LAEDC), regularly warned the public that the region was "running out of trade infrastructure capacity."[9] The Pacific Merchant Shipping Association added to the urgent call by arguing that shippers were "building their supply chains around California" because the lack of "freight supporting infrastructure" was making it inefficient and costly to do business with the West Coast.[10]

Logistics infrastructure created a new political field; the stakes included access to public funds during the neoliberal era, when social services were being slashed or privatized. Port boosters justified their access to state funding streams by claiming that logistics and infrastructure generated public benefits. Planners with SCAG, for example, cited the region's notorious traffic problems to rationalize further spending on grade separations that they claimed would relieve congestion while mitigating the negative impact of the goods movement industry on public citizens. Employees of SCAG claimed that regional leaders could improve logistics efficiencies and ease commuter traffic if they reduced "conflicts between trains and motor vehicles by separating at-grade crossings."[11] Seemingly banal discussions about grade separations and infrastructure were in fact essential to a $2.5 billion plan to extend the logistics system through the San Gabriel Valley and the Inland Empire.[12]

Government support for infrastructure projects was critical because among other things it stimulated speculative growth in the logistics industry. Larry Keller, a former executive director for the Port of Los Angeles (POLA), explained how this happened when he spoke before a congressional hearing on the Alameda Corridor project: "In the early 1980's, it was apparent an improved infrastructure would be required if the cargo transportation system serving the Ports of Los Angeles and Long Beach was to handle the predicted growth in cargo through the West Coast ports."[13] The notion that cargo was predicted to grow and that infrastructure was required became the central operating logic for logistics boosters. Official projections estimated that port capacity was at 144,500,000 tons in 1989 and was expected to reach 221,800,000 tons by 2020.[14] Port leaders pointed to the anticipated growth in Asian manufacturing, arguing that Southern California could and should establish itself as the nation's main gateway for transpacific commodity shipments.

Keller's statement reflects part of the political strategy that port boosters used to turn the region into a major logistics hub; they used speculative data to problematize the need for public spending on transportation infrastructure and proposed a strategic plan to solve this perceived problem. The logic of this argument—that growth is coming and we must therefore prepare to absorb it—became the governing ethos for a new regional development regime that rerouted public transportation funds into logistics-supporting infrastructure. Official projections performed two key functions.

First, they naturalized growth and provided a road map for port boosters to create a spatial economy that privileged logistics development. Although it is easy to dismiss boosterish claims as political rhetoric and wishful thinking, spatial ideologies can serve as powerful narratives, especially when they motivate people to act. Spatial ideologies, such as those espoused by prologistics boosters, involve what John R. Logan and Harvey L. Molotch described as "[p]eople dreaming, planning, and organizing themselves to make money" and represent "the agents through which accumulation does its work at the level of the urban place."[15]

Second, these speculative logistics ideologies necessitated new institutions to manage the expanding territorial scope and scale of development that was required to meet future projections. For example, SCAG's $26 billion Multi-County Goods Movement Action Plan (MCGMAP) called for the creation of the Southern California Institution to Execute Infrastructure Construction (SCIEIC). This new oversight body would be responsible for developing, collecting, and implementing plans to further expand the region's transportation infrastructure. According to SCAG, "No existing institution, under its current authorities, can manage the building of the wide range of infrastructure projects needed to implement the logistics-based economic strategy region wide."[16] One of the SCIEIC's key tasks was to reduce intraregional competition by facilitating collaborative funding initiatives.

Speculative data and the political discourse of eminent growth also played a key role in producing logistics as an economic category. Logistics, like all economic constructs, "is not found as an empirical object among other worldly things"; Susan Buck-Morss notes that for these constructs, "to be 'seen' by the human perceptual apparatus it has to undergo a process, crucial for science, of representational mapping."[17] The invention of logistics as an economic and spatial category by regional leaders gave that "thing" agency because the very act of labeling it turned it into a political object that could be tracked and measured. Chapter 6 gives a more detailed account of how logistics was stitched together as a container for various economic indicators. For now it is important to note that markets are produced and not naturally occurring phenomena; they are assembled and embedded in particular geographies by political actors and market forces.

Of course imagining development and actually building something are very different things. It is not enough to simply examine the discursive techniques that local political and business elites used to craft a discourse of development with the hope of luring potential investors. After all, many municipal leaders have crafted elaborate development plans only to see them languish. Just because local boosters want to turn their city into the next Silicon Valley or world-class gateway doesn't mean that it will happen. What made Southern California different was its ability to capture some of the post-1980s global capital flows while other regions suffered from economic restructuring. Before attributing too much power to the state, it is important to point out that the implementation of a logistics development path was a messy process. It is much too simple to argue that logistics development was neatly implemented and that the built environment was merely a reflection of a centralized state strategy. While the San Pedro Bay ports pursued an orchestrated strategy of port and rail expansion, other parts of the region succumbed to rampant speculative development, which was not always actively managed by port leaders. To fully understand how this happened, we need to trace how specific circuits of capital intersected with local interests to build the material spaces that enabled globalization to flourish. This requires examining how local actors aligned their development prospects with the interests of the global goods movement industry.[18]

Local actors first had to create new governance systems before they could build a territorially coherent regional distribution network.[19] The two semi-autonomous commissions that govern the Los Angeles and Long Beach ports took the lead on many of the progrowth policy initiatives.[20] Harbor commissioners had considerable power to set the development agenda by both approving individual projects and crafting longer term master plans that affected the entire region.[21] Southern California's production as a global logistics hub was orchestrated through a series of planning studies and joint funding projects that were coordinated by SCAG. These studies brought together planners and policy makers from different jurisdictions and provided a training ground for regional governance at a time when coordinated state action was unusual. The volume of policy papers, planning studies, and joint funding proposals that SCAG sponsored became a blueprint for regional cooperation and propelled logistics-based economic development.[22]

Planning for port expansion began during the 1980s with the creation of The San Pedro Bay Ports 2020 Master Plan and the Alameda Corridor project.[23] The 2020 Master Plan was adopted by authorities from the POLA and the Port of Long Beach. It highlighted three key project areas that would serve as focal points for future growth. First, port officials laid out plans to dredge the harbor to provide deeper channels for larger capacity ships. Second, some of the dredged material would be used to infill six hundred acres of harbor property, with the idea that this new area would provide enough space for thirty-eight additional terminals. Finally, the plan called for construction of an extensive inland distribution system that linked the ports with rail, highways, and intermodal facilities. Essentially, the 2020 Master Plan and later documents such as the MCGMAP used speculative port data to produce a commonsense or hegemonic rationale in which the region's economic future depended on optimizing future port capacity.[24]

While port officials planned for growth, they were concerned that worsening traffic congestion would negatively affect the region's capacity to absorb future trade. SCAG formed the Ports Advisory Committee (PAC) in 1981 to address some of these potential roadblocks. The PAC developed a series of proposals meant to improve traffic flows on roadways surrounding port terminals. Next, the PAC turned its attention to inland distribution, especially to the region's rail system. Inland distribution was particularly worrisome for port authorities because future imports would have to compete with commuters as delivery trucks and trains connected incoming container goods with transcontinental road and rail systems. By 1983 the PAC had produced the basic plan for what would become the $2.4 billion Alameda Corridor rail project. The proposed project included twenty miles of rail lines and grade separations meant to improve connections between the ports and the transcontinental rail lines located near downtown Los Angeles. The crown jewel of the project included a ten-mile-long open trench that provided traffic-free passage for freight trains traveling between the city of Carson and 25th Street along the LA/Vernon/Maywood border.

Both the 2020 Master Plan and the Alameda Corridor marked a new period of regional planning cooperation among federal, state, county, and municipal agencies, an unusual occurrence in a governance landscape normally dominated by municipal fragmentation. The corridor was a public-private partnership that, according to the California State Office of Research, was meant to "produce a sustainable economic development strategy that will effectively meet the challenges of a 21st century global economy."[25] The Alameda Corridor Transportation Authority (ACTA), which oversaw the project, created institutional opportunities to access public funds. This was especially important because regional trade corridors required multijurisdictional alliances to secure funding, gain regulatory approval, and earn stakeholder consent. ACTA had broad support from SCAG, the Los Angeles County Metropolitan Transportation Authority (LACMTA), and the San Pedro Bay Ports Harbor Commissions.

The Alameda Corridor was the beginning of a neoliberal private-public logistics regime that created new governance institutions to access public funding for port-related infrastructure. Prior to ACTA, regional transportation agencies did not have a spending category for logistics funding. ACTA's former general manager, Gill Hicks, described how the organization was locked out of public funds during a congressional hearing: "Initially, ACTA was frozen out of the competition for these funds because there was no category in which to compete. The Alameda Corridor was not a freeway project, nor a light rail project."[26] ACTA taught Alameda Corridor leaders to create new institutional mechanisms that enabled them to apply for funding from regional, state, and federal agencies. Their first move was to access funds from the Los Angeles County Transportation Commission (LACTC), the organization in charge of distributing state and federal funds for Los Angeles County transportation needs.

ACTA and SCAG also asked Heinz Heckeroth, the director of Caltrans District 7, for funding. Heckeroth suggested that SCAG "coordinate a systems-level analysis of the transportation access needs of the ports."[27] Such a plan could provide an evidence-based, comprehensive initiative that state and federal officials would view more favorably. Port leaders complied, and according to Gill Hicks ACTA set out "to develop an action plan for improving traffic conditions in the port area and to raise funds for implementing that plan."[28] One result was the creation of the PAC in October 1981, which became instrumental in redirecting public transportation funds into the Alameda Corridor project. Finally, after two years of lobbying by ACTA leaders, the regional transportation agency (LACTC and later LACMTA) adopted new funding categories and went on to provide $347 million in grants during the 1990s. Regional transportation leaders agreed to fund logistics spending "on the basis that goods movement projects such as the Alameda Corridor are essential for reducing congestion and air pollution and for maintaining a healthy economy."[29]

ACTA's biggest success occurred in 1996 and 1997, when President Bill Clinton signed a federal loan for $400 million. Clinton's decision to allocate the funds was made after regional, state, and federal actors successfully framed Southern California's logistics network as a public good worthy of federal funding. The federal loan was only granted after the Intermodal Surface Transportation Efficiency Act (ISTEA) of 1991 and the National Highway System Designation Act (NHSDA) of 1995 identified the Alameda Corridor as a high-priority corridor. Under ISTEA, those projects that were designated as high-priority corridors were eligible to receive federal financing from a special revolving loan fund. Key actors from Southern California's private and public sector lobbied for this high-priority designation. Gill Hicks claimed, "Members of ACTA's coalition and advocacy team successfully communicated the key message that the project was vital to the health of the nation's economy because it would dramatically improve a critical international trade corridor, linking every other state in the union to the largest port complex in the United States."[30]

Local port boosters also gained access to federal funding streams by capitalizing on concerns over national security after the assault on New York's Twin Towers on September 11, 2001. The LAEDC, for example, cited possible security threats when it solicited federal funds to support port operations. According to an LAEDC report from 2003, "the US Department of Defense (DoD) has designated more than 38,000 miles of rail lines—including those out of Southern California—as strategically important national assets."[31] The report continued, arguing that "these strategic rail corridors help connect military installations to ports and intermodal transfer facilities and to ensure that US military forces have the ability to mobilize heavy equipment, such as tanks and tracked vehicles, as needed." Statements such as these further rationalized state involvement in transportation systems, equating commerce with military readiness and logistics. The connection was clear in the LAEDC report, which noted, "Nearly 200 military installations require access to commercial rail lines." Logistics and the military are in fact inextricably linked; this connection can be traced back to military supply chains that stressed efficiency and speed by deploying technology and transportation systems to deliver supplies. As Deborah Cowen points out, the military roots of logistics rules out any discussion of the business of logistics without considering the role that the state has played in developing the technologies and strategies of commodity circulation.[32]

FINANCE CAPITAL AND THE LOGISTICS STATE

Jeff Holt, vice president of Goldman, Sachs & Co. and manager of the municipal finance division of the Fixed Income Currency and Commodities Group, served as the underwriter for the Alameda Corridor and articulated how public finance and regional planning were both central to the formation of Southern California's logistics regime. He attributed the project's success to coordinated regional planning that enabled the state to create new markets by developing the infrastructure that private interests were not willing to take on themselves. Holt touched on this dilemma when he told a congressional hearing committee that "the big question is always, how do we pay for the large public works projects that everyone needs but that no one agency, on its own, can afford." He also claimed that "the Alameda Corridor is possibly the best example of how multiple parties in a public/private partnership can come together to fund such large projects."[33] Again, the underlying assumption was that the state should play a key role in creating new logistics markets by funding regional infrastructure.

This ideological conflation between the market and the public good was expressed by the executive director for the POLA, who testified, "In reality, the beneficiary of the Alameda Corridor's successful completion and operation is the American public, to whom our domestic and global transportation efficiency is critical."[34] Both of these comments exemplify the mediating role that the state has historically played in mobilizing space for the advancement of capitalism when individual capitalists cannot agree to take collective action.[35] Capitalists are also buttressed by the conflation between the interests of capital and an undifferentiated "American public," a point that becomes more important when we discuss how social movement organizations contested this claim.

Cooperation and state support were particularly important to financial underwriters because they introduced greater stability and thus made the project more feasible for long-term finance schemes. Consequently, as Holt explained, Congress set aside a "$59 million appropriation for a loan-loss reserve [which] made a $400 million loan available which, in turn, made it possible to borrow an additional $1.2 billion from the capital markets to complete the $2.4 billion total project cost [for the Alameda Corridor]."[36] In total, the $2.4 billion needed to complete the Alameda Corridor came from a variety of public-private sources, including, revenue bonds (51%); Federal loans (18%); The Ports (18 %); California State grants (8%) and other sources (5%), mostly from the LA MTA.[37]

Aside from the funding, the Alameda Corridor also taught policy makers how to act regionally and how to deploy public financing to support the region's goods movement infrastructure, a lesson they would apply to future projects. In fact, the federal loan to ACTA served as a model for the Transportation Infrastructure Finance and Innovation Act (TIFIA) of 1998, a federal program that provides direct loans and lines of credit to "projects of national and regional significance." TIFIA provided "improved access to capital markets, flexible repayment terms, and potentially more favorable interest rates than can be found in private capital markets for similar instruments."[38] In short, ACTA taught local and federal actors how to mobilize the state for private-public partnerships by rescaling the spatial politics of growth. Regional cooperation was particularly important as the cost of infrastructure projects rose and local funding sources dwindled.

Federal programs like TIFIA encouraged regional coordination and created incentives for local actors to develop new institutions and governance networks. SCAG's adoption of the National Freight Gateway Strategy Agreement in 2006 marked a significant move toward greater collaboration. The agreement was established through a memorandum of understanding that encouraged coordinated efforts on transportation capacity and environmental protection. Major federal and local agencies signed on, including the U.S. Department of Transportation (USDOT), the Environmental Protection Agency (EPA), the Army Corps of Engineers, the California Department of Transportation (CADOT), SCAG, and transportation authorities for local counties.[39] The memorandum incentivized regional collaboration by giving signees access to more funding. According to the agreement, agencies pledged "to cooperate with all stakeholders in the area to improve freight throughput capacity while protecting and enhancing the natural and human environment." Yvonne Burke, Los Angeles County supervisor and SCAG's then president, claimed that "this new Southern California partnership will be vital to ensure our entire region's mutual goods movement needs, from the Ports to the farthest reaches of the Inland Empire."[40]

Each of the projects that I have outlined in this section assumed that logistics was a viable growth industry and that it provided social benefits for the region's residents. Both of these claims were part of the ideological toolkit that regional leaders used to expand the geographic reach of logistics development.

NEW REGIONAL LOGICS

Port boosters used their publicly subsidized funds to modernize shipping facilities near the docks. Many of the initial projects focused on updating existing technologies to keep up with shifts in the logistics industry. This included building new facilities that accommodated bigger shipments. In fact, the ability to accommodate massive post-Panamax ships, which can carry more than eight thousand TEUs, made the San Pedro Bay a lucrative gateway choice for shippers looking to transport large quantities of containers from Asian markets to the continental United States; something other ports, like those in the Bay Area, were struggling to keep up with. Large ship capacity is just one of the factors that enabled the San Pedro Bay ports to capture 56 percent of containerized Asian imports by 2005.[41] Port leaders also implemented strategies like the Pier Pass Program, which increased capacity by moving more traffic to off-peak hours.[42] While these changes successfully increased capacity, policy makers were convinced that the existing trade infrastructure would not meet the region's future needs.

Port expansion continued in the 2000s, but Southern California faced mounting competition from other regions, including Canada and the East Coast. Boosters cited the increased competition from other ports to further consolidate public support for regional logistics. Local leaders were especially concerned that the expansion of the Panama Canal, scheduled to be completed by 2015, would allow East Coast ports to siphon off future trade, away from Southern California.[43] Concerns mounted in 2003 when the Panama Canal Authority forged a strategic marketing alliance that openly encouraged shippers to bypass West Coast ports. The alliance was meant to "spur investment, increase trade and promote the 'All-Water-Route' (the route from Asia to the U.S. East and Gulf Coasts via the Panama Canal)."[44] Canal leaders signed memorandums of understanding with ten U.S. ports, including the Port Authority of New York and New Jersey, the Georgia Ports Authority, and the South Carolina State Ports Authority.[45] The partnership was another example of how entrepreneurial state actors competed with other regions for capital investment by forming new distribution networks.

Southern California's overland system of trucks and trains maintained its competitive advantages in the face of growing competition, especially among shippers who wanted an efficient JIT distribution system. West Coast distribution enabled shippers to reroute delivery trucks much more quickly than having to orchestrate the same task via ship, especially if market conditions changed while the goods were at sea. Instead, ships could deliver their goods to Southern California, where they could then be dispatched to the correct markets, all in a timelier manner than having to wait for ships to make their deliveries through the Panama Canal. A time advantage was especially enticing to shippers who managed high-value goods because it enabled them to avoid delivery interruptions. Overland distribution also provided greater protection from delays. If shipments for multiple markets are traveling on a single ship and that ship is delayed along the longer all-ocean route through the Panama Canal, then many more markets may be affected. Trucks, trains, and cross-dock facilities allow shippers to distribute the risk across different markets; fewer markets are affected if one truck is delayed than when an entire ship loaded with containers is delayed. Southern California ports capitalized on these flexible management techniques and gained a competitive advantage over other regions.

Nonetheless, Southern California's port boosters used mounting port competition to seek federal support for logistics development. This was especially true when Canadian port leaders—including government actors—aggressively courted shippers by launching a multi-million-dollar marketing campaign aimed directly at Southern California. In 2009 Geraldine Knatz, then the executive director for the POLA, responded to the campaign by declaring, "We're not going to sit around and let Canada steal our business."[46] Knatz's unequivocal performance—of port official as entrepreneurial agent—allowed her to jump multiple geographical scales. By invoking a foreign threat, she linked her job as a local, quasi-public representative to the ports, the region, the state, and the nation. Knatz and other regional leaders pushed for a national freight movement infrastructure policy to act as a foil against the perceived intrusion from the north, an appeal that harkened back to the Alameda Corridor project of the 1980s.

Private sector members of the logistics regime, including the National Retail Federation, the Pacific Merchant Shipping Association, and the Retail Industry Leaders Association, pursued their own federal policies because they believed that centralized strategic plans were needed to overcome fragmented, multijurisdictional planning. For example, in a plan presented at a National Freight Transportation hearing in 2008, industry leaders claimed, "Coordination within transportation corridors can only be achieved by eliminating the piecemeal action of local governments, port authorities, and regional planning organizations."[47] They argued for coordination along "an entire transportation corridor." According to industry leaders who were present at the hearing, "This systemic perspective, which only the state can provide, must be applied to the prioritization, coordination, and oversight of infrastructure projects."

Private sector calls for more centralized planning were a response to social movement organizations (SMOs) that successfully used their political capital to win concessions from local and regional state agencies. Business leaders warned that mounting labor unrest and environmental regulations were forcing shippers to route some of their goods away from the San Pedro Bay ports. Michael Jacob, vice president of the Pacific Merchant Shipping Association, argued, "We are actually on the front end of a long-term structural change of business models where people are building their supply chains around California."[48] This threat narrative was also used to warn policy makers that failure to build enough infrastructure to meet future import projections would result in the loss of tax dollars and jobs to competing cities.[49] The underlying message was also clear: business leaders warned that efforts by unions, environmental groups, and liberal politicians to rein in logistics development would result in economic disaster. Such claims sounded like earlier probusiness warnings meant to throttle progressive forces by threatening that factories would move to less-regulated terrain.[50] The threat of capital abandonment was meant to discipline both social movements and progressive members of the local state. The warning was obvious: stop your demands for environmental justice and living wages or we'll take our business somewhere else.

GREENING THE PORTS

The logistics regime embraced a green growth doctrine as a political compromise that would allow the ports to grow while dealing with some of the environmental issues that were being raised by SMOs. Several SMOs established themselves as viable opponents to the logistics regime by arguing that dogged pursuit of a port-based development policy agenda without also accounting for economic and environmental justice was shortsighted and damaging to the public good. Unions and environmental organizations used their growing political clout to challenge dominant neoliberal development narratives, including the idea that logistics represented an upward mobility path for blue-collar workers and poor residents. Instead, SMOs reframed the spatial politics of Southern California's logistics regime by casting goods movement as a dangerous and poverty-inducing industry. An example of how this occurred can be traced back to the early 2000s during policy debates about future port expansion, when some politicians began to question how logistics expansion would affect local communities, especially those located near the ports. The following exchange between Long Beach congresswoman Juanita Millender-McDonald and Executive Director for the Port of Los Angeles Larry Keller highlights how environmental concerns inserted themselves into the production of Southern California's logistics landscape:

> Congresswoman Millender-McDonald: But are you saying that right now we are going to have a 700 percent increase in cargo with the dredging of both 400 and 300 pier completed, we will go into 24 million tons of cargo? Explain that to me.
> Mr. Keller: Congresswoman, our cargo has increased 700 percent since the early 1980's and in the next 20 years—the two ports right now are putting through about 10 million containers, imports and exports. By the year 2020, we expect that number to rise to 24 million—from 10 million to 24 million. We are not, by any means, done with our development between the two ports. We have additional landfills consolidations and dredging projects in order to allow the larger ships to come in.
> Congresswoman Millender-McDonald: Uh-huh, absolutely. That is why it is so critically important that we make sure that the air, the quality of the environment is conducive to your continuing that, because we are looking forward to that, as we talk about international trade and other entities that will help us in our economic vitality.[51]

This exchange occurred in April 2001 during a congressional hearing on governmental reform. The interaction between Congresswoman Milliner-McDonald and Mr. Keller was particularly poignant because she had played a key role in supporting the Alameda Corridor project during the 1980s. More important, her comments indicated a specific political strategy that enabled future growth if port officials and private business interests paid attention to and mitigated negative environmental outcomes. This was not an antidevelopment intervention. In fact, it created a new path by linking effective environmental mitigation with progrowth policies. The result was a type of green development politics that adopted a pro-environment discourse while seeking technical solutions to possible negative effects. The underlying strategy hinted at by the congresswoman would shape how SMOs contested the unfettered expansion of the logistics regime.

Port leaders needed a green growth strategy because they were liable for environmental and health damages caused by the logistics industry. While the logistics regime touted tremendous trade growth as a positive outcome for the region, such rapid expansion also raised flags about the capacity to absorb the onslaught of new commodity shipments. The 700 percent increase in cargo mentioned by Larry Keller was an astonishing amount, because such vast quantities placed new burdens on the region's environment. Consider the amount of space required to move ten million twenty-foot containers in the early 2000s. Volume created a spatial problem. Where did they intend to put all the stuff that was being imported, and how were they going to minimize environmental health damage in a densely populated urban area? At the time, most of the vehicles used to move those containers operated on diesel fuel, a deadly and cancer-causing toxin. By 2008 approximately thirty-seven hundred Californians were dying from cancer caused by exposure to logistics-related diesel emissions.[52] Many more, eighteen thousand, died annually from exposure to ambient levels of diesel particulate matter. SMO activists used these diesel-related deaths as a counternarrative to push back against the logistics growth regime. Environmental justice activists argued that port expansion was disproportionately affecting parts of the region with high concentrations of poor, Black, and Latinx residents.[53]

The notion that logistics represented a danger as well as an economic solution became more salient in 2006, when several labor and environmental groups formed the Coalition for Clean and Safe Ports (CCSP). Key SMO leaders joined the CCSP after labor unions reached out to environmental organizations for support during a port trucker organizing campaign. While the CCSP's genesis occurred during a union organizing drive, environmental justice organizations transformed and expanded its scope and scale. The CCSP was staffed by members of the Los Angeles Alliance for a New Economy (LAANE), a policy group responsible for promoting the city's 1997 Living Wage ordinance. LAANE functioned as an intermediary among unions, community, and environmental organizations. Staff members helped to build a coalition of fifty organizations. Madeline Janis, LAANE's then executive director and a Los Angeles Harbor commissioner, cited this broad alliance as a key reason for CCSP's effectiveness. According to Janis, "The labor movement brought more political capital to the table. . . . But the environmental movement brought a lot of political credibility to the table."[54] Part of this credibility included much wider support for environmental concerns and regulations.

Members of the CCSP believed that reframing the port as a contested site, where social, economic, and environmental justice had to be negotiated, would enable them to scale up their individual and multisite organizing efforts.[55] They wanted to move beyond site- and issue-specific battles to address port expansion on a regional scale. It was a feasible strategy because the creation of a regional logistics regime, one in which SMOs could leverage some political power, enabled them to seek concessions from the state in return for greater cooperation on future growth. Geraldine Knatz claimed that even if negotiations with the CCSP on expansion projects were slowed, they were a necessary step toward cleaning up the ports. Knatz acknowledged "that some cargo has been diverted because of what we are trying to accomplish here. . . . [B]ut there is no way we would have been able to move forward with all these construction projects if not for the steps we are taking to reduce pollution."[56]

The SMOs successfully challenged the logistics regime because they increased their currency as political actors during the late 1990s and early 2000s.[57] Their influence grew as California became a more liberal electorate. Unions and other progressive political forces capitalized on California's changing demographics and mobilized their resources to elect friendly government representatives. Union and community support was especially important in electing progressive politicians, including former Los Angeles mayor Antonio Villaraigosa and Karen Bass, former leader of California's legislature. The CCSP coalition mobilized these political assets to pressure the ports into passing the San Pedro Bay Clean Air Action Plan (CAAP) in November 2006.[58] Port officials adopted the CAAP—which included environmental and labor provisions—as a preemptive strategy. The LA Harbor Commission also passed the Clean Trucks Program (CTP) in March 2008. Both the CAAP and the CTP enabled the logistics growth regime to plan for future expansion while minimizing the threat of potential environmental litigation by CCSP members.

According to the CTP, sixteen thousand diesel trucks had to be replaced or retrofitted for the port to reach 2007 EPA emission standards. The CTP also included a provision that required trucking companies to hire drivers as direct employees rather than as subcontracted labor. Members of the Change to Win Labor federation, led by the International Brotherhood of Teamsters (IBT), pushed for the provision to mitigate against federal labor law that made organizing contingent workers onerous. It was a strategic effort to bypass federal employment law by shifting the scale to local government. The move symbolized how local social movements turned to regional policy to solve some of the juridical limitations associated with national labor law.[59]

While business interests reluctantly embraced the CTP's environmental provisions, they fought hard against the labor rules. Instead they pushed for a green economy model that did not include labor rights. Company leaders balked at the provision that reclassified truckers as direct-hire employees, because the change in employment status would make it easier for truckers to join a union. Industry leaders, including the American Trucking Association (ATA), tried to drive a wedge between environmental organizations and labor unions in an effort to remove the labor rules from the CTP. A representative of the ATA claimed that environmental and community organizations had been "hoodwinked" by labor under this "very strange alliance."[60] Trucking representatives claimed that labor rights had nothing to do with cleaning the environment and launched a public campaign to undermine organized labor's policy approach. ATA spokesperson Clayton Boyce tried to split the strategic merger between labor and the environment, declaring, "We support the environmental goals of the Clean Truck Program, including the container fee for financing the replacement of older trucks, the banning of older trucks and the truck registry. . . . We have only opposed the . . . concession plans."[61] The ATA filed suit against both the ports of Long Beach and Los Angeles in an effort to overturn the CTP concession agreement. Lawyers for the association claimed that the concession plans violated the Federal Aviation Administration Authorization Act of 1994 because they "regulate the 'price, route or service' of the trucking operations at the port."[62] According to the concession agreements, trucking companies would have to obtain permits to operate at the ports, which meant that they had to comply with hiring provisions that required all drivers to be employees. In the end, even though SMOs were able to pass progressive local policies, trucking companies managed to supersede the local scale by turning to federal litigation. Court rulings effectively nullified the employment provision and dealt a blow to the labor contingent of the CCSP.[63]

If part of the logistics regime tried to push back against the growing influence of social movements, another element tried to pivot away from contentious near-port expansion fights by seeking alternative spatial solutions. Regional planners hoped to avoid the contentious politics of near-dock and thus dense logistics development by using LA's metropolitan hinterland to absorb future port container traffic. New shipping technologies and sheer volume required a more extensive strategy that included securing large quantities of additional space, something difficult to come by in LA's congested urban core.[64] Shippers, for example, began to favor integrated inland distribution networks, which allowed them to serve a dispersed consumer base.[65]

In response, the two governing bodies directly responsible for managing the ports orchestrated a campaign to build a distribution network capable of delivering record levels of imported goods to both regional and national markets. They would do so by maximizing port capacity and by extending the region's distribution complex into its inland hinterland.[66] Los Angeles's urban hinterland offered shippers and port interests a way to quickly externalize some of the constraints associated with a land-intensive industry. The president of the Southern California Distribution Management Association summed up this relationship: "[I]f you take a look at the port, they don't have land near the port, the DCs [distribution centers in the Inland Empire] offer cheap land." Planning documents described the Inland Empire as "attractive to warehousing and distribution centers because it has areas of land available for large (one million plus square feet) facilities—something that is in short supply throughout other portions of the MCGMAP study area."[67] According to SCAG planners the Inland Empire was capable of absorbing more than 50 percent of the warehouse space needed for future port expansion. The region's cheap land and labor could support an extensive inland distribution network that allowed metropolitan Los Angeles to capture a greater portion of Asian commodity shipments. Figure 8 shows how inland warehouses fit into the global distribution ecosystem.

Inland solutions posed new environmental threats to local residents, especially because they relied on diesel trucks to move goods to and from the region's warehouse ecosystem.[68] Consequently, inland residents were burdened with a disproportionate load of deadly environmental toxins. For example, the South Coast Air Quality Management District's (SCAQMD) *MATES III* study found that 50 percent of the U.S. residents who breathed

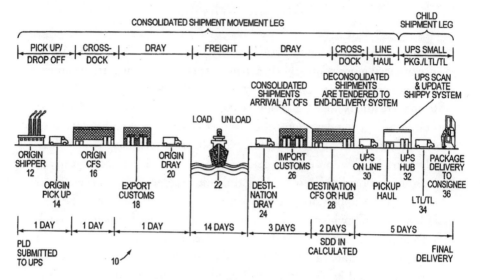

FIGURE 8. A typical integrated global shipment system. U.S. patent 7761348 B2.

unhealthy levels of PM 2.5—a diesel exhaust artifact—resided within the Inland Empire basin as of 2008.[69] Diesel trucks and trains were the main culprits.

Diesel trucks accounted for 30 to 40 percent of traffic congestion in the Southern California region at the height of the logistics boom.[70] Logistics traffic increased health risks to residents near intermodal yards, warehouses, and roadways because fine particulate air toxins are more heavily concentrated near their source. The *MATES III* study found that diesel-related cancer risks follow mobile sources like trucks, ships, and railyards. SCAQMD also found a direct correlation between increased air toxics risk and growing container volume at the ports. In total, the ports were responsible for producing 20 percent of the region's diesel particulate pollution; this made them the single largest source of pollution in Southern California.[71] Rising diesel exhaust was troublesome because it accounted for 84 percent of pollution-related local cancer risks and 83.6 percent of Southern California's air pollution.[72] Airborne pollution caused approximately 2,339 cancer cases in Southern California during 2005 (see table 1). Fontana residents had the highest pollution-related cancer risk among the ten sites that were measured by a SCAQMD study in 2007.[73]

Regional solutions like the proposed Inland Port reveal the limits of aggregate level data that fail to account for unequal burdens tied to intrare-

TABLE 1. Diesel-Related Cancer Cases, 2005

Place	Total Population	Cases Per Million	Total Cancer Cases
Riverside	1,923,731	485	933
San Bernardino	1,974,119	712	1,406
Inland Empire	3,897,850	—	2,339

SOURCE: Author's analysis of SCAQMD (2008) data.

gional differentiation. SCAG data clearly showed that San Bernardino County accounted for 24 percent of all truck miles traveled in 2003. Riverside County accounted for 18 percent, and Los Angeles captured 33 percent. Combined, the Inland Empire represented 42 percent of all truck miles traveled in Southern California during 2003.[74] Consequently, any plan to build an inland port by diverting more truck traffic to the Inland Empire would increase the region's environmental burden by pushing more deadly diesel into Riverside and San Bernardino Counties.

Environmental and community activists in the Inland Empire claimed that regional solutions—which reduced pressure on poor communities near the ports—simply shifted the toxic burden to marginalized communities in Riverside and San Bernardino Counties. A major Inland Empire environmental justice leader publicly admonished some of her coastal peers at a national gathering of port-based environmental organizations, vehemently declaring that the POLA "is not the center of the world."[75] She went on to explain her frustration with port-based growth strategies that helped protect coastal communities while failing to mitigate against the negative environmental effects of greater warehouse and diesel truck traffic in Riverside and San Bernardino Counties. Penny Newman, founder and leader of the Inland Valley–based Center for Community Action and Environmental Justice, urged social movement leaders to take a broader view of the logistics industry. She cautioned that "the port doesn't just create good jobs, the jobs in the Inland Valley are not good jobs, they are temporary, they are low wage, and they are disappearing because they are being automated." Instead of focusing on the ports, she asked the assembled labor and environmental justice activists to see goods movement as a larger system that reproduced disparities across differentiated space. Newman and other inland activists argued that Latinx communities in the Inland Empire functioned as the regional dumping ground for port-based development. Likewise, Redlands Democratic assemblyman Bill Emerson described the port-hinterland relationship by saying that while "a big part of the economy in Southern California is goods movement. . . . [W]e . . . pay the price with our health."[76]

The push to move inland was spearheaded by train and truck company lobbyists. Train-based strategies were a boon to rail companies; they supported the idea that trains provided a more environmentally and consumer-friendly way of moving goods, especially when compared to trucks. Rail companies used these claims to lobby for increased public support. Some succeeded by forming strong public-private partnerships to build integrated logistics centers (ILCs), which leveraged the state's land-use powers and public subsidies to develop large-scale projects.[77] Federal and state spending on both rail and highway infrastructure enabled rail companies to build inland ports in places like North Carolina, Virginia, Texas, and California. The inland proposal embraced rail as a solution to diesel-related community health problems because it reduced truck traffic in densely populated LA County neighborhoods. However, plans to increase near and on-dock rail did so by pushing more diesel truck traffic into inland counties. One plan in particular called for building an inland port that would process container trains from the ports and deliver them to distribution centers in the Inland Empire. According to SCAG, the proposed inland port would potentially divert between 12 and 22 percent of all port-related truck traffic away from major urban corridors.[78] Port boosters argued that fewer truck trips could increase port throughput by lowering congestion and thus shortening travel time for those trucks that remained on the local roadways. Shifting such operations to an inland port would reduce diesel emissions and road congestion for LA County residents by subjecting Riverside and San Bernardino county residents to more truck traffic and diesel pollution.

Trains remain the key to the region's transcontinental long-haul transport system. Southern California's two main rail companies are the Union Pacific and the Burlington Northern Santa Fe (BNSF). BNSF has one main artery, the Transcon, which runs from San Bernardino to downtown Los Angeles. The Transcon connects the region to all other major markets in the BNSF system. According to company representatives, BNSF invested approximately $115 million in its LA area operations during 2008. Some of these funds paid for twenty-one miles of new rail lines that expanded the company's densest route between Los Angeles and Chicago.[79] The Union Pacific has two main lines that travel through the San Bernardino and Los Angeles region. One line, the Sunset Corridor, links the region to Texas. The South Central Line connects the region to Nevada and beyond. Union Pacific's Colton Crossing facility, where its two rail lines intersect, became a major source of transcontinental and local gridlock. Logistics supporters used this crossing as an example of why public and private investment was needed.

WHEN THE BUBBLE BURST

The global financial crisis of 2008 cast doubt on the long-term viability of future port projections. Total imports declined from a national high of $2.1 trillion in 2008 to $1.5 trillion in 2009.[80] Nonetheless, port boosters were not dissuaded. Even the fleet of more than three hundred container ships that were idle in February 2009, with a combined capacity of 350,000 TEUs, didn't dampen their resolve to further expand port capacity.[81] Some used the impending crisis in their favor by doubling down on infrastructure investment and by pushing back against further environmental and labor regulations. It amounted to a strategy of persistent investment even in the face of economic crisis and based on erroneous, speculative data. Richard Steinke, executive director for the POLA, supported more investment in port capacity by arguing that "even with today's economic slowdown we foresee long-term growth in trade that will support many more trade related jobs in this region."[82] Steinke's sentiments mirrored those of private investors, who continued to press for port expansion. According to an analyst with Moody's Investor Service, "long-term expectation is that the global economy will continue to grow, trade will continue to prosper and the current downturn will really be an opportunity, or a challenge, for ports to position themselves competitively for that continued growth going forward."[83]

Steinke supported the Middle Harbor Project, which went before the Long Beach City Council in May 2009. Long Beach's Harbor Department allocated more than $1.5 billion from its reserves to pay for new expansion projects, including the Middle Harbor plan, during 2009 and 2010.[84] Likewise, the POLA announced that it too would spend money on infrastructure capacity during the economic downturn. For example, the port supported a $200 million expansion of the China Shipping Terminal to add more than 1.5 million TEUs in total capacity.[85]

Labor unions and business organizations, including the Pacific Merchants Shipping Association, applauded these port expansion projects as a long-term economic development strategy. Rich Dines, president of the International Longshore and Warehouse Union (ILWU) Southern California District

Council, cited potential jobs to encourage spending on port-related infra-structure. Dines urged Long Beach Council members to endorse the Middle Harbor project: "We know this redevelopment will not only help support the hundreds of thousands of regional jobs directly related to the ports but will add many thousands more, improving the local economy while helping fami-lies in the community and businesses both large and small."[86]

While the economic crisis did not deter port authorities from pursuing a logistics-based development strategy, it did force them to revise their once ebullient forecasts. The same 2007 projections that were used to argue that more logistics capacity was needed no longer applied in the post-2008 crisis. Port authorities had routinely argued that further infrastructure improve-ments were needed for the San Pedro Bay ports to reach a potential forty-three million TEU capacity by 2023. Yet planners were forced to revise these forecasts when port activity declined between 2006 and 2008. For example, TEU traffic for 2010 fell 36.8 percent short of the expected projections made in 2007.

The Great Recession of 2008 provided shippers with new tools to chip away at regulatory policies. Logistics analysts repeatedly blamed port fees, organized labor, and an unfriendly business climate for a 5 percent loss in market share for the San Pedro Bay ports between 2006 and 2009.[87] MAERSK, a major carrier for Walmart, cited labor negotiations and conges-tion as factors that affected its decision to move some discretionary cargo to the port of Seattle. Port authorities conceded to their critics by reducing fees and offering incentives. Both Los Angeles and Long Beach adopted per-container fee reductions for all shipments that used rail for transport to or from the port. The incentives were intended to keep any more nonlocal con-tainer cargo (discretionary cargo) from moving to other ports. It was a major incentive because intermodal rail accounts for approximately 41 percent of all TEU containers that move through the POLA.[88]

SCENE 2

Precarious Labor

ON MAY 28, 2009, A GROUP OF PEOPLE gathered around a large red truck and desperately tried to stop it from plowing into a crowded intersection.[1] The crowd was there to protect a collection of warehouse workers and community organizers who had driven a forklift into an intersection, sat down, and locked arms to block one of the busiest truck corridors in Southern California (see figure 9). Horns blared as traffic backed up onto two freeway on-ramps that fed a nearby cluster of warehouses. The truck's driver, a scruffy, middle-aged white man, grew angrier as warehouse worker supporters refused to let him through the protest line. He repeatedly revved his engine and tried to force protestors out of the way by lurching his truck forward. A short teenage girl and a weathered old priest were the only obstacles preventing the driver from plowing through the assembled demonstrators; both planted themselves directly in the truck's path.

A few protestors tried to talk the driver down by urging him to think about the safety of the men, women, and children whose bodies formed a protective chain around the intersection. Yet the more they talked, the angrier he became. After several frenzied exchanges the driver finally inched the truck forward and threatened to run over the priest and the young girl if they did not, "Get the fuck out of the way!" But they did not budge. Instead of retreating, the teenager raised her "Invisible No More!" banner higher into the air. She returned the driver's threat with a defiant glare. Meanwhile, the old priest responded by laying his hands on the hood of the truck as he whispered a series of prayers to himself (see figure 10). The driver snapped. He punched the gas and smashed through the protest line. Someone from the crowd quickly reached over, pulled the girl and the priest out of the way and kept them from being crushed by the surging truck. Protestors did not allow

FIGURE 9. "Invisible No More." Warehouse workers use a forklift to block major truck intersection. Photo by Mark Ralston, Getty Images.

FIGURE 10. Father Fernando Santillana and a small group try to stop an angry truck driver from ramming into protestors. Photo by Mark Ralston, Getty Images.

the truck to break their line. They hurriedly closed the gap left behind by the enraged driver and continued to hold the line for more than an hour, until a battalion of local riot police showed up and retook the intersection.

Disrupting the flow of traffic was only one of several goals for the action. Organizers were also trying to make warehouse work a more visible part of the logistics industry. By placing themselves in the flow of traffic, warehouse workers were challenging development narratives that cast them as cheap and malleable labor for the major retailers who had made inland Southern California into one of the largest warehouse hubs in the country. The stories in this section show that putting their bodies on the line was nothing new; they did it every day by working in dangerous conditions to deliver goods into the hands of waiting consumers.

FOUR

The Circuits of Capital

IT IS NOW TIME TO EXAMINE how global economic restructuring and the geographic expansion of commodity chains that was discussed in previous chapters affected the everyday lives of logistics workers. At its core the field of logistics amounts to the integration of physical transport modes (ships, containers, trucks) with information-based inventory control (computer tracking, order processing, delivery information). Many of the most important logistics innovations emerged from this intersection between the physical movement of goods and the efficient coordination of data.

This chapter examines how companies cut costs and added value to their logistics operations by employing new technologies and scientific labor management techniques. Among these technologies were barcodes, radio-frequency identification (RFID), and computer tracking software.[1] Retailers utilized such technologies to develop sophisticated inventory systems and point-of-sale (POS) information databases that allowed them to implement JIT production and distribution business models. While it is important to understand how these technologies functioned, I am more interested in how they transformed the nature of work. For example, in addition to new technologies, retailers and third-party logistics (3PL) companies or subcontractors also created JIT labor management practices that had a profound effect on the everyday lives of warehouse workers. Less time and more goods became the operating mantra for JIT retailers as they pursued their strategy of shorter commodity cycles and dispersed production chains by implementing new logistics technologies and flexible labor markets.

Many of the technological innovations and management practices that transformed modern retailing were invented and implemented by a skilled class of workers. These logisticians emerged as key producers of value within modern business systems because they reduced costs and maximized supply chain efficiencies. Logistics was especially important to companies that adopted a total systems analysis.[2] Such business models required more labor control and discipline to achieve tighter coordination among geographically dispersed supplies, production facilities, and consumers. Once disregarded as a nonproductive element of accumulation, logistics became a core component of corporate business models as more companies utilized extended global production networks.

Companies that adopted logistics-driven business models gained a competitive advantage by bridging the virtual world of product information with the physical spaces of commodity distribution. The most successful firms developed intricate information networks that enabled them to deliver products quickly by instantaneously matching consumer demand with dispersed supply chains. Walmart, for example, invented several distribution practices that transformed logistics work and the retail sector. The company used its supply chain innovations to achieve global retail dominance by combining lean production techniques and JIT delivery models with low everyday prices.[3] Its POS data system enabled it to maximize supply chain efficiencies by employing an inventory control regime that synchronized customer demand with product supply.[4] The system deployed technologies like bar codes and centralized computers to give retailers real-time information about which products were selling at particular stores. Computer software detected potential stock shortages when an item was selling quickly and automatically ordered more of those goods from suppliers. Its logistics system gave Walmart the capacity to maintain a dynamic inventory by ordering products that were selling well while not being saddled with slow-moving goods.

Walmart's logistics innovations gave it a competitive advantage that it used to gain market share and increase its purchasing power with suppliers. Company executives, especially under the guidance of Sam Walton, leveraged their clout to demand greater concessions from manufacturers. The retailer acquired so much purchasing power that it eventually gained the ability to decide what got made, when goods were shipped, and how they were distributed.[5] This shifting balance of power was on full display in 2010 when Walmart assumed complete control of the supply chain by forcing suppliers to use its truck fleet. Some suppliers balked at having to use Walmart trucks to deliver goods from their factories to the company's distribution centers. Walmart dismissed complaints by claiming that its trucks were more efficient. A Walmart representative explained that the decision "allowed our suppliers to focus on what they do best, manufacturing products for us."[6] The underlying message was clear: suppliers were expected to serve Walmart's needs. Manufacturers had little choice but to comply, especially when they relied on big Walmart contracts for the majority of their business. Suppliers effectively became at-will production plants for Walmart's global JIT empire. Other merchants, Target and Amazon, for example, followed in Walmart's footsteps and used their own logistics strategies to establish themselves as powerful procurers of global goods.

LOGISTICS LABOR REGIMES

Modern warehouses were among the innovations that transformed commodity circulation during the logistics revolution. Warehouses are a fusion of the old need to sort and store physical goods on their way to market with the new technological systems aimed at shortening the time that a product spends traveling between the factory and its eventual consumer. Unlike older warehouses, which served as storage facilities for goods awaiting sale, more contemporary warehouses function as distribution hubs that minimize or eliminate commodity storage.[7] Warehouse operations vary by size, sector, and company, especially because firms often rely on proprietary computer systems and corporate-specific management practices. Nevertheless, contemporary distribution centers fulfill two distinct functions. First, the cavernous megawarehouses that dominate so much of inland Southern California's landscape serve as agglomeration sites for consumer goods. When used in this way, a typical inland warehouse receives shipping containers from the port, usually delivered via diesel trucks. Workers then unload these goods and organize them into holding bins. Goods are normally stored for short periods of time and are eventually assembled into orders that are shipped to stores or individual consumers.

The second major function comes in the form of the cross-dock facility. Cross-docks are the epitome of JIT delivery because they are supposed to eliminate the storage and order picking functions that made older warehouses

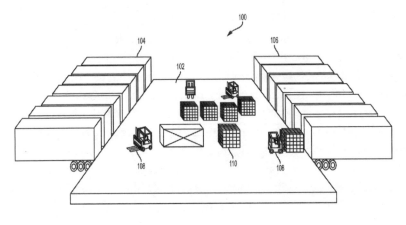

FIGURE 11. Patented cross-dock model. U.S. patent number 9367827 B1.

less efficient. Goods are delivered from the port, unloaded at the inland cross-dock, and broken into smaller batches that are then loaded with other goods into waiting trucks. A typical cross-dock facility includes receiving, sorting, and shipping functions. Trucks deliver shipping containers filled with goods to the cross-dock, and workers use forklifts or their bodies to unload those containers (see figure 11). Pedro worked at Walmart's cross-dock in Mira Loma and described a typical workday: "I loaded and unloaded boxes all day. A truck would arrive and we had to unload it, by hand. Every kind of product, shoes, clothes, microwave ovens."[8] Rather than store these goods, workers move certain items into trucks that are bound for home or store deliveries. Goods are not stored for prolonged periods; they are simply unloaded, moved across the loading dock, and put onto outbound trucks.[9] Cross-docks were especially suitable for JIT distribution systems because they applied scientific management techniques, dynamic market information, and rapid response logistics techniques to reduce redundant inventory.

Modern distribution centers and JIT cross-docks transformed the nature of logistics work. Many of the workers who were interviewed for this study pointed out that the same scientific management techniques that logisticians used to expedite the movement of commodities were also applied to human bodies. Like the Taylorist time and motion studies that dominated early industrial engineering, companies applied new surveillance technologies and management systems to monitor labor productivity among warehouse workers.[10] Modern logistics was simply the latest iteration of scientific

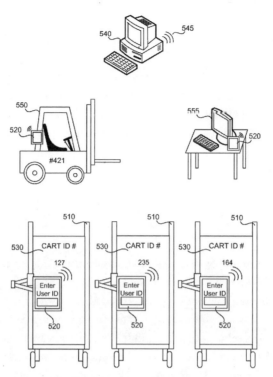

FIGURE 12. Warehouse management systems enable labor surveillance and discipline. U.S. patent application 20130211977.

management practices that, according to C. S. Maier, "extended Taylorism into all areas of labour productivity, technological efficiency, and even corporate organization."[11]

One example of how this happened was through the use of productivity quotas and surveillance. New logistics technologies let companies track individual worker production by allowing them to measure the total number of boxes that each employee moved from one place to another. Logisticians utilized this tracking information to enforce labor production quotas for individual workers. The technology made it easier for supervisors to conduct real-time monitoring. José, an immigrant warehouse worker, explained how management deployed such technologies to control labor productivity: "Well, really they don't tell us nothing because we have a computer that tells us what to do. And right there they can see through the computer who's moving fast and who's not."[12] Figure 12 shows what a typical computerized warehouse looks like. Workers like José receive instructions from mobile computers and personal digital displays that are connected to supply chain management networks. These same technologies are used to track the location of both workers and goods. Even as José hints at a hands-off management style by saying that supervisors do not give them direct orders, the ever-present surveillance of computer-enabled technologies means that today's warehouse workers are subject to continuous electronic monitoring and discipline. Warehouse workers understood that they, like the boxes they loaded and unloaded, were part of a complex supply chain that demanded breakneck speed.

JUST-IN-TIME WAREHOUSES

Human and commodity tracking technologies also made it possible for logisticians to develop flexible labor systems that delivered an adequate number of workers when and where they were needed. Cross-docking and product tracking were especially important because they made it possible for retailers to introduce high-velocity business models, which increased sales by reducing shelf life and product turnover times.[13] Toyota was an innovator in this field. It implemented a cross-docking network because company officials needed to coordinate high-frequency but low-volume supply shipments to multiple production facilities. Parts suppliers could not efficiently manage small-volume shipments to a large list of geographically dispersed production plants, a need that increased with the implementation of JIT supply chains. Cross-docking provided a solution because it allowed suppliers to ship larger batches to one centralized location. The cross-dock would then break these larger shipments into smaller ones and send them on their way to specific plants. As a result, Toyota could achieve economies of scale while maintaining a decentralized, JIT production model.[14]

The Toyota case exemplifies how JIT innovations transformed both the nature of and geographic location of logistics work. Cross-docks relocated old shipping functions like break-bulk work that was once done on the docks. Older methods required stevedores to unload ships by breaking up pallets of bulk goods and organizing them into smaller batches. Both break-bulk work and cross-docking enable small batches from multiple producers to be consolidated into one large delivery. Retailers also benefited from this arrangement because it allowed them to receive large volume discounts from vendors, while maintaining the ability to break these large orders into smaller shipments to individual stores. One result was that retailers could respond to fluctuating and dispersed consumer demand without being saddled with large orders and stagnant inventories in locations that were not selling merchandise.

Walmart implemented an incredibly successful cross-docking strategy. Its success was partly due to the company's proprietary satellite communications system and truck fleet, which provided tight integration between digital inventory information and the physical movement of goods. Consequently, Walmart could track and deliver large quantities of specific goods to stores that were not encumbered by high inventories. Cross-docking was such an innovative practice that Walmart used it to reduce costs, lower prices, and ultimately surpass K-Mart in sales. Company officials cited cross-docking as a core capability in Walmart's supply chain that allowed it to deploy a demand-driven, small-batch shipment, and low-inventory retail model.[15] Other retailers also integrated cross-docking into their business frameworks.[16] Cross-docking strategies were particularly useful to high-value and small-batch importers, who shipped more expensive commodities such as electronic gadgets into major ports and then consolidated/deconsolidated these goods into smaller shipments at regional distribution centers.[17]

Cross-docks also provided retailers with new opportunities to outsource some functions to offshore labor. For example, shippers began to subcontract their marketing and packaging operations to overseas companies. This process, known as prepacking, involves taking bulk products from suppliers and packaging them for display and sale.[18] Workers must take the bulk items that were shipped from the factory (e.g., kitchen knives), assemble them into sets or kits, and then repackage them for display. Most of this work used to be done in U.S. warehouses, but 3PL companies began offering prepacking services and gave retailers the option of sending more store-ready products to cross-docks. These store-ready products require less handling by American workers and thus cut labor costs.[19]

While the nimbler cross-dock was a significant innovation in the leaner world of JIT logistics, large-scale distribution centers did not go away. In fact, one of the most striking visual aspects of Southern California's landscape is the sheer size of newer warehouses; many are massive, windowless buildings that measure more than one million square feet. Super-sized warehouses were part of a national trend that emerged between 1990 and 2010. On average, the typical warehouse size increased from 173,592 square feet in 1997 to 308,034 square feet in 2006.[20] According to the same data, distribution centers larger than 500,000 square feet accounted for 22 percent of all warehouses as of 2008. Larger warehouses were economically feasible because new RFID tracking technologies and sophisticated computerized inventory control systems made them into efficient spaces for storing goods. The ability to track individual items on a computerized grid meant that boxes could be stored and retrieved more efficiently, even in cavernous warehouses. These same technologies also encouraged firms to subcontract more of their distribution operations to 3PLs because they could use logistics systems to track and coordinate goods without having to assume the overhead costs of maintaining and operating large warehouses. Subcontractors grew adept at designing proprietary computer software and labor systems that improved distribution efficiencies. One result is that retailers were able to shop around for the cheapest and most efficient warehouse operators. Competition increased as 3PLs tried to lure retailers by developing new ways to manage the physical space of goods with the virtual space of market information. Some 3PLs are so focused on the virtual space of logistics that they never physically touch the goods they are helping to move.[21] Greater competition eventually drove prices down and ultimately increased the power that retailers had to dictate costs and operating procedures inside warehouses run by 3PLs.

The trend toward larger warehouses meant that companies could consolidate their regional operations and therefore achieve greater economies of scale. Consolidated logistics systems helped reduce redundant inventory, which was necessary in a system of smaller warehouses. Companies that chose this path required more space and produced a form of industrial sprawl that pushed construction farther inland. Firms like Whirlpool and MGA Entertainment moved out of smaller warehouses in the more mature western Inland Empire real estate market and into bigger facilities in the eastern part of the region. The Skechers shoe warehouse in Moreno Valley (discussed in chapter 8) was meant to consolidate five smaller warehouses into one regional distribution hub.

Warehouse consolidation was just one of the strategies that companies used to create more vertically integrated logistics circuits. Another strategy involved transportation companies taking advantage of federal deregulation laws during the 1980s and 1990s to create vertically integrated, multimodal shipping services. Transportation companies tried to outcompete other logistics providers by offering door-to-door multimodal shipping services that moved goods from ships, to trains, to trucks.[22] For example, Union Pacific (UP) and CSX rail teamed up to offer a transport service from Los Angeles to New York that promised delivery in less than sixty-three hours. Similarly, Union Pacific joined forces with Schneider National Trucking and J. B. Hunt trucking to offer intermodal service between Los Angeles and Chicago.[23] New door-to-door shipping services integrated once separate logistics systems into more cohesive networks. The growth of door-to-door shipping created a new sub-market for intermodal marketing companies (IMCs), which specialized in moving data rather than physical goods.[24] The IMCs developed sophisticated information systems to manage the flow of goods and information among different transportation modes. Government officials applauded these innovations. For example, Chia Shih, the associate administrator for research, technology, and analysis with the U.S. Department of Transportation, justified federal support for the sector and said that DOT researchers were "strengthening our national economy by advancing transportation technologies and creating an efficient, effective intermodal system."[25]

The next chapter describes how all of the innovations discussed so far, including JIT supply chains, motivated some warehouse workers to organize around social justice in the logistics industry.

FIVE

Cyborg Labor and the Global Logistics Matrix

SOUTHERN CALIFORNIA WAREHOUSE WORKERS launched a series of protests in 2009 as part of a strategy to reframe the spatial politics of global commodity chains and regional development. They took to the streets and demanded that global corporations be held accountable for acts of local injustice. One of their goals included a campaign to gain public support by drawing connections among themselves, consumers, and the various sites that are bound together through the extensive global commodity chains of contemporary capitalism. Workers used the same transportation conduits to remap the hidden consequences of global commodity chains by learning to tell stories that linked their daily experiences to each other and to the public that consumes the goods they process in the region's warehouses.

Stories are more than just anecdotes. They also provide nuance and context to what traditional aggregate data can't tell us. "Stories are what we live in," and "in them" as Naomi Klein explained, "we find both our worlds and ourselves."[1] Workers' stories or testimonios provide a methodological tool to overcome hegemonic academic practices that limit who and what is valued. Chicanx scholars have used *corridos* and *testimonios* to recover history that is otherwise erased or negated by dominant narratives.[2] When combined with a more critical data perspective, the everyday *testimonios* of direct hire and temporary warehouse workers give us another way to read the global logistics landscape that transformed post-1980s Southern California.

Telling stories became a political act, because workers used their bodies to provide an alternative spatial imaginary that challenged the erasure of low-wage warehouse work. Worker stories provided counter-data that implicated diesel trucks, trains, and ships in the poisoning and premature death of poor

Black and Brown communities. They named ports, roads, and warehouses as spaces of dispossession that were made possible through their own erasure as valuable subjects. Stories were political tools because they insisted that warehouse workers had a right to live and thrive as human beings. The declaration that one is alive and present can be a powerful force in the face of a system that refuses to acknowledge one's humanity. In fact, "the power of dispossession works by rendering certain subjects, communities, or populations unintelligible," according to Butler and Athanasiou, "by eviscerating for them the conditions of possibility for life and the 'human' itself."[3]

It takes time and effort to undo the violence of erasure, especially when opaqueness is written into the infrastructure of everyday spaces. Most consumers are unaware of the vast distribution systems that have been erected by retailers to deliver today's hottest fashions and latest electronic gear. Even efforts to highlight how global production networks have subjected workers to harsh working conditions tend to leave distribution out of the equation. For example, organizations like the United Students Against Sweatshops and the Worker Rights Consortium launched campaigns to highlight appalling working conditions in places like Bangladesh and China.[4] These efforts forced some consumers and retailers to confront the symbolic and sometimes literal dead labor of factory workers that is embedded in the garments we wear and the things we consume. But workers from other parts of the global commodity chain are usually invisible in campaigns that focus on foreign and, less frequently, domestic production.

Even if they are left out of the globalization discourse, distribution workers are the invisible links in many of the global commodity chains that shape so much of our everyday lives. Workers' bodies, often burdened by heavy labor and large productivity quotas, illustrate how JIT distribution technologies and management techniques created new workflows and power dynamics on the warehouse floor. Yet as workers and organizers made clear, these bodies also possessed a spirit and desire that could be mobilized to provide alternative mappings, imaginaries that challenged dominant narratives of dispossession.

COUNTER-MAPPINGS

Individual and collective stories provide insight into how people make sense of the world. Such narratives are laden with cultural meaning and can provide the seeds for opposition to dominant systems.[5] In the case of logistics, personal narratives were critical to the construction of a warehouse worker identity that challenged the dominant progrowth discourse or the prologistics "regime of truth" by referencing devalued immigrant bodies as a foil against boosterish claims.[6] I use warehouse workers' stories as an epistemic bridge that connects Latinx studies and the theoretical tools of the testimonio to Clyde Woods's (2000) blues epistemology and Robin Kelley's (2003) freedom dreams by turning the body as a site of deprivation into bodies as sites of counternarratives and collective identities. These stories became the backbone of a campaign by the Change To Win labor federation to improve warehouse workers' conditions in the Inland Empire. Warehouse Workers United (WWU), a Change to Win organizing project, had been meeting with workers since 2008, when leaders from various national unions made a commitment to organize the distribution side of global commodity chains.

As I discovered through my interviews and informal conversations, much of what happened during the early phases of the campaign involved trying to figure out a narrative that could connect labor conditions inside Southern California's mega-warehouses to the business practices of global retailers. Organizers quickly realized that the very idea of what constitutes a warehouse worker had to be constructed from the disparate and fragmented stories of people who had different bosses, performed different jobs, and worked in isolation from one another; just because workers shared similar places in the production process did not signify class coherence.[7]

After knocking on countless doors and meeting with thousands of warehouse workers, organizers compiled enough stories to weave together a narrative that linked a multitude of individuals into a collective whole. Recounting everyday moments and learning to frame them within an economy of power was a key part of the organizing process. These alternative mappings challenged the sometimes dehumanizing relationships of warehouse work because they created spaces for workers to imagine that another world was possible.[8] Counter-mappings, according to Matt Garcia, have allowed "minorities to 'visualize a community' based on an alternative mode of human relations."[9] In this case, warehouse workers—through their bodies and their stories— held the campaign together by reintegrating the seemingly fragmented world of global logistics into the visible and experiential landscapes of their everyday lives. What is important in this case is that workers and organizers used this language to frame a new politics of commodity chain organizing. As a participant at a meeting between Walmart supply chain workers from Southern California, Louisiana, and Bangladesh explained, "when we come together as a supply chain . . . workers are reintegrating the economy. We may not be working under one factory roof, but by using new technologies we are beginning to organize across the supply chain."[10]

Framed this way, workers' stories function as alternative epistemologies that negate social and premature death. Woods provided us with an example of how culture and performance can serve as counternarratives. He showed how people used Black epistemologies, the blues, to challenge racist ideologies. He cited Richard Wright, who wrote from Paris in 1959, to demonstrate how cultural forms of expression like the blues negated the deadly forces of racism by laying claim to a basic form of humanity that refused both a physical and social death. Wright wrote, "Yet the most astonishing aspect of the blues is that, though [replete] with a sense of defeat and down-heartedness, they are not intrinsically pessimistic; their burden of woe and melancholy is dialectically redeemed through sheer force of sensuality, into an almost exultant affirmation of life, of love, of sex, of movement, of hope."[11]

By invoking a blues epistemology, Woods introduces the Black body not only as a marked being that is ready to be governed, controlled, and killed but as a site of resistance and desire. He demonstrates how culture and desire can move us to fight for class, racial, or gender justice or how it can simply encourage us to pursue new ways of life. Lefebvre makes a similar connection among the body, happiness, and the production of counterhegemonic space. For Lefebvre, space is important because it is how we experience collective identity and how we make the world that we want to live in. As such, he argues for the production of spaces that allow us to enjoy being human, including sex and sensuality. "For it is by means of the body that space is perceived, lived—and produced."[12] Therefore, he continues, "any revolutionary 'project' today, whether utopian or realistic, must, if it is to avoid helpless banality, make the re-appropriation of the body, in association with the re-appropriation of space, into a non-negotiable part of its agenda."

Warehouse workers launched a campaign to reclaim control of their bodies and their lives by challenging narratives that tried to erase them from existence. They used everyday life to craft spaces that enabled them to resist the alienation and violence of low-wage, precarious work. Similarly, these same spatial imaginaries helped to negate the deadly consequences of what can sometimes appear to be an abstract racial capitalism. The everyday lives of warehouse workers and the stories they tell demonstrate that another world is possible, and the ability to imagine alternative spaces is an important part of building that world. A former warehouse worker expressed both the hope and the angst of the American Dream represented by inland Southern California: "La situacion en el Inland Empire esta muy grave. Llegamos a este pais con toda la esperanza del mundo. (The situation in the Inland Empire is very serious. We came to this country filled with all the hope in the world.)"[13] The same stories, highlighted by economic and normative ideologies about the American Dream, that motivated people to clock into work every day also provided organizers with a way to refocus those aspirations.

One unexpected consequence of these stories is that workers who crafted alternative spatial imaginaries tossed aside old workplace-based union models and focused instead on regional notions of social justice. These social justice narratives tapped into immigrant aspirations by focusing on collective opportunity rather than on individual gain. A WWU organizer described how this unfolded: "There's conversations that you have in organizing immigrant workers where you don't even talk about the workplace." Instead "you talk about the homeland, you talk about the kids, you talk about their work, their job, and how it fits into the larger context of their narrative and why they're here."[14] The "why they're here" often referenced the economic mobility embodied in visions of the American Dream. Yet rather than focus on individualist notions, the campaign produced new regional narratives that centered on social and economic justice as a condition of development. They challenged dominant mappings that cast the region as a source of cheap land and cheap labor.

By demanding to be heard, warehouse workers were trying to undo an act of erasure that wiped them from the map of global capital flows. Instead, they rewrote themselves into the globalization discourse by moving beyond the usual confines of shop floor complaints to make a broader argument about economic justice, regional development, and global capital. According to them, the unmitigated flow of global capital—underwritten by Walmart, Amazon, and many other corporations—regularly subjected warehouse workers and local communities to poverty level wages, precarious employment, and deadly levels of diesel pollution. These interventions provided an alternative cognitive mapping that threatened to destabilize the logistics growth regime championed by regional boosters.

JOSÉ

Movement defines José Hernandez. His parents fled the civil war in El Salvador when he was young and brought him to the United States in search of a good job and a better life.[15] They settled in a mostly Latinx neighborhood on the outskirts of the San Gabriel Valley. But after a few years of living in the city of Baldwin Park, drugs, gangs, and other challenges of suburban LA life threatened José's family's immigrant aspirations and compelled them to move further into the suburban fringe of metropolitan Southern California. Like many Latinxs during the 1990s and 2000s, José and his family landed in the Inland Empire, where they found a home "right there on Baseline and Sierra, like the worst side of San Bernardino, the ghetto and all that even though I didn't think it was ghetto."[16]

José's family was part of a Latinx diaspora in which more than a million new people migrated into inland Southern California to seek out their generation's version of the American Dream. He eventually settled in and made a life for himself—going to school, getting a job—trying to reconcile his immigrant aspirations with the hard life that greeted him on the streets of the Inland Empire. He started his own family, and like his parents before him, pulled up stakes and made another move inland. The next place, somewhere other than where he was, always seemed to offer relief and hope. This time he landed in Colton, which was "nicer" than the ghetto of San Bernardino; it gave him and his girlfriend a chance to find a better life for their three sons. But even after all of the moving, the next place, the next job, never quite delivered. José managed to survive by taking up a string of warehouse jobs and filling orders for some of the world's largest retailers. Unfortunately for him, the wages were low and the benefits nonexistent.

The global logistics industry depends on workers like José; the order pickers and loaders who work inside modern distribution centers are the human link between the virtual space of consumer market information, where our desire for products is transmitted via electronic signals, and the physical space of commodity distribution, the material world that enables us to take possession of our goods. They are the workers of the global commodity chain matrix, a vast network of virtual space that links people and places in the ever-changing and always circulating movement of profit and capital. Warehouse workers are modern logistics cyborgs whose bodies connect the JIT labor of foreign factory workers to the latest desires of

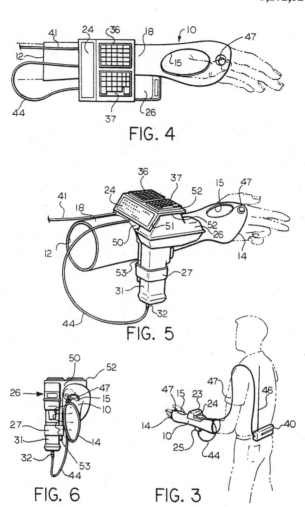

FIG. 4

FIG. 5

FIG. 6   FIG. 3

FIGURE 13. Body-worn barcode scanners turn warehouse workers into cyborg logistics laborers. U.S. patent number 5,272,324.

American consumers. As figure 13 shows, logistics workers represent the human element that enables technology to do its work. The image, taken from a patent drawing, uses a dismembered and anonymous body to illustrate how people and machines, data and flesh, combine to propel the JIT circulation of commodities. Warehouse workers like José used technologies like the hand-held scanner represented in the image to manage and redirect consumer goods through extensive global supply chains. Unlike patent drawings, which are themselves ways to protect profit by monetizing proprietary knowledge, warehouse workers used their everyday knowledge to disrupt the logistics matrix.

ANGELICA

Angelica worked as a lumper inside a major distribution center; lumpers move boxes all day long. She migrated to the United States with her husband and two children. After making the treacherous journey across the Mexico–United States border she settled somewhere in Fontana, not far from the old Kaiser mill. Angelica and her family could not afford their own place to live, so they moved in with two other families, all of them squeezing into a single-wide mobile home.[17] Our conversation was conducted at her kitchen table, while Angelica fed her children dinner and watched over them as they finished their homework. What followed was a long conversation that elucidated how warehouse workers, especially immigrants, struggled to survive within the logistics regime.

We began by talking about what life was like as a warehouse worker. Angelica laughed at the idea that warehouse workers earned anywhere near $45,000 per year. Instead, when I asked her what it was like having to raise a family on warehouse wages, she sighed, looked over at her son, and proceeded to explain how her precarious employment affected other aspects of everyday life. "Well it is very difficult because you're always under a lot of pressure because you never know when you are going to have a job and when you're going to be out of work." This is what flexible production looked like for workers like Angelica. She continued, "They can tell you one day we don't have a job for you and what are you supposed to do? I have to buy medicine and we can't pay all of our bills on what my husband makes every month. My husband would tell me, 'hey don't work we can make it on my paycheck,' but we can't."

The numbers did not add up for Angelica and her husband. "I sat down and calculated whether we can do it. He earns about $1,180 per month. We pay $490 per month on rent then $150 per week on groceries. Then we have to pay for the phone." The equation was clear: Angelica and her family could not afford to live on the unstable wages paid by the logistics industry. Yet Angelica never gave up hope. Her final statement expressed both the anguish and the possibility that something could change: "May God bless us because

I don't know what we are going to do. We have to figure something out. We'll just keep looking. Something has to come up."

MARTA

Marta spent her days loading and unloading boxes from shipping containers. It was the first and only job she got after migrating from El Salvador to Southern California in 2006. Her experience as an immigrant warehouse worker stretches beyond her individual case; she embodies how local logistics workers lived and breathed the daily realities of global capitalism. Marta's personal plight, as captured through interviews, informal conversations, and statements at public events, became a key narrative trope that she continued to craft as a prominent activist for the Warehouse Workers United Campaign. The multiscalar narrative that framed Marta's personal experience shaped the complex spatial, racial, and gendered ways that the campaign discussed the everyday life of temporary warehouse workers in inland Southern California. She exemplifies how workers used personal stories or *testimonios* as counter-narratives that challenged the discourse of development. Logistics boosters dismissed such alternative experiences by deploying aggregate data to produce an undifferentiated average logistics worker profile that was much different from the experience recounted by Marta and other workers interviewed for this project. Yet workers' stories affirmed the importance of Butler and Athanasiou's claim that "the idea of the unitary subject serves a form of power that must be challenged and undone."[18] In this case, the idea of an average middle-class logistics wage simply did not stand up as an everyday reality for all immigrant warehouse workers.

Marta left El Salvador because she thought the United States could offer her new opportunities. "Like everyone else I came for a better life. Right? To improve the life of my family. The American Dream as they say. The one people come here to work for."[19] But for Marta the United States wasn't only a beacon of hope that lured her away from home; it was also complicit in creating the conditions that forced her to migrate. She, like millions of others, fled in response to the political violence and neoliberal economic reforms that consumed Central America between 1980 and 2000. In fact, American foreign policy and economic ideology were present in many of the reasons Marta gave for why she felt compelled to leave her home. She cited economic reforms and monetary policy when describing why she felt obliged to leave:

"When the dollar came. Life got worse because everything went up from the dollar they pay."[20]

Deciding to leave was both emotionally and financially draining. While she looked forward to reuniting with family members who had migrated to the United States, leaving would create a huge rupture in her life. Even though she agonized for months about the decision, migrating meant that she would be forced to leave her young son behind. Taking him across the border would be too risky and costly. Aside from her son, the biggest challenge was gathering enough money to pay for the coyote who would smuggle her into the United States. Once everything was in place she made her way to Tijuana, where the coyote packed her into the trunk of a car and drove her across the border. Everything happened so quickly, one minute she was in the trunk and the next she was reunited with family members in the Inland Empire.

It didn't take Marta long to start looking for a job, but finding one proved difficult. Friends and family members had encouraged her to seek employment in one of the region's sprawling warehouses. They convinced her that warehouse employment was the only option for undocumented immigrants. "My husband had friends here and we heard from them that for us, our only option was to work in the warehouses or in the kitchen but it was more difficult to get a restaurant job. In the warehouse they are bringing in workers every day and getting rid of workers everyday." Marta soon learned some of the consequences of falling into categories like the "us" her friends referred to. It meant immigrant, other, and precarious.

Getting a warehouse job required her to apply through temporary staffing agencies. Marta explained that temp agencies were one of the few ways that undocumented migrants could find a decent job. "Here you can only get a job through a temporary agency. I could not go directly to a warehouse to ask if they were hiring anyone. I tried because I didn't know any better, but when I asked at the warehouse they told me that they were hiring but that I had to go through a temporary agency. They would then give us the name of the agency where we could go and submit an application."[21] Marta quickly learned the intricacies of the temporary warehouse labor market and her role in it. She filled out applications at temporary agencies and began the daily routine of calling them every morning to check whether anyone had a job for her. One of the agencies called her back a few weeks later and told her to report for work the following day. She was excited, but the thrill of finding employment dissipated as soon as she walked on the job. "I entered the warehouse and was taken by surprise." Marta quietly explained her first day as a warehouse worker. "Because when I first came to the United States when you look at it from the outside everything looks beautiful. But when I went into the warehouse it was something very different.... I remember the first time when I went in and I saw the Walmart name."[22]

It was a familiar name that brought back memories of hard labor and low wages. She had felt Walmart's presence long before settling in Ontario. The memories went back to when she was sixteen years old and took a job in El Salvador's garment industry. Like many other Central Americans and Mexicans, Marta was swept into the wave of development that transformed garment production in the 1990s, when neoliberal free trade agreements turned parts of Latin America into low-wage textile manufacturing zones.[23] She spent years making denim jeans and jackets for Walmart's retail stores. These vivid memories compounded the harsh experience of her first day as a warehouse worker.

Even though working in a Walmart warehouse involved a different type of labor, the pressure to perform and the bad working conditions were very familiar. Marta explained that garment work reminded her of the harsh conditions inside Walmart's Southern California warehouse. "It is very hard work. They used us like we were robots.... We felt the same kind of pressure when we were making that clothes in El Salvador, the same kind of pressure I felt here in the warehouse." She went on to compare the working conditions and the quota systems in both places. "There we would go into work at 7 in the morning, work all day and night until we met our quotas. I come here and it's the same thing. The first day that I came to work we didn't get to eat the entire day." Her first day and the traumatic flashbacks it evoked were emotionally and physically exhausting. "I was in shock. When I finished the day I had to drag myself home."[24]

The idea of the American Dream that drew her to the United States was slowly replaced by the everyday insecurities of precarious work. Any romantic notion she had had about finding a job, working hard, and achieving success was replaced by the more complicated reality of warehouse work. The shock of what she found inside Walmart's American warehouse was transformative, because it peeled back the glistening hope that had framed her immigrant narrative. If her immigrant aspirations were shaken by what she experienced inside the warehouse, the anger she felt when she discovered what was inside Walmart's retail stores was part of the reason she became involved in the warehouse worker campaign.

Marta's anger toward Walmart was palpable when she explained why it was impossible for her to shop at one of the company's stores. "No, because when I first arrived from El Salvador, my husband took me there and I saw some shirts that we had made in El Salvador." Those shirts helped Marta understand the circuitous nature of global commodity chains. "Nosotras hicimos esta ropa! Me dio coraje porque sabia yo las chingas que nosotros nos llevabamos haciendo esa ropa. (I told him, 'we made this clothes' and I got angry because I worked like hell to make that clothes.)" She was angry that Walmart was making a large profit on her and her coworkers' backbreaking labor. "For 35 pieces they paid us 15 cents. But just think about how many shirts we had to make each second to earn what we did, sometimes we earned as little as 5 dollars per day." Low wages were matched by brutal working conditions inside Walmart's space and time economy. "We worked ourselves so hard that we wouldn't even go to the restroom because they would put a price on the order and then encouraged us to compete with one another so we didn't dare go to the restroom or our productivity would go down." She had asked her husband to take her home, and she told me, "I never went back to a Walmart store again."

Marta's ability to connect her experience as a garment worker in El Salvador to warehouse work in Southern California enabled her to create a new narrative of how immigrant workers hold global supply chains together. The shirts triggered old memories and helped her realize that the pressure she felt and the injuries she sustained were tied to an elaborate labor regime that stretched across space and time. It was clear that no matter how far she had traveled, she had once again entangled herself in Walmart's global web of production and distribution.

Even as workers like José and Marta regularly blamed major retailers for poor warehouse conditions, Walmart and other companies tried to insulate themselves from such claims by arguing that they were not legally responsible for what happened inside contracted facilities. A Walmart spokesman defended the company by claiming, "We hold all of our contractors and their subcontractors to the highest standards and expect and require them to comply with all applicable laws."[25] The same spokesperson downplayed abuse allegations by arguing that third-party warehouses were a relatively small component of Walmart's overall operations.

WALMART'S HIGH AND TIGHT SYSTEM

Major retailers control such a large share of the commodity market that they can dictate how distribution centers operates by establishing productivity guidelines for their subcontractors. In fact, logistics became so vital to core operations that retailers could not afford a laissez-faire relationship to 3PLs. Instead, they built extensive systems and meticulous workflows to structure and manage logistics operations. Retailers monitored warehouse operations to make sure they were in compliance with corporate productivity goals. An employee at one of Walmart's Chino warehouses explained how this type of surveillance worked by recounting a warning that she received from one of her supervisors. The supervisor warned that she should be careful with someone named David. He routinely walked around the warehouse to make sure that the facility was running smoothly. According to the supervisor, David was the boss. The warning confused her because she thought that Ed, the person in charge of the 3PL company, was the head of warehouse operations. The worker then explained how she tried to clarify the power hierarchy inside of the warehouse. "I asked him, who is he? He said, 'he's the boss, el mero mero'. And I said, isn't Ed the boss? The bald guy up in that office [referring to the 3PL]? No, he said. 'David is Ed's boss. He is Walmart'." The encounter was indicative of how warehouse workers had to negotiate complicated webs of power and control on a daily basis. While managers with the 3PLs clearly exerted direct power over workers, the warning that Walmart was always on the prowl revealed the power that retailers maintained to surveil and discipline. When company representatives like David spoke, everybody listened.

Retailers also used production quotas to monitor and discipline warehouse workers. Quotas varied across different warehouses but usually spelled out the number of boxes that workers were supposed to label and load onto shipping containers. Some workers reported having to move more than two hundred boxes per hour, all by hand. One particular worker explained how quotas were enforced at his facility. "They would give us about 25 boxes per half hour, depending on how many items each box has. Each box can have between 10 to 25 items. For example, if each box had 25 pieces they would give us about 8 boxes per hour. They would just be hanging out looking at the clock."[26] Each box had to be unpacked, labeled, and loaded onto a truck.

Supervisors and leads were under tremendous pressure to enforce daily production quotas. A lead at Walmart's Chino facility reported that managers required them to attend daily productivity meetings and pressured them to increase output. Leads and supervisors had to report fifteen to twenty minutes before the beginning of the shift. Managers used logistics data to review worker productivity and claimed that "they were getting complaints [from Walmart] because we weren't making our workers work hard enough, that we weren't meeting our quota."[27]

Another worker at the same facility explained how managers systematically enforced quotas. "They would count all of our boxes at the end of the day and then they would compare our productivity and say, 'hey if so and so produced this many boxes why did you make less if you were given the same amount of work? Why is there a difference?'"[28] The ability to monitor individual output meant that any human body not able to meet standardized productivity levels was subject to discipline or dismissal. In the case of temporary workers, failure to meet productivity quotas often meant that they weren't invited back to work the following day.

Tensions were especially high whenever Walmart placed what supervisors called "hot orders." These exceptional orders required expedited attention, and managers exacted harsh punishment if they were not fulfilled on time. Leads were often threatened if their crews didn't meet the expected quota. "They would yell at us, 'You didn't go on break because you haven't worked hard enough. Don't you understand that this is a hot order!' They didn't do that when we had orders from other stores."[29] Such meetings often ended in threats. The message from 3PL managers was clear: "If you don't feel capable or willing to do the job tell us, we have hundreds of applications to take your place." Leads understood that they were expected to exert power and discipline over their crews. "They did that so that we could pressure the workers."[30] Several workers were suspicious of special hot orders. They hinted that 3PL managers routinely labeled something a hot order even if a particular shipment remained at the warehouse after it had been loaded for delivery. One worker accused managers of using hot orders to create a sense of crisis that compelled everyone to work harder. Whether this was true or not, hot orders did function as moments of exception because they required workers to perform above and beyond regular production quotas.

Hot orders were part of Walmart's attempt to meet JIT market demands. They were also examples of how retailers exerted power to increase value along the logistics chain. One of the workers observed, "Walmart gives us quotas and deadlines. If Walmart didn't pressure the company [3PLs], then they wouldn't put so much pressure on us. The pressure comes from the top, from the owners. Walmart has the responsibility because most of the products we move belong to them and the work we did for them was more difficult and there is more pressure and they pay us less."[31] Other workers suggested that even if the quotas did not directly come from Walmart, 3PL companies implemented demanding labor regimes because they were afraid of losing their Walmart contracts. Managers and workers were keenly aware of

Walmart's power to control their livelihoods. A former lead explained the difference between Walmart and other retailers. "When we would put together orders for Macy's, we didn't feel the same type of pressure. We would be told, 'Here is an order for Macy's, make sure to get it done when you can, but prioritize Walmart'."[32]

Quotas and hot orders were just two of the techniques that Walmart's logisticians crafted to enforce specific work standards. Another was the implementation of something called the "high and tight" rule. According to workers, managers constantly pressured them into quickly squeezing as many boxes as possible into shipping containers. Some workers tried to ease the physical burden of the high and tight rule by placing boxes on pallets that they then moved onto the container with a forklift. Jaime explained how workers used "perfect pallets" to ease the workload. "Some of the products come wrapped really tightly on pallets. We call them perfect pallets, because they don't have to be broken down into smaller orders. Loading a truck with those was easy because we just used a pallet jack."[33] This method avoided the strain of having to load an entire container by hand, box by box. But a standard pallet (which measures 48 by 40 by 6 inches) takes up precious space inside a shipping container, and supervisors banned the perfect pallet practice once they discovered what workers were doing. As Jaime continued to explain, "they told us that if we used those perfect pallets, it was costing us space. That if we broke them down and put the boxes on the floor, box by box, instead of on the pallets, we could fit more stuff on the trucks, we could ship more boxes and more weight."[34]

The high and tight rule was a clear example of how scientific management of abstract space trickled down to warehouse workers. Supervisors explained this decision to maximize space as a logistics calculation. In the end, Jaime summed up the logic of power that justified such a decision. "That is what Sam White [Walmart representative] does. He figures out how to put more stuff in the shipments, they call it 'high and tight.' They want those trucks full, all the way to the top and very tightly packed. The more weight and boxes you put on a truck, they win."[35]

Besides the obvious extra burden that the high and tight rule created for warehouse workers, this brief synopsis encapsulates how workers could decipher the logic of power and control that retailers used to shape everyday life on the warehouse floor. It also reveals how cheap contingent labor is vital to reaching the logistics efficiencies that are central to retail business. Because squeezing every bit of space and time efficiency out of each shipping container is such an important component of contemporary capitalism, the labor regimes put in place to service this need are clear and readily enforced by both Walmart and its logistics subcontractors. Workers, including a former lead at a Walmart cross-dock, noticed how this chain of power worked. "Well, if David [Walmart representative] talks to Ed [3PL manager] and tells him, 'you aren't loading those trucks the way they need to be done,' Ed then tells the supervisor, so the supervisor tells us, 'I want them to burst! High and tight'; that is what we always heard."[36]

SIX

_____

Contesting Contingency

WHEN UNION STAFF CHOSE TO BLOCK an intersection off the 60 freeway (CA Route 60) in the unincorporated town of Mira Loma, they were
making a political statement by rewriting low-wage warehouse workers into
the regional narrative of logistics development. Warehouse Workers United
chose a public action to broadcast how logistics workers in urban fringe communities like Mira Loma prop up global distribution networks for some of
the largest retailers in the world. Collectively, warehouse workers move millions of boxes from the backs of diesel trucks into neatly sorted piles that are
then delivered to consumer homes or local retail stores. Their trace—their
sweat and labor—is often undetectable in the things we buy. Nevertheless,
their labor is critical for the lean production systems such as JIT manufacturing and distribution that make up modern capitalism.

The WWU campaign provides an opportunity to examine how workers
challenged the dehumanizing nature of capitalist space by producing regional
counternarratives. These opposing accounts represented a discursive tactic
that social movements sometimes deploy to organize against hegemonic
development norms. Efforts to change the narrative through direct actions
invoked what Helga Leitner and her colleagues call the "imaginaries, material practices and trajectories of contentious politics."[1] Workers and organizers with the WWU campaign used their position as immigrant laborers to
craft spatial narratives that mapped racial and economic justice onto the
regional and global logistics industry. The ensuing conflict over who got to
decide the scope and scale of port development illustrates the important role
that competing cognitive mappings can play in actively shaping how space is
contested, defined, and produced.[2]

Inland warehouse workers posed two organizing issues for WWU staff. First, the growth of mostly nonunion inland warehouses was part of an old geographic problem for organized labor that began when shippers moved goods distribution work away from the heavily unionized ports. The invention of the shipping container in 1956 had made it easier for companies to shift distribution and packaging operations for large quantities of goods to inland facilities, where shippers could use cheaper, nonunion labor to break loads into smaller batches. For example, high-velocity retail strategies have increased the use of transloading facilities and inland distribution networks. Transloading, which involves transferring goods from international to domestic shipping equipment, allows companies to maximize efficiencies because U.S. standards allow for larger container capacity. Companies have also used transloading to make en route distribution changes that are responsive to market corrections, which can be made via continually updated sales information. Goods can be transloaded and shipped to markets that were not originally planned as final points of destination. Most transloading facilities used to be located closer to the ports in places like Carson and Compton; many are now located in the Inland Empire.

Longshore unions responded by trying to force shippers to keep the loading and unloading of goods near the docks, where they could more easily claim them as union jobs.[3] Labor leaders made, as Herod claims, a strategic choice "to produce industrial space and shape labor markets as a means of confronting the threat posed to the livelihoods of its members by containerization and off-pier consolidating."[4] The strategy ultimately failed, as cargo steadily moved inland. More important, union efforts to limit the goods movement industry to the location of the ports prevented organized labor from adapting to the expanding geographic scale of the logistics sector; union leaders ultimately chose a defensive strategy when they decided to protect the shrinking number of dock-based jobs by forgoing any significant attempt to organize new inland distribution facilities.

Some union leaders argued that the failure to organize inland logistics workers contributed to the creation of a racialized labor aristocracy in the goods movement sector. An officer with the ILWU explained how he tried to convince the union to organize workers beyond the docks to reduce the racial wage gap: "If I pose it to them as, well we have economic apartheid, you're making thirty-three dollars an hour here [on the docks] and this worker here [inland warehouse] is a Latino immigrant making you know eight-fifty an hour and no benefits."[5] Longshore workers were not moved by such arguments. Union leaders could not convince longshore workers because some feared that they might have to trade their gains at the bargaining table in exchange for access to new warehouse members. Some ILWU members were also concerned that low-wage immigrant warehouse workers might drag down wages and benefits for all members of the union's bargaining unit. Instead, the ILWU anchored itself to the docks and chose not to organize the inland distribution spaces of a modernizing logistics industry. This spatial strategy condemned the union to a patch of shrinking territory as corporate managers used new technologies to extend the geographies of logistics work while reducing port-based jobs.

The second challenge that union staff faced was the need to develop a strategy for organizing a global logistics industry that operated across multiple geographic scales while addressing the needs of warehouse workers who were embedded in a particular place. The WWU leaders tried to resolve this spatial dilemma by speaking in broad terms about global commodity chains while addressing the local specificity of racialized low-wage labor markets. This broader framing enabled union staff to extend the scale of the campaign beyond individual warehouses and occupations. A WWU lead staff member explained how this worked by claiming that they needed "to make this a moral movement, kind of like a crusade."[6] They did so by arguing that "the region is being screwed by companies that are taking value and not giving much back."[7] What happened to temporary warehouse workers was particularly egregious, according to campaign staff, because regional logistics boosters deliberately tried to write low-wage workers out of existence by making their plight invisible to the public.

LABOR IN THE TIME OF FLEXIBILITY

The WWU campaign was an experiment that gave union staff an opportunity to develop new organizing approaches for an industry they knew relatively little about. This experimentation took place while key factions of the labor movement debated whether union strategies and institutions—remnants of Fordist manufacturing and craft unionism—could be effective bulwarks against the expanding power of the neoliberal state and a highly flexible twenty-first-century capitalism.[8] National unions like the Service

Employees International Union (SEIU) and the Hotel Employees and Restaurant Employees (UNITE HERE!) responded to deindustrialization by focusing on service sector industries. Other unions, especially the International Brotherhood of Teamsters and progressive worker centers, chose to focus on supply chain workers. Partnership for Working Families (PWF), a national network of leading regional advocacy organizations, began work on a national supply chain campaign in 2009. The executive director for one of PWF's anchor organizations thought that a "from trucks to dumps" strategy could engage different members of its national network at different points along the supply chain.[9]

Union leaders were pressed into action during the 1990s and 2000s because organized labor was dwindling. Key national union leaders had begun to question whether labor could survive mounting manufacturing job losses and neoliberal policy reforms that threatened their ability to maintain collective bargaining agreements. There was enough dissent to trigger a reform movement within the country's major labor federation, the AFL-CIO. Reformers installed John Sweeney in the national leadership of the AFL-CIO in 1995. Sweeney and his coalition pushed for institutional reforms they believed would help unions regain membership.[10] One of their strategies was major new organizing campaigns.[11] They focused on emerging economic sectors as a way to recapture some of the members lost when heavily unionized manufacturing industries like steel and auto began to decline after the 1980s.

Several unions, including the Service Employees International Union, adopted more radical reforms during the early 2000s.[12] SEIU's executive vice president called for drastic changes because he believed that the labor movement was "becoming dangerously close to being too small to matter."[13] Powerful labor leaders, SEIU's Andy Stern in particular, argued for a more centralized decision-making power structure because they claimed that union governance models and organizing techniques had proven inadequate for the challenges that were introduced by flexible production and extended commodity chains.[14] They argued that labor had remained stagnant while capitalism had evolved. This new generation of union leaders blamed inadequate organizing strategies, insufficient institutional capacities, and an unfriendly conservative regulatory climate for labor's continued decline.[15] Stern and other labor leaders wanted a more streamlined structure and claimed that decentralized union locals did not have the institutional capacity to confront global capital. Rank-and-file activists and some local union leaders countered by arguing that such top-down strategies were antithetical to democratic unionism.[16] Instead, dissidents claimed that local autonomy and democracy, not centralized leadership, was the key to a vibrant labor movement. Reformers responded by asserting that union locals were complicit in labor's decline because they had failed to organize workers in the growth sectors of contemporary capitalism. In an attempt to solve this problem, some unions created super locals that stretched across multiple cities and regions to encompass all workers in a particular industrial sector. The SEIU's multicity Justice for Janitors union was one example of this strategy.

Some of the struggles between labor reformers and more traditionalist union leaders were evident in the efforts to gain broad support for the WWU. For example, Change to Win's (CTW) Washington, D.C.–based leadership chose to fund and staff the warehouse campaign because they felt that local union leaders could not organize the region's growing logistics sector. Organizing staff, most of whom were brought in from other national campaigns, faced resistance from local unions. The campaign's commodity chain approach and regional strategy challenged the workplace-by-workplace model that many local unions used as an organizing strategy.

Tensions between local and national labor leaders included ongoing struggles to reform moribund central labor councils (CLCs). These administrative bodies are often organized at a regional level and serve as spaces for local unions to coordinate with one another. Reformers argued that CLCs could revitalize organized labor by providing support for organizing drives and political campaigns. Perhaps the most well-known case is that of the Los Angeles County Federation of Labor (LA Fed). Under the direction of Miguel Contreras, the LA Fed became a powerful political voice that successfully placed working-class issues in local and statewide policy debates. Key local unions and the LA Fed turned Los Angeles into a hotbed for reform-driven organizing campaigns during the 1990s and 2000s; they succeeded by leveraging union resources along the changing demographics to elect a new generation of more progressive political leaders. Labor tried to reproduce the success of the LA Fed in other CLCs. For example, some of the same leaders who helped to reform the LA Fed were also involved in reorganizing the Orange County CLC during the mid-2000s.

The same did not happen in the Inland Empire, where the head of the CLC, Laurie Stalnaker, was sometimes forced to ally herself with the conservative politicians who controlled regional politics. She chastised a visiting labor leader who questioned the CLC's leadership on progressive issues, exclaiming, "You people in Los Angeles want to come here and have people marching in the street; we don't do that here, sometimes we have to support Republicans in order to survive."[17] Critics argued that Stalnaker's moderate stance provided political cover for a CLC leadership team that was more interested in maintaining the status quo than in championing the cause of the region's low-wage workers. While other CLCs launched campaigns to organize workers in expanding economic sectors, many of them occupied by immigrant workers, the Inland Empire CLC did not. Stalnaker's invocation, "we don't do that here," naturalized geographic difference and never accounted for the role that the CLC played—by not providing more progressive leadership—in producing the Inland Empire as a conservative space. A local Teamsters leader expressed frustration with the CLC's inability to support regional organizing, especially in the logistics industry. When asked at a goods movement conference hosted by the University of California, Riverside, why union leadership was not leading the charge to organize warehouse workers, the Teamsters leader responded, "The CLC has failed in its job, has not looked at the long term. They either need to get out of the way or die."[18] Several other union staff claimed that CLC leaders were standoffish when approached for support by the WWU and other immigrant worker organizing campaigns.[19] A group of unions, led by the Teamsters and the Communication Workers of America, made a bid to replace Stalnaker as head of the CLC in 2004. Key unions such as UNITE-HERE rallied to Stalnaker's defense and helped her maintain her leadership position.

Leaders with the WWU campaign sidestepped Stalnaker's political and institutional indifference by building their own social movement support network.[20] They provided financial and organizational support for a new batch of organizations like Clergy and Laity United for Economic Justice (CLUE), PWF, and the Inland Valley Labor Action Network (IVLAN), with the goal of gaining community support for worker organizing and progressive policy campaigns.[21] The WWU organizing staff believed that the organization's long-term effectiveness was dependent on changing the social and political environment of the region. A senior WWU staffer reiterated this point during a strategy meeting: "There needs to be an approach to the region right, not just the workers."[22] The lead research and policy person concurred with the regional approach: "We need a plan to improve this region's economy. Are the jobs that are being created good jobs or bad jobs?"[23] This regional framing extended the campaign beyond the workplace. Staff were trying to win by making warehouse workers part of a larger discussion about regional economic development and social justice.

Union leaders arrived at a regional social justice strategy after determining that other approaches were not feasible. They spent months digging for financial and regulatory tactics to pressure the logistics industry. Their efforts were part of a high-road strategy that unions had developed in other industries across the country. The goal was to pressure key companies to sign neutrality agreements that allowed unions to organize workers with less interference from antiunion consultants. Labor leaders viewed such high-road strategies as more effective and less costly ways to organize large numbers of workers; traditional shop-floor organizing was thought to be too risky and expensive.[24] Nonetheless, WWU organizers determined that the Inland Empire was too conservative and lacked the type of civil society infrastructure necessary for a high-road strategy to be successful. For example, none of the region's regulatory bodies was willing to pressure companies into signing neutrality agreements or living wage pay scales in return for the approval of new warehouse construction. An exasperated staff member summed up the decision to abandon the high road: "We looked at regulatory, we looked at legislative, we couldn't find anything so we decided that we had to organize the workers."[25] Simply put, the region's conservative political infrastructure meant that they had to build a grassroots movement.

Most of the WWU's senior staff was very familiar with a grassroots organizing model. In fact, they were experts at crafting an organizing narrative that focused on immigrant, mostly Spanish-speaking workers. I raise this point to note that union staff played a key role in shaping the campaign's organizing narrative and the production of a collective warehouse worker identity. Most of the staff had previously worked for low-wage service sector unions and were predisposed to crafting specific types of narratives. It is important to remember that organizers bring particular skills and practices to a campaign. In this case, cultural capital and institutional practices embodied in the union staff fundamentally shaped collective worker identities. Union staff embraced the immigrant warehouse worker narrative because it fit with their institutional organizing experience. It was easy for organizers to make immigrant temp workers into the face of the campaign; they occupied the most marginal positions within the logistics industry. A staff researcher explained why temporary workers were the primary target of the campaign: "The biggest thing wrong with this industry is temp workers, [we] need to get rid of temp employment in the warehouses."[26]

Sometimes staff wanted to mold the workers into a collective identity that fit their organizing model even when workers fell outside these comfortable categories. Organizing staff acknowledged this and recognized that their narrative sometimes excluded members of the labor force who did not fit their profile. When asked whether the campaign should only be focused on temp workers, a lead staffer with the WWU replied, "We should figure out a way to target the industry, the big companies and not just the temp agencies."[27] Organizers initially thought that native-born workers would be more difficult to mobilize because they occupied a privileged status within the warehouse employment hierarchy. According to staff preconceptions, this would make them more complacent and unwilling to associate themselves with immigrant temp workers. Instead, they found a group of young workers who challenged both the campaign narrative and organizer assumptions. Organizers called this group the Lost Boys.

Lost Boys were native-born workers who, according to union staff, made up 25 percent of the labor force in specific warehouses.[28] Keith was a typical Lost Boy. He was young, Black, and an eager participant in the campaign. An organizer described Keith as "our ultimate lost boy, he had the piercings on his lips, he was into punk, had a long list of jobs, bad warehouse jobs." The organizer recalled how he first approached Keith about the campaign: "We're like we just want to kick shit up and we want to take the industry on. He was like, 'I don't give a fuck, sign me up'."[29] WWU staff discovered that many of these Lost Boys had arrest records, which made it difficult for them to find jobs. Temp agencies—especially those that did not perform background checks—gave them access to jobs; as they did for undocumented workers, small temp agencies provided major companies with cheap labor by funneling marginalized workers into logistics jobs.

Lost Boys were more than a rambunctious agitation crew; they also represented a counterpoint to the immigrant worker narrative that defined the public face of the campaign. The angry and rebellious Lost Boy image was perhaps less palatable than the hopeful optimism that framed the campaign's immigrant warehouse narrative. A WWU organizer explained this contrast: "This whole Lost Boy thing, there's a lot more anger out here. I talked enough to the immigrant workers to know that there may not have been simmering anger, cause there wasn't, but there was a shitload of hope." Here is how the same organizer discussed the motivational framework for immigrant workers in contrast to the angry rebellion of the Lost Boys: "Immigrantes, you know they come with their hope. Right? And there's nothing they wouldn't do, perhaps not for themselves but for their kids." Immigrant narratives of hope, sacrifice, and success—all metrics for the American Dream—became the dominant voice of the campaign. At the same time, the Lost Boys and the challenge they presented to normative notions of success slid into the shadows.

"FUCK THE HIGH-END JOBS"

Despite public complaints from workers about the harsh conditions inside the region's warehouses, many civic leaders were loath to charge the industry with any wrongdoing. This is part of what made a high-road strategy unfeasible. Instead, logistics emerged as a darling of regional boosters because it was one of the few growth sectors in the region that could not easily pick up and move elsewhere, like so many of the manufacturing jobs that relocated offshore after the global economic shift of the 1980s and 1990s. Consequently, policy makers of all stripes lined up behind the idea that logistics was an economic solution for the region's sagging job base. SCAG played a key role in crafting this pro-goods movement rationale and assembled a network of policy makers, business interests, and economists to spread its vision.

One report in particular, "Logistics & Distribution: An Answer to Regional Upward Social Mobility," argued that goods movement could deliver the region's growing ranks of blue-collar workers into the middle class by paying an average yearly wage of more than $45,000 per year.[30] Policy and economic leaders used these figures to argue that Southern California's ports provided the building blocks for a more sustainable and diverse economic future. The report provided an ideological foundation for a regional logistics strategy. Its author, John Husing, became a champion for the regional goods movement economy. He claimed that the lack of infrastructure hindered the region's economic prosperity. According to Husing, "If the area's economic power is to be unleashed, its economy must be freed of the constraints imposed by lack of truck, rail and airport infrastructure." For Husing, it was the state that should be involved in securing such infrastructure. He laid out this vision for the state, claiming that "investment in these projects would have the beneficial effect of allowing the region's logistics sector to accelerate, providing a growing base of good paying jobs which its marginally educated workers can learn via on-the-job experience and learning." Husing's vision for a state-subsidized regional logistics economy was predicated on the idea that goods movement was the only economic engine that could improve the standard of living for blue-collar workers. As the report argued, "This would appear to be the only route that the region has available to helping those workers achieve growing standards of living while simultaneously correcting the recent deep slide in Southern California's relative prosperity vis-à-vis other major parts of the country."[31]

Husing's ideas were influential and gained traction with local policy makers and regional boosters. Paul Granillo, president and CEO of the Inland Empire Economic Partnership (IEEP) since 2010, credited Husing's development ideologies for shaping his organization's advocacy efforts. The IEEP supported economic development and advocated pro-business growth through entrepreneurship, policy, and educational programs. Husing served as the chief economist for the IEEP. Granillo and Husing pushed a blue-collar approach to regional development. As Granillo explained, "I think what we're saying is, we are a blue-collar region, so let's be the best blue-collar region we can be and if we do that well then we will grow and we will become something else, but for the longest time, I believe, there [sic] has been a real hesitancy to say we're blue-collar." This approach differed from other regional efforts to lure white-collar workers and high-tech development. Husing added, "You constantly hear this, 'well where are the high-end jobs?' Excuse me, fuck the high-end jobs, we have a blue-collar population." Granillo tried to massage Husing's comment by quickly chiming in, "That needs some nuance." To which Husing said, "I'm not sure but it's true."[32]

How do we reconcile SCAG's prologistics discourse with the everyday reality of warehouse workers like José, Angelica, and Marta (discussed in the previous chapter)? First we must understand that the goods movement industry has been produced as an economic and political apparatus by a specific set of actors and institutions. As Giorgio Agamben argues, this apparatus functioned as "a kind of formation . . . that at a given historical moment has as its major function the response to an urgency."[33] In this case, logistics became the apparatus that was supposed to solve the blue-collar middle-class crisis caused by multiple rounds of globalization.

Economists built the logistics apparatus by creating a coherent industry out of eight different North American Industry Classification System (NAICS) codes.[34] The model enabled policy makers, business interests, and community members to develop a common language about how port activity affected the local political economy but it was also imprecise because it did not fully capture all of the logistics sector.[35] SCAG's decision to use this economic model skewed some of the public benefits that it touted for the region. To begin with, SCAG's model relied on industry-wide wages that lumped

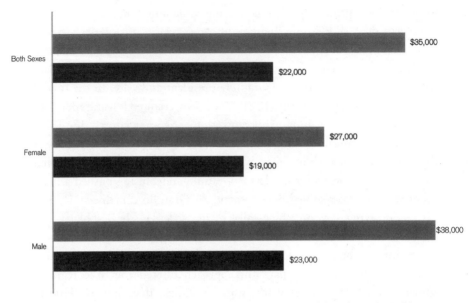

■ Non Blue-Collar Jobs   ■ Blue-Collar Jobs

FIGURE 14. Blue-collar warehouse wages. Author analysis of data from the Public Use Microdata Sample, American Community Survey, 2007–2011.

white-collar and professional occupations like pilots and train engineers with blue-collar warehouse workers. This meant that a warehouse worker was classified in the same category as a computer logistician, without factoring in how education and skill level affected job mobility. SCAG's economic model also excluded temporary workers from its industry figures. Consequently, the reserve pool of immigrant labor that enabled companies to use flexible distribution strategies was erased from debates about logistics.

My wage model uses the American Community Survey's Public Use Microdata Sample to determine a more nuanced and accurate pay scale for warehouse workers. According to these data, blue-collar warehouse jobs paid a median annual income of $22,000 per year between 2007 and 2011, which assumes that they worked full-time and year-round (see figure 14).[36] Female workers accounted for 33 percent of blue-collar warehouse occupations and earned $19,000, roughly $4,000 less than men. What explains the wage difference between men and women? Several women mentioned that they were often excluded from higher wage occupations. For example, while women were usually assigned as lumpers and labelers, few were ever given the opportunity to take higher paying forklift driver jobs. Finally, race also factored

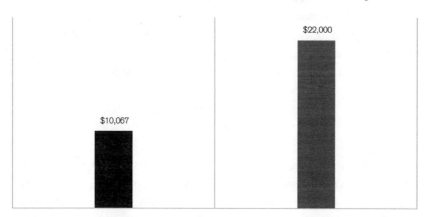

FIGURE 15. Temporary worker wages. Author analysis of data from the Public Use Microdata Sample, American Community Survey, 2007–2011.

into wage differences within the sector. While both Black and Latinx logistics workers earned more than they would in other sectors, white logistics workers earned significantly more than Latinxs.[37]

Wages were even lower for temporary warehouse workers. According to the Bureau of Labor Statistics, the average full-time temporary worker earned $19,965 in 2012; this was for all industries.[38] But temporary warehouse workers earned far less, especially when compared to direct-hire employees. Temp workers—who were hired to do the same jobs as direct-hire employees and worked at least twenty hours per week—earned a median income of $10,067 per year (see figure 15). What explains the wage disparity? To begin with, many temp workers were placed in relatively low-wage warehouse occupations. These positions were more susceptible to market fluctuations and provided less regular employment. Approximately 70 percent of all temp workers in warehouse occupations reported working less than forty weeks (roughly less than ten months) in a year. When they did find work, close to 40 percent of temporary workers in warehouse occupations worked less than thirty hours per week.[39]

Logistics boosters cast temporary warehouse workers as an exception to the otherwise exemplary goods movement economy. Husing was dismissive when asked to account for low wages among warehouse workers. He told a reporter, "The people who throw that stuff around are ideologues. They don't want that sector to survive because they consider it to be dirty."[40] Such denials formed the backbone of a spatial politics that enabled public and private boosters to mobilize the region for logistics development by emptying the landscape of low-wage warehouse workers. Their erasure was a political gesture meant to stabilize the good jobs narrative by removing anything that might contradict boosterish depictions of the industry.

FLEXIBLE RACIAL LABOR

Boosterish claims aside, low-wage logistics workers cannot be easily dismissed; they are important links in the global supply chain. Temporary warehouse labor was especially critical for companies that adopted flexible production and distribution systems. In fact, temporary labor facilitated the switch to the rapidly fluctuating labor needs called for by JIT delivery and shorter product cycles.[41] This occurred in part because labor-intensive secondary sectors, like temp warehouse agencies, employ lower waged workers who have less permanent employment and whose unskilled relationship to capital makes them more expendable. Retailers could therefore use contractors to access flexible labor without having to incur the higher overhead costs associated with direct-hire employees.

As retailers turned to more flexible business models, they handed over many of their day-to-day warehousing and logistics functions to a growing array of third- and fourth-party companies. This labor switching meant that retailers could maintain flexibility without being bogged down by capital investments in facilities and labor. Contingent employment expanded during the economic restructuring of the 1990s.[42] The temporary staffing industry grew at even faster rates in less-unionized sunbelt and right-to-work regions. In the Inland Empire, temporary employment grew by 390 percent between 1990 and 2006 (see figure 16). Temp agency establishments jumped from 60 in 1990 to more than 270 by the end of 2007. By the height of the economic boom of the mid-2000s, temp agencies employed more than forty-one thousand workers in inland Southern California.[43] This represented a disproportionately large share of the region's overall employment when compared to Los Angeles and the rest of the state.[44]

Available wage data do not let us determine exactly how many of the region's temporary workers were employed in local warehouses. Nonetheless, even if temporary workers made up only a fraction of the

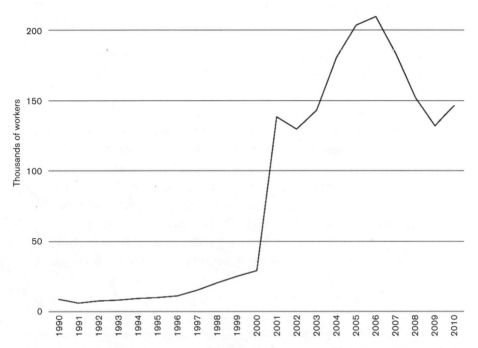

FIGURE 16. Growth in temporary employment. Author analysis of data from the Bureau of Labor Statistics, 1990–2010. https://data.bls.gov/.

warehouse workforce, they certainly played a vital role in the logistics economy. Some of the biggest names in retail, such as Amazon and Walmart, used temp workers to operate their facilities. When Amazon announced that it would hire workers for two new distribution centers in Chattanooga, Tennessee, company officials said that three thousand out of the forty-five hundred total employees would be seasonal or temp workers.[45] Amazon was not alone in its use of temp workers. Of the eleven dedicated Walmart distribution centers that I identified in the Inland Empire, nine employed temporary workers.[46]

Major corporations contracted with temporary agencies because they performed two critical roles as labor market intermediaries.[47] First, they served as conduits through which a low-wage, flexible, and largely undocumented labor force was funneled into goods-movement jobs. Second, they protected the industry's access to cheap labor by taking advantage of labor laws that made it more difficult for logistics workers to organize into collective bargaining units. Temp agencies essentially functioned as human resource offices that funneled immigrant labor into the local logistics industry. It was common knowledge among the region's immigrant networks that temp agencies were one of the few places where they could seek employment. This was especially true as immigration control policies—for example, E-Verify—increased employment barriers for immigrant workers. Immigrants were forced into more precarious labor conditions by such tighter labor controls.

While access to hiring agencies and increased immigration controls attracted undocumented immigrants, who learned to decipher local barriers to employment. One worker explained: "Most workers like us [undocumented] know that if you want a job you go to the agencies. Everyone knows which ones don't use instant verification; if they have that sticker on the window, you move on to the next one."[48] "That sticker" was a reference to the federal E-Verify program, which was expanded in 2007 to block undocumented immigrant access to employment. Nevertheless, undocumented workers figured out how to play the legal status game, often with help from temp agency staff. Another worker explained how she gained access to temp warehouse jobs: "We filled out the [job] application and they could clearly see that we did not speak English and all of that, they knew that we did not have papers (papeles)." Workers understood that certain staffing agencies allowed counterfeit documents, "because when they saw other workers who had work permits (micas) that looked obviously fake they would tell them to go get one that looked more legitimate. . . . Obviously it's a counterfeit, but everyone uses them. It isn't a problem with temp agencies."

Those who gained access to temporary employment often became locked into dead-end, precarious work. Their experience contradicted social science research and port boosters alike, who claimed that labor market flexibility and contingent work offered workers, particularly white-collar labor, freedom to choose among the best employment scenarios. This was obviously not the case for most blue-collar and low-skilled clerical temp workers, who preferred permanent full-time jobs.[49] Instead, temporary warehouse workers were trapped in a flexible labor market built on precarious employment. When asked why, after working at a Skechers warehouse for over a year, she was never offered a more permanent position, one worker summed up her experience this way: "Skechers has a different policy. They don't want to hire people directly. The only people who are hired by Skechers are managers, supervisors and some of the leads that are training people. But no one else."

Some companies did provide a path to direct-hire work, but undocumented workers were typically locked out of this opportunity because of their legal status. Felipe, a forty-something immigrant warehouse worker, explained how this happened to him. He worked for two years as a temporary laborer at a local warehouse before his supervisor offered him a direct-hire position. Felipe explained how happy he was after submitting his direct-hire paperwork to human resources, because they informed him that he would receive a substantial raise. A few weeks later his supervisor called him into a private meeting and told him that there was a problem with his Social Security number; the system had bounced the number back as invalid. His supervisor told Felipe that he needed to submit valid documentation to prove that he was authorized to work. But Felipe explained that he could not provide proper documentation because he was undocumented. The supervisor quickly responded, "Well, if you can't submit valid papers then you should go back to the temp agency and tell them I want you here tomorrow; you can have your old job back [as a temp worker]."[50] What happened to Felipe confirmed what other warehouse workers claimed: that employers knowingly used temp agencies to circumvent legal employment obligations.

Labor market vulnerability also routinely exposed temp workers to management techniques that used precarious status as a tool to extract more value from workers. Cash cards are one example. Some temp agencies used cash cards, like prepaid credit cards, to pay their workers. They did so because new financial services companies created a cash card payroll market that gave employers a way to reduce overhead costs by outsourcing part of their human resources operations. In return, payroll service companies generated revenue from the contract and from each transaction. The use of cash cards was part of a larger trend to integrate financial service companies into payroll management and human relations for the contingent employment sector. Some temp workers were given the option of having their paychecks placed in bank accounts via direct deposit or in a cash card account. It wasn't really a choice for those immigrant workers who, either because they were unfamiliar with the U.S. banking system or because of their undocumented status, did not have access to direct deposit bank accounts.

Warehouse workers felt that cash cards were yet another way that agencies nickel and dimed them. They hissed and booed whenever a union staff member displayed a cash card during an organizing meeting. Workers were openly hostile because they were forced to pay transaction fees when making cash withdrawals on their own income. They also had to maintain a balance on their cash card to keep the account open and to ensure future payment. This meant that workers could not withdraw the entire amount of what they were paid. One union organizer summed up the situation, comparing cash cards and other management tools: "Global cash card systems, like, they're making interest off of the pooled workers meager shitty pay checks; it's really bad. This is so fucking backwards, I can't even believe it's 2009."[51] Organizers compared this payment relationship to the use of company scrip, in which employers would extract further profit from workers by locking them into a dependent economy of production and reproduction. "It's bad enough that you get paid peanuts, but once you do, you can't pull out all your money or you can get charged for taking out all your money? Or you have to leave a certain balance there? Or you don't know how much money you got paid and for how many hours because they won't give you a check stub for that."[52]

Temp workers were routinely exposed to other predatory hiring practices, such as the shape-ups that once defined dock work. Employers used shape-ups to control the local labor supply. These occurred in two ways. First, staffing agencies used physical shape-ups to visually assess potential workers and to decide who would be hired for the job. The process was described by a union organizer as follows: "The staffing agency person shows up at 9 am and looks the crowd over and will hand-pick the 10 best workers, who they feel are the best workers right, and send the rest home. I mean that's a shape-up."[53] Second, shape-ups were often hard-wired into regular hiring practices. A typical worker registered with several temp agencies to increase his or her odds of being hired. The worker was then told to call every morning to confirm he or she was available for work. Failure to call meant the worker was not placed on the list of potential employees. Even if workers were called and asked to present themselves for work, they were not guaranteed employment. Temp agencies deliberately created a labor surplus by routinely asking twenty workers to show up even if only ten employment slots were available. They had an incentive to create such a surplus because it guaranteed that they would have access to an adequate number of workers. The logic behind this practice was described by a union staff member: "They don't want to lose that contract with the warehouse so if that warehouse needs ten people, they call twenty ... so you have folks, twenty folks that will show up outside of the staffing agency, standing there for almost two hours."[54] Those temp workers who reported for work but who were not offered employment were sent home without compensation.

Agencies also used other tactics to secure a JIT labor force. For example, workers complained that they were routinely told to report to work but were then ordered to wait around, off the clock, before being assigned to an actual job. A normal day went something like this: "You have to sign in when you get to the place. So you get in line, you sign, you get the [scanning] gun, once you have all your equipment, including your work list, that includes all the merchandise you are responsible for, after all that then they let you clock in." This process usually took anywhere from fifteen to twenty minutes, all of it off the clock.

Some workers had to wait much longer for a job, especially when companies were responding to the ebbs and flows of JIT logistics. A longtime temp worker explained that workers often had to wait around for trucks to show up. "If they called in 70 people because the goal is to have 80 to 100 trucks, but if there are only 10 trucks, then they aren't going to employ all of the lumpers." Prospective workers were familiar with the routine. "So they get 20 lumpers out of 60 people that includes drivers and lumpers, the other 40 to 50 people that are there, they have to stay there without clocking in, they have to wait until there is more work."[55] The wait was usually anywhere from twenty minutes to three hours, all of it off the clock and without pay.

Working off the clock was also not uncommon. Supervisors sometimes made employees work off the clock as punishment for not meeting their daily quotas. The process unfolded as follows: "The supervisor would say, 'because the work didn't get done and you didn't work fast enough, you are going to clock out and then come back to work because Walmart and the company did not approve overtime'." Anyone who refused could be threatened, "They would say, 'you have to stay to finish it because if you don't get it done, then you won't have a job tomorrow.' Sometimes we wouldn't be done with work until 9pm."[56]

Managers also extracted surplus labor and maintained labor discipline by subjecting women to gendered management techniques. Many of the women I interviewed made direct connections between on-the-job sexual harassment and their vulnerable status as undocumented temporary labor. For example, supervisors and temp agency staff routinely promised future job security in exchange for sexual favors. This promise of job security for sex was simply another way that precarious employment made women vulnerable in the JIT distribution world. Some women reported that even personal conflicts were often gendered, because female workers often occupied the lowest paid positions. According to Marta, the worst treatment she ever received while working in a warehouse occurred while she was pregnant. She thought that her condition would give her some breathing space and that supervisors would stop harassing her. But rather than show concern, supervisors used her pregnancy to ramp up the work pressure. Her assumption that supervisors would show compassion because of the pregnancy fell to pieces; she explained how they completely disrespected her as a human being. "When I told them I was pregnant, they made me feel like I didn't have a right to get pregnant. They told me, 'you come to this country to work not to have children.' On and on like that." Their admonition, that she was first and foremost a worker, resonated with Marta. She explained how shocked she was to be stripped of her humanity by supervisors who used her immigrant female body to impose gender and labor discipline. This same vulnerability, as an undocumented transnational mother, was also what gave her strength to reclaim her humanity by negating the alienating identity imposed by warehouse supervisors. This nexus between gender and class power was clear in her description. "My supervisor. They didn't respect me. They supposedly lay off people who come out pregnant. But I needed the work, I have a son in El Salvador [begins to cry]. I have a 12-year-old son. He's the reason I put up with it all. Even through all of the heavy work. I would fall down sometimes and grab my stomach, I was big when this happened. They would sometimes send me to load containers and some of my coworkers would say, 'hey she's pregnant.' The supervisors would say, 'We don't have special treatment for anyone.' And they would send me to load containers. I would grab my stomach when I bent over to pick up the empty pallets and carry them outside. I would just grab my stomach. I was so big at that point that it bothered me. They didn't want to let me stop working."

She was afraid that taking extra time off would mean losing her job. So she kept working, stopping only eighteen days before she went into labor. Marta had less than a month to recuperate from her cesarean section before getting back to the hard work of lifting boxes and moving pallets. She went in to work only because she now had two children to look out for, and her immigration status limited her job options. When asked about her son in El Salvador and why she hadn't brought him with her, she became emotional. Her voice softened, her eyes watered, and she said, "I don't have the money to bring him, or I would have brought him over already. I've never been able to save even $100. The money I earn disappears." Little changed when she returned to work. Now the harassment and taunting focused on her physical appearance. Some of the supervisors mocked her for wearing a special body brace that protected her childbirth incision. Marta's story exemplifies how gender, class, immigration status, and economic precarity combined to shape the everyday lives of warehouse workers.

SCENE 3

The Reterritorialization of
Race and Class

HUNDREDS OF PEOPLE GATHERED ON THE STREETS of Murrieta, a small city in southwestern Riverside County, to block three buses from delivering their human cargo to the local border patrol station in July 2014. Many of the protestors draped themselves in American flags, held up signs that read "Stop the invasion of illegals," and shouted slogans like "Send them back."[1] Local and national camera crews rushed to capture the drama that erupted as a group of mostly white protestors planted themselves directly in front of the border patrol buses and refused to budge. Immigration officials responded to the standoff by ordering the buses to turn around and leave Riverside County. The buses eventually made their way to a border patrol station near San Diego, but tensions continued to rise over the next several days as pro-immigrant activists converged on Murrieta to challenge the hostile, some argued racist, environment.[2] Angry exchanges between pro- and anti-immigrant sides harkened back to the contentious politics of immigration that had dominated California elections in the 1990s.[3]

Scenes like these were no longer supposed to happen in California. A March 2013 poll showed that 72 percent of registered voters supported a path to citizenship for undocumented immigrants, and 53 percent claimed that they had a mostly positive effect on the state's economy.[4] Unlike people in Arizona and more conservative southern states like Georgia and Alabama, Californians were thought to be more comfortable with and accommodating to the immigrants who had transformed the state's ethnic landscape. Southern California in particular came to represent an iconic immigrant metropolis leading up to the turn of the twenty-first century. Nonetheless, what happened in Murrieta showed that the state's old political order, which had given life to strident anti-immigrant propositions like 187 and 229, had not disappeared into the shadows. All the media attention made Murrieta a flashpoint in the ongoing national debate about immigration. Central American refugee children were simply the latest phase in a much older border conflict between the United States and its southern neighbors.

SEVEN

Mapping the American Dream

WHEN HENRY KAISER BEGAN CONSTRUCTION on his steel mill in April 1942, he had to bulldoze the remnants of what had been the largest hog farm in the world. Construction crews were literally forced to push aside some of the fifty thousand pigs that had once made Fontana Farms one of the region's largest agricultural producers. Pigs and the rural landscape that the mill dislodged became iconic elements of Kaiser's public image. Company literature routinely depicted an army of pig laborers operating various parts of the new mill.[1] The transformation was a symbolic gesture that represented what was to come, one economic regime replacing another. In fact, much of the agricultural industry that dominated inland Southern California's landscape between 1880 and 1940 was slowly being plowed under by the region's transition to postwar industrial manufacturing. The building of the mill—along with the opening of two new military bases and a railyard—marked inland Southern California's growing relationship with a war-related industrial economy and provides us with an opportunity to examine how space, race, and power were mapped onto the landscape. This chapter begins by describing the landscape of the Inland Empire, then examines the role the inland area has played as a development region for metropolitan Los Angeles. It also shows how the Kaiser mill contributed to the territorialization of new racial and class relations that affected the region's politics long after the mill had succumbed to global restructuring.

DREAMING IN THE SUBURBS

From the air, the Inland Empire is a patchwork of gray, windowless, warehouse boxes; green, curvy, suburban cul-de-sacs; and dry, undeveloped lots.

Large tracts of middle-class homes and endless rows of massive warehouses now stand on land once given over to orange trees and dairy cows. Both the old and the new versions of the Inland Empire are what Joan Didion described as "an alien place: not the coastal California of the subtropical twilights and the soft westerlies of the Pacific, but a harsher California, haunted by the Mojave [desert] just beyond the mountains."[2]

Sprawling vistas and distance from some other center are often used as a metaphor for what seems like a giant cultural gap between Los Angeles and the people of the Inland Empire. For example, while inland locals embrace the suburban and rural landscape as a refuge from the problems and complications of city life, coastal county residents have invoked the same dusty images to describe it as a backward place. Residents of Orange and LA Counties were so abhorred by their inland cousins during the population boom of the 2000s that they mounted social media campaigns to keep the "meth labs, cows and dirt people" associated with the inland 909 area code away from their pristine and peaceful beach communities.[3]

Even if inland Southern California seems to be a spatial paradox and a regional antipode to Los Angeles and Orange Counties, one cannot be understood without the other. They share a symbiotic relationship.[4] The latest example occurred during the housing boom of the 2000s, when scholars, policy makers, and residents claimed that inland counties could keep the American Dream alive in Southern California by extending homeownership to a new generation.[5] Inland counties were supposed to provide an alternative for members of the aspiring middle class because the suburban landscapes of post–World War II Los Angeles were either too expensive or no longer desirable for a new wave of home buyers.

Inland Southern California has routinely served as a frontier region for metropolitan Los Angeles. White settlers repeatedly used it to fulfill the spatial and racial fantasies of Manifest Destiny during the nineteenth and twentieth centuries.[6] These white settlement narratives were present when Joan Didion wrote that "the San Bernardino Valley would draw a kind of people who imagined they might live among the talismanic fruit and prosper in the dry air, people who brought with them Midwestern ways of building and cooking and praying and who tried to graft those ways upon the land."[7]

Who were these people, and what types of spaces did they create by trying to "graft" their ways onto the region? The first significant round of white migration, or what Didion refers to as "Midwestern ways," took place during the second half of the 1800s, when white families descended on the Inland

Empire in the immediate aftermath of California's transition from Mexican to U.S. control. They built a regional citrus industry that made the Inland Empire one of the most important agricultural centers in the country.[8] Citrus, speculative capital, and race combined to produce a regional political culture in which a white agricultural elite held political power over a highly racialized Mexican, Chicanx, and Asian labor force.

A second round of migration occurred during World War II, when a manufacturing surge led by Kaiser Steel, railyards, and military bases drew new migrants into the region. Thousands of African Americans, Asians, Latinxs, and working-class whites moved in to find work and buy homes during and after the war. Both of these migrations reterritorialized race and class relations. The first migration erected a white capitalist shrine by displacing the indigenous and Mexican spatial orders that came before it. The second integrated inland Southern California into the bowels of American empire by dragging it into the Keynesian economy of postwar geopolitics.

The most recent wave of inland migration, which occurred between 1980 and 2010, was decidedly different. To begin with, the sheer number of people moving into inland counties not only eclipsed earlier migration figures, it also made the Inland Empire one of the fastest growing metropolitan regions in the United States. The most spectacular growth period occurred during the 1980s, when the Inland Empire's population grew by 66 percent, or more than one million people.[9] White residents accounted for 45.9 percent of this growth, and Latinxs made up 38.4 percent. This mix changed during the 1990s, when Latinxs accounted for more than 80 percent of the population growth (see figure 17). The Latinx population surged once more between 2000 and 2010. While Latinxs maintained their nearly 80 percent share of the total growth, Asian and Pacific Islanders (APIs) grew at a faster clip, rising to 13 percent. No other major metropolitan area gained more Latinxs between 2000 and 2008. In addition, the region ranked third for API growth during the same period.[10] Immigrants accounted for some of the population growth. Approximately 933,000 immigrants lived in Riverside and San Bernardino Counties by 2010, giving the Inland Empire metro area the ninth largest foreign-born population in the country.[11] Immigrants made up 22.1 percent of the total state population, up from just 7.8 percent in 1970. Among the foreign-born population, approximately 71 percent were Latinx and nearly 18 percent were APIs. Not all ethnic groups expanded; the region lost 72,000 white residents to out-migration and low birth rates.

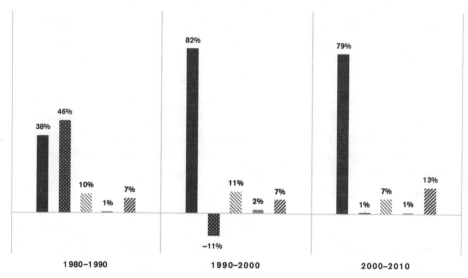

■ Latino ▨ White ⬝ Black ⬝ Native American ⧄ Asian/Pacific Islander

1980–1990
38% · 46% · 10% · 1% · 7%

1990–2000
82% · −11% · 11% · 2% · 7%

2000–2010
79% · 1% · 7% · 1% · 13%

FIGURE 17. A Latinx region in the making: share of population growth by race, Riverside and San Bernardino Counties. Author's analysis of U.S. Census data, 1990, 2000, and 2010.

Even as overall ethnic diversity increased, segregation continued to shape the region's largest cities. Established major cities like Riverside, San Bernardino, Fontana, and Ontario all had majority or near-majority Latinx populations. Some of the fastest growing cities, especially those that marketed themselves as upscale, white-collar communities, had relatively large white populations. Temecula and Murrieta, for example—both located in southwestern Riverside County—often identified with their whiter and more affluent neighbors in Orange County rather than the Inland Empire. Other fast-growing and outlying cities—Moreno Valley, Corona, and Victorville—had larger Latinx populations. African Americans were most heavily concentrated in San Bernardino, Moreno Valley, and Victorville. Asian and Pacific Islanders were concentrated in Rancho Cucamonga, Corona, Temecula, and Murrieta, all cities with relatively large white populations and smaller numbers of Latinxs.

FIXING RACE AND SPACE

Inland Southern California's war-era migration is particularly revealing because it illustrates how race, class, and political power were grafted onto the land during the expansion of American capitalism's golden age.[12] Kaiser's mill was but a subplot in the bigger story of capitalism's expansion into the American West. The war was a pretext for what Henry Kaiser really wanted, which was to build a steel empire that could provide construction material for the expansion of the American West during the postwar period. According to Kaiser's plan, Fontana would be converted "from wartime products into [a] well-rounded, integrated range of peacetime products, enabling it not only to survive, but to be a strong, independent competitive force in the West and in the whole steel industry."[13] Kaiser believed that he could earn a fortune if the region continued to develop and if he could provide the steel needed for the expected construction boom. Yet he lacked the capital to build the type of facility that could compete with Big Steel, the East Coast monopoly that controlled most of the country's steel production.[14]

Japan's bombing of Pearl Harbor gave Kaiser an opportunity to secure funding for his project by convincing the federal Reconstruction Finance Corporation (RFC) to expedite a loan.[15] Kaiser framed the loan as a private-public partnership that would produce enough steel to arm the Pacific Fleet. Big Steel tried to hamper Kaiser's plans. East Coast steel executives pressured members of the RFC to require that all new facilities be built fifty miles inland; this would—according to the new provision—protect them from Japanese bombing raids. Fontana provided a spatial solution to Big Steel's roadblocks. The dusty inland town gave Kaiser access to relatively cheap land that was far enough from Japan's warships yet close enough to a robust transportation network that connected it to Los Angeles and the Bay Area. It also benefited from access to ample sources of water and power, remnants of earlier investments in the agricultural industry. Kaiser's mill eventually propelled the United States toward victory by producing enough steel to build a steady supply of navy warships. Fontana's workers made most of the steel used at Kaiser's seven West Coast shipyards.

Big Steel's opposition to Kaiser did not end with the mill's construction. In fact, U.S. Steel successfully negotiated favorable postwar terms with government lenders and managed to purchase a steel plant in Geneva, Utah, for twenty cents on the dollar. Kaiser responded by launching a public relations campaign to secure better financing terms on a renegotiated federal loan that he argued would allow him to compete with Big Steel's efforts to expand into the West Coast. His supporters in Congress rallied to Kaiser's defense by framing the mill as a symbol of economic sovereignty for western states. California congressman Chet Holifield described Kaiser's struggle against

U.S. Steel as "a mighty struggle between the power of huge companies and the economic freedom of the West."[16] Kaiser also appealed to consumers by claiming that a new mill would produce 750,000 tons of finished steel that "could be rolled into critically-needed hot and cold-rolled sheets to make consumer goods, home appliances, stoves, refrigerators, farm equipment, freight cars, and automobiles."[17] To deny Kaiser meant subjecting U.S. consumers to scarcer and more expensive goods. Kaiser's publicity materials declared: "America cannot afford to subscribe to an economy of scarcity and indecision."[18] Kaiser's transformation into a producer of steel for commodities marked a transition to the postwar era's consumer society. The mill became an icon of postwar standardized production and mass middle-class consumption.[19]

If the crisis of war convinced federal lenders to support the mill's construction, direct appeal to consumers and commodities was the clear driver of further government support for the Fontana plant. In fact, at the height of its production cycle the mill became the largest steel manufacturing plant west of the Mississippi. It drew iron ore, manganese, and fluorspar from California's mountains and coal from mines in Utah. The 2.25 million tons of iron ore needed to operate three blast furnaces were shipped in from an open-pit mine at Eagle Mountain. Kaiser had to go farther to secure another key ingredient—labor—for his steel plant.

The inland region posed a labor problem that could not be solved by the army of imaginary pigs that was popular in company literature. Kaiser's promise to supply navy warships meant that he had to staff the mill in a relatively short amount of time. In the absence of other significant steel-producing facilities on the West Coast from which he could recruit, he had to train a new labor force or import skilled workers. Company executives decided that they didn't have enough time to train workers during the middle of a war. Instead, Kaiser recruited them from other steel-producing regions. Experienced steelworkers from the East Coast and Midwest flocked to the Inland Empire when the mill was first built in the 1940s. These mostly white families moved west because Kaiser provided a solid economic foundation that allowed many of them to buy new homes, get good jobs, and pursue their suburban American dreams. This was a familiar business practice for Kaiser, one that company officials had used to recruit workers to its Richmond and Portland shipyards in the early 1940s.[20] Kaiser executives lured skilled white workers by providing a social safety net that included affordable health care and housing. These incentives were an important part of producing an attractive space, especially in boomtown areas, where the local infrastructure was not adequately set up to provide a comfortable living for young families. Kaiser's need to attract skilled white workers meant that company officials had to produce Fontana as a desirable place to live.

Henry Kaiser's efforts to recruit skilled white workers earned the company a reputation as a liberal employer. Consequently, skilled white workers enjoyed benefits that fell along racial lines. While the company did not have a de jure policy of segregation, racial tensions were built into the division of labor. Economic opportunities were institutionalized through Kaiser's hiring practices, which depended on imported skilled white workers, who were the first to be hired. The rest of the jobs were distributed to Kaiser's multiracial blue-collar workforce. A former Kaiser worker explained how this worked: "You basically had three types of mill workers. They either called you nigger, wetback, or white boy."[21] Many of the worst jobs were reserved for African American and Latinx workers. For example, those who got stuck working in the dangerously hot and dirty coke oven were mostly Black and Latinx, or as another former white worker put it, "that's where the ex-felons and foreigners worked."[22] Ex-felons was a code word for Black, while foreigner was a code word for Mexican.

Even though Kaiser developed a liberal reputation, race and gender progressivism weren't always present in the company's labor policies. For example, the Fair Employment Practices Commission (FEPC) responded to complaints from the National Association for the Advancement of Colored People (NAACP) and found that Black workers were routinely paid lower wages than their white peers at Kaiser's shipyards.[23] When the FEPC urged Kaiser to promote more Black workers by appointing them to supervise integrated work crews, Kaiser officials balked, claiming that such a move would lead to a race riot. The mix of imported white workers from conservative regions like the Midwest and South with Black and Mexican workers created mounting tensions both in and outside of the workplace. Kaiser's plants were officially desegregated, but dining halls and other common areas were divided along racial lines. Racial divisions were palpable and volatile inside company housing. In one episode, after "a black worker kept his radio on despite complaints, three hundred whites gathered at Hudson House, bent on violence. It took a vanguard of police to prevent bloodshed, or even a race riot."[24] In both cases—the specter of a race riot if Kaiser appointed Black workers to supervise integrated work crews and the threat of racialized violence by white workers to discipline and control a Black worker—race and class were mapped onto everyday spaces. Racial violence was also written into the geographies of Southern California's postwar industrial landscape, including Fontana and the Inland Empire. For instance, O'Day Short, his wife, and two children were killed by an arsonist who set their Fontana home on fire in December 1945. Mr. Short had moved his family into a segregated white neighborhood; his neighbors responded by threatening to hurt them if they did not leave.[25] The assault on the Short family took place in the same industrial spatial order and political culture that was erected by postwar capitalism in inland Southern California.

CLAIMING SPACE

Fontana, like Maywood, is an example of what happened to suburbs during the transition from a postwar Keynesian spatial order to one based on flexible accumulation. By the 1980s Fontana had become a staging ground for the type of economic and ethnic transformation that was taking place in many cities across the American West.[26] Kaiser Steel, for example, announced that it would shut down part of its Fontana operation and reduce the labor force by three thousand in November 1981. The mill, the largest in the region, employed approximately seven thousand workers at the time of the initial reduction. Some local residents responded to economic decline by blaming job losses on the region's changing racial demographics. Such claims echoed Samuel Huntington's argument that Mexican immigrants posed an economic threat to the United States.[27]

Racial explanations for mounting economic hardship were implicated in a series of violent attacks against Black and Latinx residents during the 1980s and 1990s. One of the most violent attacks took place on July 1, 1980, when Dovard Howard was repairing a telephone cable off a side street in Fontana. Witnesses would later tell police they saw a white man drive up to where Dovard was working, get out of his car, shout a racial epithet, and shoot him in the back with a shotgun.[28] Mr. Howard survived, but doctors were forced to remove one of his lungs. Just over two hours after Howard was shot, and not far from where his blood seeped into Fontana's streets, the Ku Klux Klan held a march and public rally.[29] Klan members denied any responsibility for the shooting. One exasperated KKK member tried to deflect blame, saying, "You know what gets me? A nigger gets shot, and bam, sure as hell, they blame the Klan."[30]

FIGURE 18. Ku Klux Klan members march through residential streets in Fontana, CA, November 28, 1981. Photo by Mike Mullen, Herald-Examiner Collection, Los Angeles Public Library.

Nonetheless, Howard's family and local African American community leaders blamed the KKK for establishing a climate of racial hostility that provoked and sanctioned anti-Black violence. Reverend William D. Dunston, head of the Rialto NAACP, a city immediately east of Fontana, cited the attack on Dovard Howard and other violent acts, claiming that "many Black people are living in fear."[31] To Dunston and other community members who organized a Black Solidarity Rally at Fontana's City Hall, what happened to Howard was part of a more expansive cycle of racial violence, which defined the Inland Empire as a hostile space for Black and Brown people. The threat of racial violence during the 1980s and 1990s was so pervasive that Fontana gained a reputation as KKK territory.[32] As figure 18 suggests, KKK members tried to inscribe themselves onto the region's suburban landscape by staging public performances in which they marched through the streets to claim Fontana as a white space. Tensions ran high enough in the aftermath of the Howard shooting that the LA-based Nation of Islam sent fifty men from a special self-defense unit to patrol Black neighborhoods in Fontana, Rialto, and San Bernardino.[33]

Increased KKK activity during the 1980s was a violent response to a feeling of white dispossession. White supremacists capitalized on growing social and economic malaise by producing a narrative of loss and displacement that depicted white blue-collar workers as victims of globalization. Tom Leyden, a Fontana native and former leader of the violent skinhead group the Hammerskins, attributed rising racist acts to white working-class economic and social displacement. "I think the Klan took total advantage of that as the mill shut down," he said.[34] In fact, KKK leaders produced a white working-class narrative of the Inland Empire that connected manufacturing job losses to a narrative of white displacement. According to Tom Metzger, a former KKK grand dragon for the state of California, the Inland Empire's down-and-out blue-collar identity, embodied in a place like Fontana and the Kaiser mill, made it prime recruiting territory for white supremacist groups.[35]

While some narratives of loss and dispossession were framed in blatant racial terms, others were more nuanced. For example, white suburban melancholia framed loss and dispossession by lamenting the disappearance of a more rural or agricultural landscape.[36] According to this narrative, the Inland Empire that once existed as an antiurban space removed from LA's urban core was in danger of being lost. Rapid population growth, changing racial geographies, and the disappearance of an old agricultural order were all blamed on the incursion of the big bad city. Lamenting this lost antiurban idyll effectively meant calling for the return of the highly racialized economic and political structures that held such a society in place. This cognitive remapping of racial and economic displacement was meant to rally white residents who might have felt their homes and old ways of life were slipping away.[37] Such a conflation among a sense of belonging, power, space, and privilege is similar to what Paul Gilroy refers to in his discussion of postcolonial melancholia, a condition in which colonial powers yearn for the charmed lives of their imperial pasts and try to recapture nostalgic feelings by reproducing old relationships of dominance.[38] Postcolonial melancholia provides an elegant way for us to connect statecraft and the economic logic of colonialism with the emotional and cultural forces tied to Williams's work on structures of feeling. In the Inland Empire, lamenting the loss of particular landscapes involved a melancholic nostalgia for the types of segregated spaces and charmed lifestyles that O'Day Short's white neighbors were trying to keep for themselves when they set fire to his house and killed his family.

The KKK's invocation of a racialized working-class spatial imaginary—grounded in what Metzger referred to as the "White workers of Fontana"—

firmly rooted racist organizing in the city's industrial past and the defunct Kaiser steel mill. As Metzger told a reporter, "One of the main reasons for it [KKK activity] was because it wasn't long before the steel plant closed down. . . . There was a lot of integration of the neighborhoods going on and there were a lot of blue-collar white people there."[39] Whether or not this occurred at any significant level is not certain, but what is important is that this narrative became part of the mobilization strategy for racist social movements. For Metzer and those who supported his cause, the Inland Empire was part of a white cultural narrative that linked the region to the Kaiser mill and the social relations embedded in the production of Fontana as a racially exclusive space.[40] He argued that the name "Inland Empire" was an extension of the KKK's claim to the region and used it to characterize inland Southern California as a symbolic white refuge.[41] Such mappings, or "representations of space," sanctioned racial violence by invoking an emotional call to protect a sense of territorial entitlement.

Metzger's mapping of blue-collar economics and racial politics was on full display during the lead-up to a 1988 Martin Luther King Jr. birthday parade. Local white supremacists discovered that Martin Luther King III was scheduled to speak and chose to use the parade as a rallying point.[42] They were apparently outraged over the appearance. Metzger posted a message to his Aryan Update telephone hotline to warn the world that the "White workers of Fontana" would demonstrate if King marched on city streets.[43] The president of the White Mafia used the shuttered Kaiser mill and rising unemployment to justify his opposition to the King march. He declared to a small gathering of reporters, "Whites have rights, too, . . . can't even get a job around here."[44] This invocation of racial and class oppression is a familiar trope among skinhead groups. Some have used the image of a crucified skinhead to embody white working-class oppression.

Although membership in racist organizations was not numerically significant, these racial mappings were pervasive.[45] According to the Center for the Study of Hate and Extremism at Cal State San Bernardino, the Inland Empire had one of the highest concentrations of hate groups in the country, approximately one dozen. For many African American and Latinx residents, Fontana became synonymous with white supremacy. Draymond Crawford, a Black associate pastor at the Loveland Church, summed up this feeling: "These people can thrive openly here. . . . A lot of people tend to have similar philosophies, but they're hidden."[46] In fact, references to Fontana as "Klan territory" were pervasive in 1997, when the Mexican American Political

FIGURE 19. Vandals paint KKK graffiti and erect a cross on the home of Anthony Alexander and his mother, Ora Angel, San Bernardino, CA, 1984. Photo by Paul Chinn, Herald Examiner Collection, Los Angeles Public Library.

Association (MAPA) and the Rainbow Coalition protested and filed complaints against what they claimed were racist teaching practices in the Fontana School District after an African American student claimed that a teacher had tried to convince students slavery had a positive impact on the United States and that slaves were treated well.[47]

The notion of an underlying presence in the landscape, the pervasive specter of the KKK, was echoed by Tom Metzger: "It's more secretive than the old Klan was because we have so many individuals who do not identify themselves and don't wear uniforms and don't go to marches. [But] that undercurrent is still there."[48] To the region's growing African American and Latinx residents, this racialized white geography was cognitively mapped as "Fontucky" and effectively linked the Inland Empire to the racist legacy of the American South.[49] Scenes of racial violence were proof that the racial past was very present in the landscape (see figure 19).

Even if Metzger was inflating the KKK's presence to remain relevant during a time when his organization was in disarray, the fact remained that many people continued to identify Fontana as KKK territory precisely because they mapped an underlying feeling of racial antagonism onto the region. In fact, this feeling was so pervasive that Shougang managers warned their Chinese workers against straying far from their hotel during the year they spent dismantling the Kaiser mill. Workers were told that they should beware of what managers called "the three Ks." They were also told to be on the lookout for skinheads and roving members of the Hells Angels.[50] Managers used the threat of white violence to control the movement and behavior of their imported Chinese labor force.

Racist mappings of the Inland Empire were increasingly challenged as more Black and Brown people moved into the region during the 1980s. We can see elements of this in the King march mentioned previously, during which Metzger invoked the "White workers of Fontana." Incidents like those mentioned prompted Black and Latinx community leaders to form People Against Racism (PAR) to challenge acts of white supremacy. PAR repeatedly appeared at and countered events organized by the region's KKK-affiliated and neo-Nazi splinter groups. Perhaps more important, they also attempted to produce new racial mappings that moved beyond the constraints of white spatial imaginaries by redrawing the Inland Empire as a space that was open for Black and Brown bodies. The very presence of Martin Luther King III on the streets of Fontana challenged the notion of the city as a white space. In fact, the march was as much about claiming Black space as it was about the white supremacist racial order. Marchers used their bodies to claim the streets as an inclusive public space and to challenge the white racist imaginary represented by cognitive mappings of Fontucky and the KKK. Reverend David Rodrigues evoked this spatial claim when he said, "We think it's a big step forward for the city. It's a message for all those people who didn't think we were civic-minded or open to all people."[51] During a church service after the march King said, "Fontana used to have a bad reputation, not any more, not after today."[52]

Dovard Howard's bloody entanglement with white supremacists and the other acts of racial violence previously mentioned cannot be separated from the social and economic context that shaped Fontana and the rest of inland Southern California. Most attempts to understand racism focus on linking discrimination to specific acts that isolate race from other factors. Such a surgical and ahistorical definition "suggests that racism can be eliminated on its own, because it is readily extricable from everything else."[53] But racism is an ideology distinct from discrete actions. As Laura Pulido argues, "while it may be possible statistically to separate and analyze 'racial' and income groups, such a procedure does not necessarily help us to understand the racialized nature of our economy, including the process of class formation, the division of labor, and poverty."[54] One way to approach this understanding is to look at social actors and networks and to determine who they were, what motivated them, and how they organized themselves to wreak havoc. The forensic work of mapping these racist actors and networks must be left for another project. Nevertheless, it is important to note that these actors represent only one level of the much more complex and multilayered set of forces that produced Fontana as a racialized landscape. Fontana and other parts of inland Southern California will help us understand how racism evolved through and with specific regimes of power and money. Even if the KKK represents only the most extreme aspect of this sentiment, nostalgia and melancholia caused some residents to fight for older orders. Anti-Black sentiments quickly turned into anti-Mexican discourse as the Latinx population grew. A former Kaiser worker characterized this shift thus: "The place went from being Fontucky to being FonTijuana."[55]

EIGHT

Land, Capital, and Race

MARCIA NAROG, A FIERY, MIDDLE-AGED white woman, stood before the Moreno Valley Planning Commission in January 2009 and claimed that her rural way of life was under attack.[1] She and some of her neighbors had pushed city leaders to include equestrian trails in land use policies like the general plan.[2] Now she was among more than six hundred people who had shown up to participate in a crowded public debate about whether the relatively small city of 200,000 would become the next development frontier for the global logistics industry. The public hearing was an opportunity for opponents and supporters to express their opinions on whether city leaders should allow the construction of a 1.8-million-square-foot Skechers shoe warehouse. People were drawn to the meeting because it also represented a struggle between groups with seemingly opposing ways of life. Anti-warehouse activists were concerned that the proposed warehouse project would clear the way for large-scale development that would encroach on their pastoral lifestyles. Not everyone opposed the warehouse. A large contingent of warehouse supporters wore white T-shirts with the words "Jobs Now!" printed in bright orange lettering; they erupted in raucous applause when anyone made a point in their favor. It was a heated debate, and commission members were forced to extend the meeting deep into the night to accommodate everyone in the audience who wished to speak.

Many of the speakers alluded to racial and class differences to explain what appeared to be wide ideological gaps between opponents and supporters. On the surface, the racial differences were obvious. For example, while 88 percent of those who spoke against the warehouse were white, supporters were overwhelmingly Latinx.[3] What was more interesting is how the Skechers warehouse became a proxy struggle between groups with different lifestyles and approaches to what constituted a valued way of life. The Skechers debate ultimately became a struggle over who had a right to shape the city and provides an opportunity to examine how global capital must sometimes negotiate locally embedded histories of race and class to establish new territory.[4] More specifically, horses and warehouses served as proxies for a broader contest over how city space would be produced during a period of economic and demographic transition. Public comments about the growing blue-collar labor force and the upscale nature of economic development were direct references to the demographic changes that transformed Moreno Valley and the rest of the region between 1990 and 2010. For example, the city's white population plummeted from 57 percent in 1990 to less than 20 percent in 2010.[5] At the same time the Latinx population increased from 23 to 54 percent.[6] Warehouse supporters cited the demographic shift to argue that the new Latinx majority needed blue-collar warehouse jobs. Those who wore the "Jobs Now!" T-shirts during the planning commission meeting were signaling that Moreno Valley's Latinx population had a right to shape the city in a way that met their perceived interests. The Skechers case was unique to Moreno Valley, but the arguments were not. Many of the points made during the debate could have applied to other communities, especially those that were forced to confront the challenges wrought by global economic restructuring while also adjusting to rapid demographic changes.

DON'T WORRY, IT'S A NICE BUILDING

One of the evening's key speakers was Ido Benzeevi, head of Highland Fairview Properties. Benzeevi's company had signed an eleven-year, $100 million lease with the Skechers shoe company and needed the planning commission to approve the project before construction could begin.[7] Benzeevi's pitch included an elaborate multimedia presentation that used computer animations to downplay any negative consequences linked to projected truck traffic. He also claimed that the new distribution center would help alleviate the economic crisis by creating jobs and improving the city's quality of life.[8] He defended his project from critics who claimed that the proposed warehouse would dump more diesel truck traffic into neighborhoods that were already overburdened with dangerous levels of air pollution. Instead, his presentation focused on the aesthetic qualities of the building and suggested that the city's mountain vistas would not be harmed by the new warehouse

FIGURE 20. Skechers warehouse in Moreno Valley. Courtesy Skyphotos Aerial Photography.

(see figure 20). He called the new distribution center a "world-class" facility with a good design pedigree because the architectural firm was based in Orange County, a reference meant to imbue the project with upper-class status.

Benzeevi's reference to "world-class" design produced a narrative of beautiful exceptionalism, in which aesthetics were meant to downplay the potential deadly environmental consequences of the project. He described how clever design techniques would mask the distribution center's presence in the landscape. For example, a row of trees and a lowered elevation would partially hide the warehouse from those driving along the freeway. Benzeevi claimed that the design would make the warehouse nearly invisible. ProLogis first vice president Mike Del Santo asserted that landscape design and architecture would mask some of the more unsightly elements of a modern warehouse. Del Santos argued that the design was so effective, "You'd think they were a community recreation center or a community cultural center."[9] These same aesthetic design cues were cited by politicians, who argued that the upscale nature of the warehouse development somehow set it apart from other distribution centers in the region. Council member Bonnie Flickinger, for example, rejected the comparison of Moreno Valley to the high pollution levels of Mira Loma and suggested that good building design could prevent environmental problems: "There's no relation in the development standards we impose and those that created that mess over there."[10] What might seem like mundane land use decisions were in fact contentious episodes in the ongoing struggle between local and global forces to shape the production of space. Such *choques* or confrontations, "are not merely localized arenas in which broader global or national projects of neoliberal restructuring unfold." Instead, these contested spaces are, as Neil Brenner and Nik Theodore note, "increasingly central to the reproduction, mutation, and continual reconstitution of neoliberalism itself."[11] They illustrate how local development fights are embedded in multiscalar relationships among economics, social status, and culture. Simply put, the forces and actors involved in the Skechers debate were also producing a new territorial regime that made it possible for global capitalism to expand and evolve.

Global investors were forced to rely on local intermediaries like Highland Fairview to help negotiate contentious land use politics. Highland Fairview was particularly valuable as an intermediary because company leaders had developed an extensive political network that could help clear the way for controversial development projects. Benzeevi gained political clout by building a new inland growth regime that framed logistics as vital to the collective interests of a growing Latinx population. One consequence of this political strategy was that logistics space was produced through the modalities of racial and class politics.

THE POLITICS OF GLOBAL AND LOCAL SPACE

Benzeevi's political apparatus would have to defeat an old governing bloc that included people like Marsha Narog. He began chipping away at the old regime by making a series of relatively large contributions to school board and city council races during the 2004 election cycle.[12] He also created an economic council that involved County Supervisor Marion Ashley, City Planning Commissioner Michael Geller, Moreno Valley school board member Tracey Vackar, and several other business leaders. All of these efforts were part of a strategy to gain political support for future development projects.

One way that Benzeevi's political apparatus provided value to global and national logistics companies was its ability to negotiate the complicated labyrinth of local development politics. Skechers senior vice president of distribution Paul Galliher alluded to this when he explained how Highland Fairview used its relationships to shepherd the project along: "We are very pleased we were able to secure an agreement with Highland Fairview Logistics at their Rancho Belago development. . . . The city manager and his team have been extremely helpful and supportive."[13] Such support included Mayor Bill Batey's decision to shorten the public review period for the Skechers warehouse from the normal thirty days to only ten. The mayor cited the city's high unemployment rate of 15.5 percent to justify his decision and defended his action by telling the local press: "I don't want to see 1,000 jobs going to another city if we have an opportunity to land them here."[14] Even with stout support from local political officials Highland Fairview could not snuff out all dissent. Some council members, environmental organizations, and residents questioned whether a few jobs were enough to offset the negative outcomes that were outlined in the environmental impact report. Critics were particularly aggrieved by the mayor's decision to shorten the review period because it gave them less time to mount a legal environmental challenge.

Any elected officials who challenged the Skechers project faced a substantial backlash from Benzeevi's political apparatus. When council member Charles White questioned Benzeevi's efforts to rename part of eastern Moreno Valley, the developer contributed money to White's political opponents. Benzeevi's personal contributions were amplified by his political machine. For example, the same Michael Geller who sat on Benzeevi's economic council was also the head of the Moreno Valley Taxpayers Association (MVTA), which received a $263,000 contribution from Highland Fairview during the 2008 election cycle.[15] Charles White and Frank West, both of whom expressed opposition to the warehouse development, were ousted in 2008 by candidates who received major contributions from the MVTA. By the time Highland Fairview signed a lease with Skechers, Benzeevi was assured that his project would be approved by the newly reconstituted and more development-friendly city council.

Benzeevi's political network included key leaders of Moreno Valley's growing Latinx population. His financial contributions helped Jesse Molina become the only Latino to sit on an otherwise all-white city council.[16] Benzeevi's personal relationship with Victoria Baca, who sat on the school board, also gave Highland Fairview access to her network of Latinx community activists. Baca served as Molina's campaign manager and as head of the Moreno Valley Parent Association (MVPA), a group that was very active in education and immigrant rights issues. When Baca spoke in support of the warehouse before the planning commission that night in 2009, she identified herself as a Latina community activist. She did not mention her professional and political ties to

Highland Fairview. These community activists helped Highland Fairview broaden the Skechers debate by positioning the warehouse as a vital economic boost to the region's growing blue-collar Latinx community. For example, several of those who spoke before the planning commission, including members of the MVPA and the Mexican American Political Association (MAPA), cast the anti-warehouse camp as an elitist group that was out of touch with the economic interests of the city's growing working class.

Raul Wilson, a MAPA leader and longtime activist, claimed that the Skechers fight marked a deeper social conflict "between the rich and the poor."[17] For Wilson, a seventy-something Latino with thinning hair and dark mustache, Skechers was a line of demarcation, with working-class families lined up on one side and wealthy families on the other. He explained, "We are a divided city based on social class and income." Wilson described the divisions thus: "There are a few rich people in Moreno Valley, probably less than 100 families that always get their way in what happens . . . while the rest of us struggle for the bread crumbs we get in order to survive and provide for our families." For Wilson the "100 rich families that have organized the fight against Skechers and the jobs it will bring here" were part of the governance bloc that had reproduced racial and class privilege by writing it into local development policy.[18]

Supporters argued that access to blue-collar warehouse jobs meant economic opportunity for local residents. Accordingly, denying people access to logistics jobs for the sake of protecting a pastoral lifestyle amounted to class warfare against the city's growing working class. The result was a type of moral spatial economy that linked the success of the logistics industry with the economic welfare of the Latinx population. Warehouse supporters invoked social justice language and political performance to emphasize their claims. At one point Norma Cortez, a senior partner at a local staffing agency, tried to rally the overflowing planning commission audience by turning to them and shouting, "What do we want [gesticulating at the audience with both arms]? Jobs! And when do we want them?" Audience members answered with an emphatic "Now!"[19] Cortez's call for jobs adopted the language and performance routinely used by unions and other SMOs. It was a point that activist Raul Wilson hammered home when he declared during the planning commission hearing, "We want Skechers. We want jobs and we want them now." Warehouse supporters thus repositioned logistics development as a common good that stood in contrast to the antidevelopment lifestyles of an elite pastoral ruling class. Their argument echoed regional boosters who claimed that logistics was as an economic solution for the region's struggling blue-collar workforce.

Moreno Valley became the testing ground for a new brand of racial and class politics that connected the official logistics development discourse (described in previous chapters) with a pro-jobs Latinx political coalition. The warehouse fight provided a platform for Latinx political actors to mobi lize the growing population by performing a type of ethnic politics that tied political power to support for the logistics regime. Victoria Baca exemplified how this transpired when she argued that the region's Latinx workers, many of whom had low education levels, needed the entry-level jobs that were promised by logistics boosters. According to her, to deny warehouse construction amounted to an anti-Latinx agenda. Jobs were deployed as a shield against critics who argued that warehouse development would harm local communities. A prominent warehouse critic worried that speaking out against Skechers would mark someone as anti-Latinx and anti-jobs.[20] Yet it was never clear how many jobs were at stake during the Skechers debate. Highland Fairview remained noncommittal about the actual number of new jobs that would be created, but industry estimates suggest that modern warehouses produce only nine employees per acre that is developed.[21]

Warehouse supporters tried to paint the opposition as a rich white elite that was insensitive to the needs of other residents, but the presence of middle-class homeowners like Vivian Galvan complicated this image. Galvan had been lured into eastern Moreno Valley by slick marketing materials that promised a pastoral lifestyle. She told commissioners that she had moved to the area because developers had guaranteed her a home with access to natural vistas and pastoral landscapes. Galvan held up a development brochure during her public comments to emphasize this point. She raised the brochure above the podium and exclaimed, "When I bought my home in this area I was promised Rancho Belago, a beautiful community." The sales brochure claimed that she would be "able to ride my horse, I was going to be able to walk on the trails. . . . [T]his is not beautiful [pointing to an image of the proposed warehouse]."[22] Inland cities like Moreno Valley provided an opportunity for many middle-class Latinx, Asian, and African American residents like Galvan to buy a house that they could not otherwise afford in the more expensive coastal cities of Los Angeles and Orange Counties. Their presence in the Skechers debate complicated long-standing racial and class alignments, in which poor meant Latinx and rich meant white. Vivian Galvan and other members of the region's racially diverse middle class therefore challenged the notion that a racist white elite was trying to deny jobs to poor Mexicans and Central Americans by framing their opposition as an effort to maintain an antiurban lifestyle.

Even if the racial and class differences were more nuanced, warehouse supporters cited people like Margie Breitkreuz, a member of the Moreno Valley Recreational Trails Board, to argue that antidevelopment activists routinely used coded racial and class language to devalue logistics development. Breitkreuz claimed that she opposed the Skechers warehouse because "Rancho Belago is supposed to be upscale."[23] The notion that warehouses were not "upscale" underpinned a spatial economy that attached moral and economic value to pastoral landscapes. Marsha Narog referenced this moral spatial economy when she declared, "People that are wanting these jobs do not necessarily live or appreciate the values that we appreciate in the 92555 zip code area and I think condemning us to a lifestyle we don't want is irresponsible."[24] Stopping Skechers meant protecting their ability and perceived right to pursue a good life, which was dependent on negating those who did not "appreciate the values" that they held dear. Narog's comments marked anyone who wanted access to a warehouse job as an outsider and therefore discredited their right to shape the city's development path. The racial and class implications of this insider/legitimate versus outsider/illegitimate dichotomy became more evident throughout the evening.

Louise Palomares—a self-identified community activist—challenged the anti-warehouse spatial economy by arguing that Skechers would be a valuable addition to her community. Ms. Palomares told the planning commission, "This is gonna be good for our students, when they get out of school and they graduate cause a lot of them ain't ready to go into colleges, a lot of them ain't ready to go into the trade schools. And we don't have no jobs."[25] Palomares was in fact arguing that blue-collar warehouse jobs were part of an economic plan to provide employment for the region's growing young Latinx population, a claim that echoed SCAG's and Husing's logistics discourse. In their view, warehouse jobs represented a greater public good and thus a moral logic that justified their opposition to elite pastoral landscapes. Warehouse supporters were so successful at reframing the debate that other issues like the environment and traffic were drowned out. Some speakers did address increased traffic and pollution concerns, but the major arc of the debate was centered along racial and class lines.

Marsha Narog and her allies responded to these critiques by claiming that warehouse supporters were engaging in "a gross discrimination against people with visions of a different lifestyle."[26] Narog described how these "visions of a different lifestyle" were codified into local policy. "We worked long and hard for the General Plan to have a business park there, we wanted to have an overpass where people could walk or ride their bikes to work." What Narog referred to as "visions" were in fact spatial ideologies that informed the city's politics. Spatial ideologies served as a cognitive map of what should and should not exist in the landscape. This mapping was clear when Narog testified, "We had a vision, we have a dream too. Our dream did not include warehouses, our dream did not include extra semi-trucks, our dream did not include a lot of what Ido Benzeezi's dream is."[27] These "dreams" were important rhetorical tools that contesting sides used to give moral weight to their arguments about how space should be produced. Warehouse supporters dismissed such claims by arguing that local policy simply reflected the racial and class aspirations of a dominant class. Pastoral lifestyle policies were, according to warehouse supporters, discriminatory spatial practices that were inscribed into law and sanctioned by the state. The morality and value attached to an equestrian way of life was therefore nothing more than an exercise of racial and class power.

Raul Wilson's and Marsha Narog's exchange was a political performance meant to rally support to either side. What is fascinating and insightful about these performances was that both sides positioned the construction of a single warehouse as a spatial competition between contesting ways of life. It is especially revealing that horses became a marker of racial and class antagonism, because equestrian identities have a long history of serving as proxies for race and class in the American West, where, as Laura Barraclough describes, "the horse is simultaneously a symbol of the American frontier experience and a marker of wealth, status and political power."[28] Post-1940s suburban activists in Southern California's San Fernando Valley used horse-keeping to protect their white privilege without having to talk explicitly about race. Instead, the horse-keeping lifestyle became a color-blind pastoral trope that enabled activists to maintain their power over the landscape without having to wave the banner of "explicit white supremacy."[29]

The historical lesson is that color-blind pastoral tropes have been used to produce idyllic portraits of the countryside that obfuscate the power and violence required to produce racial and class difference. What might seem like a lovely, pastoral idyll is often made possible by the dispossession of land and by exploitative labor systems.[30] Warehouse supporters were referencing this much longer history of power, identity, and space when they framed equestrian lifestyles as manifestations of hegemonic power.[31] For activists like Raul Wilson, building the Skechers warehouse meant challenging the ability of local elites to create spaces that condemned working-class Latinxs to economic and political disenfranchisement. When trying to make sense of why anyone would oppose the warehouse, he characterized the fight this way: "So why are these rich people, living high in the hills, fighting against Skechers? Simple, because they don't care about the poor. They've always looked down their noses at us. They don't care if our families have jobs."[32] The implied spatial distance was analogous to Wilson's own moral economies, in which class and human value were intrinsically linked. "We live in different worlds and the people fighting Skechers don't care about ours. So they use their scare tactics and act like they care about our children, but they don't fool us. We know they don't care about us. They never have and they never will. Can we really hold that against them? Not really. It's just who they are."[33] For Wilson, spatial difference, what he called "different worlds," was equivalent to a moral economy of human value in which those with power produced landscapes that exposed poor and marginalized groups to economic and social precarity.

While Wilson's separation between the rich and poor made for a dramatic rhetorical gesture, these seemingly separate worlds were in fact woven together by a complex and multilayered spatial order. One could not exist without the other. Marsha Narog's reference to the general plan as a document that enshrined her community's desire for low-density development and equestrian landscapes affirmed claims by warehouse supporters who argued that existing policy documents simply reproduced the ruling elite's power to shape the city in their interests. By challenging the equestrian lifestyle, warehouse supporters were going after the institutional and political infrastructure that enabled a specific spatial and racial order to exist. They were chipping away at the state-sanctioned property rights that codified and protected racial and class privilege.[34] Perhaps more important, they were also challenging the moral spatial economy that sanctioned and reproduced precarity. The issue was, as Raul Wilson noted, much bigger than the Skechers warehouse, because it implicated a more expansive struggle over land use and the right to the city.[35]

BUILDING THE GOOD LIFE ON SOUTHERN CALIFORNIA'S DEVELOPMENT FRONTIER

The Skechers debate was part of a wider effort by local policy makers to move away from the region's agricultural economy, while maintaining symbolic elements of the nonworking rural landscape. Rural aesthetics were particularly important to this strategy because local land use policies had historically favored nonurban development. Regional planners during the postwar period, for example, used low-density land policies to produce an antiurban region for white homeowners who were fleeing post-segregation-era urban Los Angeles. Inland cities tried to make the region more attractive to potential settlers by avoiding the type of high-density development that defined racialized urban living. Instead, they implemented low-density growth by setting aside large amounts of land for single-family housing and retail development. This pattern extended to the 1950s and 1970s, when San Bernardino County allocated 40 percent of all usable, level land to low-density housing.[36] An additional 25 percent of the remaining land was set aside for streets and highways. Only 8 percent was designated for industry and utilities. Low-density development on the urban fringe, what some would call sprawl, was a deliberate political and economic choice.[37]

Economic changes during the 1980s prodded Inland Empire policy makers to change course. They responded by rezoning agricultural land into more profitable terrain for logistics and residential housing development. More than 178,000 acres of farmland were converted to other uses in Riverside and San Bernardino Counties between 1984 and 2014.[38] San Bernardino County supervisors endorsed this move away from agriculture by opening the Chino Dairy Preserve to real estate investment in 1993. Their decision allowed the cities of Ontario and Chino to annex more than 14,000 acres of former dairy land.[39] Other agricultural land was also converted into residential and industrial real estate during the warehouse and housing booms of the 2000s. Table 2 shows how pervasive this trend was across the Inland Empire. Most of the converted farmland was set aside for housing development, but warehouse developers also benefited.

Local developers and municipal leaders quickly drew up plans to turn the former dairy and other agricultural land into large master-planned communities, but pushing the cows out was a slow process. Approximately 290,000 cattle still roamed the preserve in 1999, making it one of the highest concentrations of dairies in the United States. By 2006, 80 percent of the 160 dairies that remained in operation either had been sold or were in escrow.[40] City leaders in Ontario and Chino adopted plans to replace the cows by adding more than 140,000 residents on the annexed dairy land. New development projects were given names like "The Preserve" and the "New Model Colony." The Chino City Council created an official vision for The Preserve project

TABLE 2. Former Farmland Converted to Housing and Warehouse Development, San Bernardino County, 2004–2006

Project	City	Conversion Type	Acres
Sorrento Housing	Redlands	Housing	55
Unnamed	Redlands	Housing	45
Ashley Furniture Warehouse	Redlands	Warehouse	45
California Palms Warehouse	Redlands	Warehouse	20
Power Plant	Redlands	Power Plant	15
Water Treatment Plant	Redlands	Water Treatment Plant	10
California Street Landfill	Redlands	Landfill	10
Mission Lane Homes	Loma Linda	Housing	60
Barton Vineyard Apartments	Loma Linda	Housing	25
Crafton	Yucaipa	Housing	50
Braeburn	Yucaipa	Housing	35
Citrus Estates	Highland	Housing	70
The Reserve Condos at Empire Lake	Rancho Cucamonga	Master Development	75
Kumho Tire Warehouse	Rancho Cucamonga	Warehouse	55
Town Square Shopping Center	Rancho Cucamonga	Retail	25
Sycamore Hills	Fontana	Housing	100
New Homes	Fontana	Housing	50
2 Distribution Centers	Fontana	Warehouse	100
Total			**845**

SOURCE: Data from California Department of Conservation Farmland Mapping and Monitoring Program, http://www.conservation.ca.gov/dlrp/fmmp.

that described it as "a contemporary community that captures the spirit of historic home town America combined with a respect for the agricultural heritage of the people who shaped the City of Chino and a commitment to cooperatively restoring and preserving a major piece of one of the Southland's most significant habitat resources."[41] The description hints at the strategies that local boosters and developers used to produce a marketable pastoral destination to middle-class homebuyers like Vivian Galvan. In fact, land conversions were part of a larger plan to remake the region into a place that catered to upper-middle-class residents and white-collar business sectors who sought relief from LA's crowded urban landscape.

High-value developers first had to convince potential customers that former dairy lands and uprooted farms could be transformed into desirable and valuable luxury developments. During his tenure as Ontario's city manager between 1997 and 2010, Greg Devereaux explained this logic: "We don't have the upscale and more urban kinds of housing that managers and owners want to live in. . . . And if they can't find someplace to live here, they won't locate here."[42] In other words, to lure white-collar development, the city needed a spatial strategy that included remaking itself into a desirable destination for a particular type of resident. Developers and boosters used spatial ideologies and regional narratives to increase the speculative value of inland Southern California by appealing to what Deveraux called "upscale" potential residents. White-collar workers were the literal and figurative embodiment of a regional development trajectory that included luxury housing, upscale shopping, and suitable professional employment opportunities. If warehouses represented the region's blue-collar future, then white-collar development was the antithesis. City leaders, especially those who no longer favored having mega-warehouses within their jurisdictions, tried to lure white-collar workers by approving master-planned lifestyle spaces for the upwardly mobile.

These white-collar development dreams were part of a longer historical arc in which pastoral tropes have been used to increase value and desire for white settler economies in the American West. Ido Benzeevi propagated such settler geographies as a strategy to increase real estate values. In fact, prior to the Skechers warehouse, Ido Benzeevi's biggest project had been the twenty-nine-hundred-unit, upscale Aquabella retirement community. The project included million-dollar tract homes aimed at the region's upper-income baby boomer population. Aquabella was supposed to be built on farm land that once served as an agricultural field station for the nearby University of California at Riverside. The field station's replacement by upscale housing was yet another example of how the region's agricultural space was slowly being plowed under by the expansion of residential construction and logistics. Benzeevi tried to increase the value of his rural real estate holdings by convincing Moreno Valley council members to rename a large section of the city Rancho Belago. According to the development's website, "Belago is a word meaning beautiful lakes, loosely translated from Italian and pays homage to the Southern California explorer De Anza and the cultural and natural heritage of this area."[43] The name is of course a fanciful invention. It follows the pattern of other master-planned development projects that have used European aesthetics and frontier narratives to produce marketable landscapes.[44] While it's easy to dismiss the Rancho Belago name change as boosterish hyperbole, its invocation of white settler spatial imaginaries—De Anza's plundering of indigenous lands—clearly demonstrates how developers continue to use pastoral narratives that erase and therefore glorify racial violence. Instead of dismissing Rancho Belago's name as an overreaching sales ploy, it should be taken as a serious attempt to produce an ideological normative space that is deeply implicated in the mutually constituted racial histories attached to white settler colonialism and American capitalism. Again, the key point here is that race, space, and capital are tightly woven into the production of everyday landscapes.

Frontier narratives like those referenced by the Rancho Belago website have functioned as ideological roadmaps for white settlement; they operate by clearing out troublesome racialized bodies. This emptying out of space produces a new landscape that is rendered open and conquerable. Performances and practices that invoke a Spanish fantasy have been key elements of this process. A fantasy heritage has enabled white settlers to appropriate land and culture while erasing what David G. Gutierrez described as "the actual historical producers of the culture that Anglos ostensibly celebrated."[45] Yet settler stories obfuscate the political and economic logics at work by erasing the racial violence that enabled frontier development.[46] They often exclude the critical role that the state, speculative investment, and real estate markets played in shaping the material landscape.[47] Cultural erasure, especially from the landscape, was a form of racial violence that cleared the way for new normative spatial and social orders, all built on exclusive access to private property rights.

One of the key functions of the fantasy heritage is to normalize white settler colonialism through the celebration of symbols and spaces that rationalize European conquest. Rancho Belago's website is one example. Another is the annual Ramona pageant, held less than twenty miles from eastern Moreno Valley. The pageant is an interpretation of Helen Hunt Jackson's novel *Ramona*; it romanticizes life in the aftermath of U.S. expansion into Mexican California. Hunt's novel was meant as a Progressive Era liberal critique of social discrimination against Native Americans. Yet the play's reformist slant also justifies cultural and territorial dispossession by never challenging white racial supremacy and power. Instead, the play proposes a compassionate liberal solution that reproduces white capitalist society by extending the American Dream to new subjects.

Jackson's novel reproduced the same settler narrative that was present in the Rancho Belago and Skechers debate. For example, middle-class homeowners who lamented the loss of a Spanish pastoral landscape—as viewed through the eyes of De Anza's Rancho Belago trope—were complicit in reproducing speculative settler economies. Both *Ramona* the play and Rancho Belago as Spanish fantasy landscape were marketing tools that were produced by developers to increase real estate values. The play was created in 1923 by the Hemet-San Jacinto Chamber of Commerce to attract real estate investment on what was once part of the Estudillo Mexican land grant. Condido Hopkins, a self-identified indigenous man who wrote to the U.S. Department of the Interior to complain that Native Americans should share in any profits related to the production of the play, described it as "primarily a publicity scheme on the part of the real estate interests."[48]

Rancho Belago was part of this same tradition. Developers located its genesis in the region's incorporation into the Spanish empire. "Three centuries ago, as the explorer De Anza surveyed inland Southern California for the Spanish king, he came upon the area known as Rancho Belago," reads the description on the development's website. According to the site, De Anza "was awestruck by its natural beauty and majestic landscape as he noted in his personal diary, 'as the most beautiful place' he had ever encountered."[49] Rancho Belago developers used De Anza to construct a landscape that rendered nature as a bountiful place. De Anza's imperious gaze was the first step in building a social system and spatial logic that turned the region's "natural beauty" into a profit-making landscape by making it available for a new generation of consumers.[50]

This effort to transform rural agricultural landscapes into upscale residential spaces required a cognitive and material remapping of the region. Rancho Belago's website, for example, included an image of a middle-aged white woman, dressed in fashionable workout clothes, walking briskly through tree-lined streets and under a French-themed, wrought iron street sign emblazoned with the words "Rancho Belago."[51] The ornate signs were part of a $350,000 streetscape plan meant to evoke the affluent lifestyle associated with Beverly Hills.[52] Rancho Belago's signs were so convincing that Beverly Hills threatened to sue it for trademark violations. An attorney for Beverly Hills argued, "[The sign] connotes an image of prestige and exclusivity that is the essence of the Beverly Hills brand."[53] There we have it. Elaborate street signs are nothing more than cultural techniques that developers use to make sense of and add value to commodified landscapes. Exclusive street signs and aspirational website images served as a narrative framework that developers hoped would connect individual home buyers' aspirations to the material spaces required to realize those fantasies. Culture, desire, and political power are part of the toolkit that developers routinely use to shape local real estate markets.

What does Rancho Belago teach us about race, space, and capital? First, it is a reminder that the idea of landscape is "inseparable from the construction of capitalist geographies based on," as Mitchell writes, "the full commodification of the land (and thereby the 'freeing' of labor) and the subsequent need to represent ownership (or non-ownership) as a natural order of society."[54] Rancho Belago's reference to an imperial gaze acted as a powerful ideological force that added value to new territory and therefore made it available for development. Second, cultural mappings and moral economies about what constitutes value and thus a good life play a key role in defining how local capitalisms develop. This means it is important to pay attention to normative or ideological processes in addition to other capitalist social relations like land and labor. For example, cognitive mappings and representations of the American West were crucial to the expansion of U.S. imperialism. Travel writers and explorer narratives provided ample material for people on the East Coast and in the Midwest to produce the West as a landscape of opportunity. "In producing these landscapes," Brady notes, "these writers initiated capitalism's work of rationalizing (normalizing and abstracting) space, making it available for measuring, assessing, selling."[55]

If De Anza's gaze represented the narrative that rationalized settler colonialism, regional builders embodied the financial machinery that turned inland Southern California into one of the country's largest housing markets. More than 54 percent of California's new homes were built in the Inland Empire during 2006.[56] National homebuilders in particular transformed local real estate markets when they invested vast amounts of capital during the 2000s building boom. Companies like Lennar, Pulte, Centex, and D. R. Horton invested heavily in the Inland Empire's real estate market. Table 3 lists California's top homebuilders. Several of the biggest builders expanded their market share by aggressively pursuing new projects in the Inland Empire.[57] Much of this housing boom was underwritten by banks and other financial institutions that also targeted Riverside and San Bernardino Counties. For example, Citigroup expanded its Inland Empire mortgage and refinancing operations to compete with local lending campaigns by Wells Fargo and Washington Mutual.[58]

Together, the speculative logics of finance capital and the cognitive remapping of the region transformed Southern California's landscape. As I have argued, fantastical cognitive mappings continue to do certain work that must be acknowledged, not as nostalgia, but as part of the reproduction of new topographies of power and money. Rancho Belago's imperial gaze provided a

TABLE 3. Top Homebuilders in the Inland Empire

Builder	Net Sales	Market Share	Number of Projects	Single Family
Lennar Homes	6,872	7.7%	198	81.00%
D.R. Horton	6,574	7.4%	141	65.73%
KB Home	5,175	5.8%	149	84.46%
Centex Homes	4,963	5.6%	136	88.80%
Pulte Homes	2,716	3.1%	74	82.33%
Shea homes	2,398	2.7%	71	80.69%
Standard Pacific Homes	2,151	2.4%	94	83.73%
K. Hovnanian Homes	1,996	2.3%	70	76.20%
Pacifica Companies	1,943	2.2%	28	0.00%
Richmond American Homes	1,536	1.7%	77	99.48%
Total	36,324	40.9%	1,038	—

SOURCE: Hanley Wood Market Intelligence (January–December 2006), http://www.hanleywood.com/tag/market-intelligence.

powerful psychological link between race and the political economy of state-sanctioned development. These individual and collective spatial imaginaries were underwritten by a state apparatus that created enough territorial coherence to enable capital investments in vital infrastructure. Like other frontier narratives, the renaming of eastern Moreno Valley as Rancho Belago enabled new settlers to craft the Inland Empire as a place where they could pursue their version of a good life.

SPECULATIVE LOGISTICS AND THE HUNT FOR LAND

Former agricultural land provided new investment opportunities for the booming industrial real estate market of the 2000s.[59] More than 159 million square feet of industrial space was built between 2000 and 2008.[60] Inland Southern California eclipsed Los Angeles County as the center of warehouse construction during the 2000s. More than 80 percent of all Southern California industrial space under construction as of June 2008 was in Riverside and San Bernardino Counties; Los Angeles County was second, at 12 percent.[61] Three factors contributed to the warehouse boom. First, inflated port projections created speculative demand for more warehouse space. Second, new finance products and innovations, including publicly traded real estate investment trusts (REITs), increased the amount of funding for industrial real estate. Finally, standardized logistics practices enabled developers to speculate on potential warehouse needs by erecting a portfolio of nonleased, build-on-spec distribution centers.

Modern warehouses are land-intensive projects. Roughly 50 percent of the land required for a new warehouse project is used for the actual buildings. If, for example, a development company wanted to build a one-million-square-foot warehouse, it would need a two-million-square-foot land parcel.[62] A combination of large land parcels, access to transportation infrastructure, and accommodating local state institutions made inland Southern California prime territory for industrial warehouse development. Developers were especially keen to pursue inland projects because they gave them a head start on the building approval process. Some local jurisdictions courted speculative warehouse construction by developing planning tools such as site-specific plans to clear environmental regulations for a proposed land parcel before anyone had submitted plans to develop that property.[63] These entitled projects could then be sold at a premium to companies that did not want to wait for the usual yearlong environmental approval period.[64]

Most of the industrial warehouse market was in the hands of national and international real estate developers. Major companies like ProLogis and AMB emerged as significant warehouse developers because they were publicly held REITs that could tap into growing pools of finance capital. Investors were particularly keen to buy stock in industrial warehouse REITs because profit margins for this sector reached 25 percent during the height of the building boom.[65] As Table 4 shows, ProLogis, Majestic, and Hillwood quickly became the largest industrial property owners in Southern California. Other national players like Panattoni and SARES-REGIS also expanded their Southern California operations.[66]

ProLogis exemplifies how finance capital markets transformed warehouse space in Southern California. The company owned or managed approximately eighty distribution properties in Riverside and San Bernardino Counties, which accounted for more than thirty million square feet of building space in 2008.[67] It distinguished itself by creating lucrative business practices that yielded higher profits and thus attracted larger amounts of investment capital. For example, ProLogis formed joint venture companies that allowed it to secure capital from pension funds and institutional investors. Under this model, ProLogis would develop a new property, sell it to a joint venture firm that it partly owned, and then continue to draw revenue

TABLE 4. Largest Industrial Warehouse Developers in the Inland Empire, 2009

Owner	Rentable Building Area (millions of sq. ft.)
ProLogis	32,698,945
Majestic	23,752,906
Hillwood	11,833,065
American Realty Advisors	7,371,771
Space Center, Inc.	7,061,678
Panattoni	6,414,945
SARES-REGIS Group	5,004,784
California Steel Industries Inc.	5,000,000
First Industrial	4,322,996

SOURCE: CoStar Group, "CoStar Industrial Real Estate Market Data," www.costar.com (2009).

by serving as the property's manager.[68] Investors rewarded ProLogis for such innovations by providing it with access to deep financial pockets, which it then used to outbid other developers in the region's inflated land market. Much of this funding was used to build speculative warehouse space. Speculative development—building a property without having a signed lease from a prospective tenant—gave developers an opportunity to gain market share. Highland Fairview was one of the few local developers that had enough real estate assets and political capital to build speculative warehouse projects. It was a relatively small player when compared to ProLogis and other REITs. Nonetheless, the Skechers warehouse received a tremendous amount of public attention because it marked an important political effort to extend logistics development into new territory.[69] The project was so politically significant that then governor Arnold Schwarzenegger and Secretary of Labor Victoria Bradshaw joined Iddo Benzeevi in the middle of an empty field on March 12, 2010, for the ground-breaking ceremony. Benzeevi used his political influence to fast-track the warehouse construction by chipping away at zoning regulations. For example, when the city council approved the 1.8-million-square-foot Skechers warehouse, they obligated the developer to build a dirt trail for horses, bikes, and joggers. Highland Fairview cited this trail during the public debate leading up to the city council vote. Benzeevi claimed that the trail would contribute to the overall aesthetic appeal of the project.[70] Yet after construction had begun, Benzeevi petitioned the city council in May 2010, arguing that the trail should be delayed or eliminated from the final plans. The council agreed to delay the construction of the trail and vowed to return to the issue because some members were not convinced that attaching trail requirements to development projects was sound policy for a growing city. According to then councilman Richard Stewart, "I don't think mixing horses with diesel trucks is a good thing."[71]

It was unclear whether Skechers would ever deliver on the promise of jobs. Paul Galliher, the senior vice president for Skechers' global distribution, told the city council that the Moreno Valley facility would provide between nine hundred and twelve hundred jobs. Likewise, Ido Benzeevi claimed that the project would generate $1.4 million in annual tax revenues. But in February 2012 the company employed only six hundred people, well below what it had predicted.

NINE

Latinx Frontiers

RAMON GRANADOS WAS AMONG THE 1.7 MILLION new Latinxs who moved into Riverside and San Bernardino Counties during the thirty-year period from 1980 to 2010. Like many others, he packed his bags, gathered his family, and set off to find a good job and a nice home somewhere on LA's metropolitan fringe. Some of the new arrivals came from other states and countries, but many migrated from Southern California's coastal regions. Between 2000 and 2006 more than 450,000 residents of Los Angeles and Orange Counties migrated inland.[1] They headed inland because, as Granados described, "There was tons of work—new apartments, new construction. Everybody wanted to come to this part of California."[2] Such rapid population changes are typical of frontier development regions like the Inland Empire. These places represent the spatial embodiment of boom and bust capitalism. For Ramon and millions like him, inland Southern California offered employment and housing opportunities at a time when rising rents and exorbitant home prices pushed many working-class and upwardly mobile people out of Los Angeles.[3] Indeed, the Inland Empire provided a spatial solution for a new generation of Californians.

The first part of this chapter examines how key elected leaders responded to the region's changing demographics by cultivating an anti-immigrant narrative that tied the Inland Empire's growing Latinx population to the national discourse on border enforcement and undocumented immigration. They did this by casting the Inland Empire as a migration hotspot that needed to be defended from the onslaught of new migrants. One consequence was that anti-immigrant politics often ensnared native-born Latinxs into the same pot of racialized politics that subjected legal and undocumented immigrants to social precarity. The second half of this chapter examines how SMOs cultivated a brand of spatial politics that challenged the fixing in place of specific racial and class hierarchies. They did this by disrupting the boundaries of citizenship and belonging that constituted normative iterations of the American Dream.

PROBLEMATIZING MIGRATION NARRATIVES

Migration narratives like Ramon's (above), Marta's, and Jose's (see chapter 5) cast the Inland Empire as a development frontier for a new generation of Californians. Such stories are integrative because they explain migration within the context of an American middle-class normative experience. For example, a spokesperson for then San Bernardino Republican congressman Jerry Lewis rationalized the influx of Latinx immigrants by framing them as a new constituency with familiar aspirations. When explaining why the Latinx population grew in such large numbers, the congressman's spokesperson claimed that many of them came from "the Hispanic suburbs of LA County." He went on to describe them as good citizens who "came for the same reasons that almost everybody else comes out here. The housing is much, much cheaper. The school districts tend to be a little less chaotic."[4]

This is a nice story, but the narrative must be interrogated because it aspires to validate and reproduce the economic, social, and territorial infrastructures of white settler colonialism. The story tries to legitimize the new arrivals as part of the pattern of U.S. colonial settlement in the American West without problematizing the underlying history of racial contradictions and violence that made such a process possible, including the bloody entanglements among white settlers, Mexicans, and indigenous populations. Recent immigrants are thus swept up into the imperial racial logics of why "everybody else" migrates to the inland region. It is an ahistorical explanation that ignores the role of the racial state and of capital, including the role they had played in producing earlier rounds of migration. Instead, it is important to interrogate how the production of illegitimate subjects as racialized others was central to past and present migrations.

ILLEGITIMATE SUBJECTS

Victoria Baca was part of the Latinx diaspora that fled Los Angeles in pursuit of another future. She moved to Moreno Valley in the early 1990s after being convinced that purchasing a tract home would allow her to buy her way into the American Dream. Her decision to move "started with the affordable housing, that's why people move out here. Cause I certainly didn't move out here for a job, there were no jobs. I was commuting from here to LAX. That was a sacrifice that I made, thinking that it would be better here."[5] "Better" meant escaping from the everyday challenges of growing up in a poor urban community. "What I was trying to get them [the children] away from was the gangs. My nephews were always getting beat up, they weren't gang members, they weren't taught to fight. I wanted something different for them than the way I grew up."[6] She quickly realized that extending the privileges of American citizenship to her children required more than simply paying her mortgage. "When we moved out here I think like most people we want better for our kids. But we really don't know what we're getting ourselves into." Her children felt like outsiders in the very institutions that were supposed to help them integrate into society. "It was hard for them in school. They didn't feel welcomed. The teachers looked down on them and they suffered because of that. That was the difference from East LA to Moreno Valley, the schools were not ready for us."[7] What did it mean for her to say that "the schools were not ready for us?" Victoria felt that the schools, like other local institutions, were racially exclusive and hostile. "There were atrocious things going on in the classroom, with public humiliation. I questioned myself, 'Where did I move to?' You're moving sixty miles east, but you're moving into a whole different world and it was very hard to deal with."[8]

Local police were also cited as an example of a hostile institution that made Latinx residents feel like illegitimate citizens. According to several residents I interviewed, local political leaders used a hyperracialized law-and-order narrative to implement policies that targeted the Latinx population. For example, top law enforcement officials created a set of narratives and policies that enforced national borders by leveraging local assets to arrest and detain undocumented immigrants. Latinx residents often felt targeted by these practices.

The politics of race and immigration were clearly at play when Riverside County decided to expand its cooperation with the federal Immigration and Customs Enforcement (ICE) agency by continuing to implement its 287(g) program.[9] The 287(g) program was part of the Illegal Immigration Reform and Immigrant Responsibility Act (IIRIRA) of 1996. Under section 287(g) of the IIRIRA, local law enforcement agencies received delegated authority to act as immigration agents, especially at county and city jails.[10] Riverside

County supervisors signed a memorandum of understanding with ICE and supported 287(g) as a crime-reduction measure. Supervisor Jeff Stone argued that Riverside County residents would gladly pay for any immigration-related policing costs because greater deportation rates resulted in a safer climate. In fact, crime data have not supported the claim that reduced crime rates are tied to higher deportation rates through the 287(g) program.[11] Supervisor Stone echoed proponents of immigrant-related policing who argued that more police would improve public safety, as he declared during a meeting: "In plain English, I fully support to identify and return illegal aliens, especially those that commit crimes, back to Mexico."[12] His statement not only deputized local law enforcement as border patrol agents, something not normally within the purview of police officers; he also produced undocumented immigrants as racial subjects by categorizing them all as Mexican.

Stone's equivalence between "illegal aliens" and "Mexico" was indicative of how anti-immigrant activists discussed immigrants and Latinxs as an indistinguishable category. A community organizer explained that Stone's description was a commonly held perception: "Because of the demographic change, there's a supposition that most [Latinx] people are undocumented—meaning illegal—meaning criminal—meaning should be treated like criminals. It serves as a justification for abuse."[13]

The same spokesperson for Congressman Jerry Lewis who had compared recent migration to earlier rounds of suburbanization also claimed that as Latinxs (with no distinction made between immigrants and native born) moved into the region, sometimes to escape the perceived problems of Los Angeles, they brought urban criminal elements with them.[14] Other government leaders made similar connections between Latinxs and undocumented immigrants. Leaders of the Inland Regional Narcotic Enforcement Team made a series of high-profile arrests in 2009 and claimed that Riverside and San Bernardino Counties had become a major distribution and logistics hub for the La Familia Michoacana Mexican drug cartel. Drug traffickers and criminalized immigrants were thus deployed as dangerous subjects who needed to be tracked down, contained, and deported. Local policy makers acted on this criminalization narrative by sponsoring legislation and policies that expanded border control and enforcement. Congressman Lewis opined that immigration-related enforcement policies—such as 287(g) agreements—maintained public safety by helping to get rid of dangerous criminals.[15] He also pushed to expand the federal E-Verify program, which was supposed to prevent undocumented immigrants from securing legal employment.

Anti-immigrant advocates used this criminal-immigrant discourse to target social services and public institutions, especially if those institutions served the growing U.S.-born Latinx populations. This strategy produced a racialized alien subject who could be locked out of public goods. The move was drawn from an old playbook, which was meant to cut public spending by linking social services to illegitimate racial subjects. For example, conservative supporters of Ronald Reagan's austerity programs deployed Black women dressed as Cadillac-driving welfare queens to justify social spending cuts.[16] Criminal aliens became the equivalent comparison that policy leaders used to slash social services.

In the case of immigration, the racialization of Latinxs made them into suspect citizens whose rights could be suspended. This too was part of an old nativist strategy that had resulted in the deportation of immigrant and native born alike during the 1930s. Alicia R. Schmidt Camacho notes that "the practice of law enforcement did not distinguish between the rights of lawful citizens and undocumented migrants" because both were part of "the same racialized community." This equivalence meant that "local and federal authorities deported Mexican Americans along with Mexicans to deny them access to federal relief benefits."[17] Juridical and material expulsion from the nation was made possible by an ideological choice to produce immigrants and U.S.-born Latinxs as illegitimate bodies; those who stayed could support the region's precarious low-road development strategy without burdening the state with the costs of social reproduction.

Riverside County supervisor Bob Buster used this political strategy of precarity and exclusion during the economic crisis of 2008, warning against public spending on programs that might benefit immigrants. Buster cautioned that "with the recession, everybody's watching the dollar [and debating which] people we should be spending money on."[18] His separation of people into legitimate and illegitimate categories enabled Buster to expand the neoliberal agenda of defunding the social welfare state by using the racialized anti-Latinx discourse to produce a questionable deserving public.

LATINX FUTURES AND THE POLITICS
OF RACIAL NOSTALGIA

Such exclusive policies were not always obvious. Some cities contributed to racial and class inequality by embracing a politics of nostalgia that denied social services to the region's growing Latinx population. The city of Redlands provides an example of how municipal leaders deployed a politics of racial denial by servicing a nostalgic white public that was no longer present. Redlands is, as described by Husing, "a town that thinks it's old and has all these programs for seniors."[19] The reality is that the "number of people 10 to 19 is double the number 65 plus."[20] In fact, those over age sixty-five made up only 13.1 percent of Redlands's population in 2010, while those under eighteen made up 23.7 percent.[21] Latinxs represented 37 percent of all children in Redlands during 2009, while white children amounted to 46 percent. Finally, the number of Latinx students increased from 28 percent of all Redlands Unified enrollments in 1993 to 43 percent by 2009.[22] Cities like Redlands tried to hold onto a racialized white founding myth by refusing to acknowledge the needs of new residents; this focus on an imagined white public reproduced racial privilege through the apparatus of the local state. Demographic denial resulted in funding disparities. Husing criticized Redlands for having "no recreation program in the city. They have one guy working for the police department and that was their recreation outlet." His point was that the city was directing most of its services to the aging white population while ignoring the city's Latinx future.

Redlands was like many other cities in the region. Young people, both immigrant and native born, represented a significant part of the population growth that transformed the Inland Empire between 1990 and 2010. Of the region's significant youth population, 44 percent of all Inland Empire children under the age of eighteen—approximately 500,000 in total—had at least one foreign-born parent.[23] In addition, approximately seven out of ten children in Riverside and San Bernardino counties were nonwhite in 2010; almost the exact opposite of the senior population. The state's graying and overwhelmingly white baby boomer population, when combined with the mostly Latinx and Asian young population boom, created a cultural generation gap with serious racial consequences that can be measured by looking at policy decisions and social spending.[24] Paying attention to youth was especially important because, as the head of the IEEP explained, "Redlands Unified is predominantly Hispanic but nobody wants to say it."[25] The consequences of racial denial were devastating. Local schools ranked among the worst in the state when measured by government-mandated testing scores. Fifty-eight percent of all schools within the San Bernardino City School District ranked below average on California's Academic Performance Index when compared to similar schools throughout the state in 2010; the figure was 74 percent for the Colton Unified School District.[26] In addition, 402 of the region's schools were placed on the No Child Left Behind Act of 2001 sanctions list for failing to bring all student groups up to federal standards.[27]

Poor education outcomes were compounded for immigrant and second-generation students, many of them classified as English Language Learners (ELLs). The number of ELLs nearly doubled, from 93,162 in 1995 to 182,652 by 2010, a growth rate of approximately 96 percent.[28] More than 94 percent of the Inland Empire's English learners spoke Spanish as their first language. Some 38 percent of San Bernardino County ELLs and 39 percent of Riverside County ELLs performed at the advanced or early advanced levels on the 2010 California English Language Development Test; the statewide average was 37 percent.

Local school board members admitted that most local teachers were not trained to meet the needs of ELL students.[29] According to these officials, the majority of teachers in local schools had not earned state-mandated English language teaching credentials (also known as BCLAD and CLAD). This lack of institutional readiness was perceived as an act of systemic racism by community activists. Moreno Valley parents believed Latinx Spanish-speaking teachers were systematically denied jobs in the school district. One of these parents was Victoria Baca, who eventually got elected to the school board. As she explained, "We said give us the numbers of everyone with a Spanish surname, with credentials and who was qualified and applied for a teaching position here in Moreno Valley." Baca and her parents' group believed that qualified Latinx candidates were wrongfully denied jobs. As she explained, "I think they gave us 120 applications and I think they hired 9 or 10. We knew that people were applying but they weren't being hired."[30]

Baca led a protest in 1996 at Vista Heights Middle School to protest racist hiring and discipline policies. Hundreds of students walked out of the school and passed out fliers that demanded Chicanx and Black studies classes; they also asked for a more racially diverse teaching staff.[31] Baca and her group believed that the system's overwhelmingly white senior staff did not prioritize the needs of the growing Latinx population. Data from the California Department of Education show that white teachers constituted 70 percent of all Moreno Valley Unified teaching staff in 2000; by 2010 they made up 62 percent. During the same period, Latinx teachers increased from 14 percent of all Moreno Valley teachers in 2000 to 23 percent in 2010.[32]

Institutional negligence manifested itself in inadequate funding for programs and services needed by the region's young and diverse population. A

San Bernardino school board member described how state funding cuts forced local communities to make tough educational choices. "Just like in every other school board, it's the budget. We have a $4 million deficit, so we're just looking and seeing what we can cut."[33] The old education system that had sustained California's postwar economy was—like the factories— being gutted. A board member described the consequences: "What we're going to end up with is just the basic K-12 program with no extras. We're looking at getting rid of busing, we're looking at getting rid of class size reduction, we're looking at getting rid of pregnant minor programs, the adult education program. We're just wiping everything out."[34]

SECURE COMMUNITIES

Local jurisdictions, including the Riverside County Sheriff's Office, angered community activists when they began integrating police enforcement with the U.S. Border Patrol's deportation program. The border patrol launched a series of raids throughout the Inland Empire between 2008 and 2009. Immigrant advocates argued that the raids were the direct result of a new quota system that provided incentives for agents to boost apprehensions and deportations.[35] Border patrol agents responded to the quotas by expanding the scope and scale of their activities. They initiated regular sweeps of Latinx neighborhoods, including sites where day laborers congregated for work. Activists were particularly aggrieved because they claimed that local police departments violated their mandates by actively participating in coordinated immigration sweeps with border patrol agents.[36] A spokesperson with the Justice for Immigrants Coalition of Inland Southern California (JICISC) explained why her group chose to protest how local police partnered with the border patrol: "These agents are not using probable cause. They're not searching for criminals. They're not at the border. They're just driving up to a street corner and asking everybody for identification and taking everybody."[37]

Deportation quotas, according to regional activists, also encouraged innovation among border patrol agents. One example was a pilot program called BP Alert, which local agents were testing for potential nationwide deployment. One of the region's leading immigrant activists described how the program worked: "There was a program called BP alert providing 'assistance' in translation and identification for police or sheriff departments."[38] The program built closer relationships between border patrol agents and police officers; the agents would regularly hand out cards to local police officers. "So if I'm a police officer," the activist continued, "I can call the Border Patrol and say hi I don't speak Spanish come and talk to this worker for me and translate for me and by the way they are also undocumented." Border patrol officials reported that a four-day test of the BP Alert program resulted in 130 immigration arrests in the Inland Empire.[39]

Greater cooperation between local and federal agencies was systematically enabled through national policies that enticed and pressured police agencies to act as surrogate immigration enforcement agents. The ICE's Secure Communities program, for example, created new requirements that compelled local police to cooperate with federal immigration enforcement. Under Secure Communities, anyone booked into local jails was automatically scanned through the Department of Homeland Security immigration database. If the database listed someone as undocumented, local police agencies turned that person over to ICE. A day labor organizer described how this worked: "There's a major detention center located in Rancho Cucamonga called West Valley Detention Center. If you're arrested by the Sheriff you're gonna go to West Valley and ICE is all up in there. They do videoconferencing with deputized Sheriffs, have immigration hearings, and deport people."[40]

Police leaders in other parts of the state were critical of programs like 287(g) and Secure Communities because they believed that such cooperation damaged their ability to serve immigrant communities. However, Riverside County sheriff Stanley Sniff defended the programs. In fact, Sheriff Sniff was a leading opponent of the TRUST Act, a bill in the California legislature that would have limited police powers to deport arrestees. Sheriff Sniff and other police leaders in Riverside County gained a reputation as aggressive anti-immigrant agencies because, according to a regional leader in the immigrant rights community, they had "increased their informal cooperation with the Border Patrol."[41] The same activist listed the BP Alert program as an example.

Local police used other methods to target undocumented immigrants. Activists with the JICISC and the Latino Roundtable claimed that police departments in San Bernardino, Moreno Valley, Ontario, Pomona, and Coachella used regular sobriety checkpoints as a de facto policy that targeted undocumented and unlicensed drivers. In fact, ICE agents routinely showed up at sobriety checkpoints and arrested dozens of people who were suspected of violating immigration rules. Officials with the Riverside County Sheriff's

Department acknowledged that they notified ICE of the raids and welcomed their help as interpreters.[42] Undocumented immigrants were particularly vulnerable to this practice, because the law prevented them from obtaining a valid driver's license. Consequently immigrants who were caught in the extensive web of sobriety checkpoints were detained and had their cars impounded. While police officials justified checkpoints as a public safety measure that helped to reduce drunk driving, community advocates claimed that the automatic thirty-day impound given to unlicensed drivers was an undue burden on immigrants; many of those who lost their cars had to pay thousands of dollars in towing and impound fees.

Activists argued that police used sobriety checkpoints to generate police revenues, and that this practice racially profiled Latinxs and immigrants.[43] Data from both the Riverside and San Bernardino Sheriff's Departments seemed to support such claims, showing that most checkpoints were conducted in neighborhoods with large Latinx populations. For example, Moreno Valley police conducted thirty-seven checkpoints between 2007 and 2009 in the city's three voting districts that contained a large concentration of Latinxs. At the same time, only five checkpoints were conducted in the city's remaining two mostly white districts.[44] Police claimed that checkpoint locations were based on traffic levels and dismissed accusations of racial bias.

The checkpoints contributed to a growing distrust between Latinx residents and local police. Even if the checkpoints were not explicitly racist, community distrust made them a contentious issue. Immigrant groups and more mainstream middle-class Latinx organizations mobilized against the checkpoints; they claimed that police used drunk driving as a cover for racial profiling. Anti-checkpoint organizers were able to mobilize native-born and immigrant residents alike because many people, especially Latinxs, felt that police stops treated them as racialized subjects. An organizer with the regional anti-checkpoint coalition explained why people felt compelled to act: "This drew out a lot of non-immigrant community people to support because either they had been harassed or they saw family members or people who are close to them who had been affected." According to him, people were skeptical about police claims and asked, "Why are police doing checkpoints in the morning? Why are they doing checkpoints at noon? Why are they doing them near schools?"[45]

Activists, teachers, students, and other residents began defying the checkpoints by diverting traffic away from the stops. They used roving human billboards and social media to both inform people of particular checkpoint locations and mobilize a regional network of pro-immigrant activists. Mounting pressure eventually forced some local police agencies to change their impound policies. For example, community pressure convinced Cathedral City in Riverside County to end automatic impounds; instead, unlicensed drivers were given fifteen to twenty minutes to arrange for a licensed driver to take possession of their vehicle. The anti-checkpoint movement was important because it marked one of the first efforts by immigrant activists to organize on a regional scale.

Two key alliances, the Justice for Immigrants Coalition (JIC) and the Rapid Response Network (RRN), were formed because of the policing practices and immigration raids outlined here. While these groups included many of the same members, the two alliances had different organizing philosophies and used different tactics. JIC was spearheaded by the Inland Empire's Catholic diocese, which was under the leadership of Bishop Gerald Barnes. The bishop had decided to integrate immigrant rights into the church's core mission after he was appointed to head the 1.2-million-member diocese in 1996.[46] It was a continuation of his earlier work as chairman of the U.S. Bishop's Committee on Migration and Refugee Services, during which he spearheaded the Justice for Immigrants campaign to change immigration policy. Bishop Barnes wanted to incorporate immigrants and immigrant issues across all ninety-four of the diocese's congregations. He attempted to do so by creating an institute to train lay members for new leadership positions. The bishop appointed Auxiliary Bishop Rutilio del Riego as head of the Ministry Formation Institute and charged him with creating a core training curriculum that included an immigrant component. Bishop Barnes, according to his senior staff, ran the only diocese in California that included a full-time staff person who worked on immigrant justice projects.

Yet even with Bishop Barnes's leadership, church leaders struggled to implement his pro-integration message across all the Inland Empire's parishes. Only a few parish leaders adopted the pro-immigrant message. Diocese staff felt that priests were reluctant to advocate for immigrants because they were afraid of a conservative backlash from members of their congregations. This was the case in 2005 when a relatively white and wealthy Riverside parish was entrusted to priests from the Philippines. According to one of the parish priests, many of the white congregants complained about the new priests' accents.[47] These same members also objected to the growing Asian and Latinx presence in the congregation. Tensions boiled over when the church began to expand its Spanish-language services to accommodate the immigrants, who made up an estimated 25 percent of its membership. Eventually, several of the most influential donors and volunteers left the parish. Unfazed by the exodus, the new priests continued their campaign to remake the church as a space that reflected and welcomed the growing Latinx and Asian populations. Some of the white parishioners returned after a few months, but the hostile reception showed church leaders that they needed to navigate the contentious cultural and spatial politics of immigration in the Inland Empire.[48]

As Bishop Barnes built the infrastructure to strengthen the diocese's internal capacity he also developed alliances with immigrant advocates outside of the church. Several interview respondents credited the church with fortifying the region's integration ecosystem by lending legitimacy to the JIC and for holding the coalition together. The JIC launched a series of marches and political lobbying campaigns to roll back federal and local enforcement programs like 287(g). JIC leaders thought they could convince local agencies to modify or abandon 287(g) agreements during the Obama administration's mandate to renew local-federal memorandums of agreement in 2010. Catholic auxiliary bishop del Riego and other JIC leaders met with local police leaders and encouraged them to withdraw from the 287(g) program.

Advocates eventually concluded that outright rejection of 287(g) was unlikely and instead adopted a reform agenda to modify existing agreements. JIC members called for a public stakeholder committee with oversight on enforcement, removal of nonfelons from the program so that only convicted felons would be screened, and greater public transparency. None of these proposals was ultimately adopted, but JIC members used the process to establish regular communication with law enforcement, something relatively new for the immigrant community in the region. JIC members also used their work on the 287(g) renewal to establish better regional coordination among themselves. Such networking and relationship building provided valuable space for new alliances and partnerships to develop. For example, members of the JIC used the network to connect Pomona Habla—a community-based organization located in eastern Los Angeles County—to fledgling groups in Cathedral City, Moreno Valley, Coachella, and San Bernardino, which were all organizing around the effects of police checkpoints on immigrant communities.

Another regional alliance, the RRN, formed in the aftermath of a 2008 immigration raid on a Palm Springs area bakery that resulted in more than fifty-two arrests by the local border patrol station. The network included a broad coalition of service providers and community organizations. It was a crisis intervention organization that deployed people to help before and after immigration enforcement raids. One of the group's key members credited the JIC for helping to build the collaborative infrastructure for the RRN to emerge. He explained that "through the connections that we had already developed, as the raids were happening there were people protesting . . . my people were working with the Mexican Consulate to try to get people released, and some of the church-based groups were working on trying to raise money."[49] RRN members deployed mobile response teams to places where they knew a raid was going to take place; enforcement agencies sometimes informed RRN members of an impending raid. During one such mobilization, the rapid response team prepared day laborers for an imminent raid by informing them of their rights and instructing them on how to respond if confronted by a border patrol agent. Most of them avoided arrest. RRN members also joined forces to document enforcement abuses at day laborer sites throughout the region; they used video footage to support their claims that local police agencies were violating the intent of established 287(g) agreements. Network members used their experience with raid victims to organize protests against further sweeps and worked with the Mexican consulate to pressure enforcement agencies into reducing the volume of deportations. These activities and mass organized regional protests raised questions about border patrol policies and local police cooperation. Activists linked these charges to the border patrol quota system and demanded that it be shut down.[50]

Unlike the JIC, RRN members embraced protest politics and civil disobedience. Members of the RRN repeatedly said that more grassroots social movement tactics were needed because they felt disempowered by the legislative approach to comprehensive immigration reform. One of the region's key day labor leaders described the difference thus: "The diocese has the interest in legal services for immigrant citizenship . . . the idea that once reform passes then we're going to have to help all these people adjust their status. But that's kind of taken a back seat at this point because . . . there's no reform." The inability to pass comprehensive immigration reform at the federal level meant local activists focused "more on enforcement related issues that are sort of day-to-day experiences that people are having and that need to be dealt with right now, you know. And something that we actually have maybe more power over . . . something we can actually change, whereas immigration reform seems really big and out of our league."[51]

Frustration over the lack of comprehensive immigration reform triggered debates among activists. Should they pursue a pragmatic politics of reform or push the debate by giving voice to more radical solutions? What about the difference between passing reform policies versus doing the work of ensuring that the implementation of such policies addresses the issues at hand? Labor organizers and community-based immigrant rights groups used the RRN and the warehouse worker campaign to expand the fight for juridical rights by extending notions of citizenship to include economic justice. They organized a raucous region-wide May Day march that gained wide community support and shook up the normally serene streets of downtown Riverside.

Church officials disagreed with the confrontational approach taken by RRN members against border patrol activities and argued for a more focused juridical approach to citizenship rights. Yet many of the activist-based members of the RRN pushed for a direct action approach to immigration that included a broader social justice message. Labor union involvement contributed to a more direct and confrontational approach. Several national labor unions put immigrant workers on the political radar by launching regional organizing campaigns in the residential construction and warehousing sectors during the 2000s. While these immigrant-focused campaigns received little to no support from the local labor council, they did build alliances with community-based immigrant groups like the RRN and JIC.

Labor's involvement in regional immigrant advocacy networks helped to frame immigration as an economic justice issue. This pro-immigrant labor voice was expressed in at least two significant ways. First, by engaging in direct actions and public organizing campaigns, immigrant workers introduced the idea of economic justice into the debate on regional development. It was an important intervention in a region where most leaders clamored for more jobs without a serious discussion about living wages and community benefits. Workers could craft a pro-integration vision for the future by framing jobs and economic development as a long-term strategy for economic mobility. Second, the organizing campaigns enabled national unions like CTW and LiUNA to team up with grassroots immigrant-based organizations like CLUE and the National Day Laborers Organizing Network (NDLON).

Union staff members also took active roles in organizations like the JIC. Members of the coalition believed union participation was important. Yet several community advocates said they were initially cautious of organized labor's interest in immigrant workers, because local unions had been mostly hostile or absent. They acknowledged, however, that labor participation could strengthen the immigrant social justice movement by providing funding resources, organizers, and campaign knowledge. Unions also emphasized a regional organizing model.

The new labor-immigrant coalition suffered a setback when the 2008 recession stymied efforts to ramp up worker organizing. Most of the union staff who participated in the immigrant network were employed by the national organizing office. For example, even though LiUNA had Inland Empire locals, it was the national organizing staff—through the regional campaign—that took a leadership role in conducting citizenship fairs for the immigrant community. When unions began cutting staff, their participation in regional immigration coalition work also shrank. Some unions, such as the Warehouse Workers, continued to participate. Even with the setbacks, labor and immigrant organizations both felt that their alliance was crucial to a strong regional social movement.

Conclusion

THERE HAS BEEN A PROFOUND lack of political leadership in inland Southern California. The region's low-skilled and undereducated workers have had to fend for themselves against the devastating flows of speculative capital while the evangelists of neoliberalism have cut back the safety nets of the Keynesian state. Members of the logistics regime were complicit in this. They convinced themselves and tried to convince everyone else that goods movement represented economic salvation for a region suffering through the job losses of deindustrialization. A sense of economic crisis justified spending on roads, bridges, and rail. At the same time, low wages and cancer-causing diesel pollution were written off as collateral damage. Yet the 2,339 estimated people who get cancer from diesel exposure every year in the Inland Empire and the many more who suffer medical problems that lead to premature death cannot be written off as unfortunate consequences of development; premature death is an "intolerable failure," not an unfortunate happenstance.[1] Even if I personally do not believe that the deadly logics of racial capitalism I have discussed here can be massaged into a more compassionate system, I do think that it's necessary to create political spaces that amplify the voices of dissent and hope.

Few of the policy makers who pursued logistics jobs in the name of economic prosperity ever raised questions about whether the industry provided living wages and safe living conditions for inland residents.[2] Unlike coastal California, where SMOs worked with local policy makers to implement living wage ordinances and community benefits agreements, leaders in inland Southern California did not pursue such proactive policies. Instead, inland leaders fell prey to a classic tool of hegemonic ideology: they held fast to the idea that port-based development was in "the general interests of all citizens, not just particular interests."[3] This is how hegemony works, by convincing people that there are no other feasible options.

Many of those who provided the stories for this book proposed a counter-mapping of the American Dream by placing racial, social, and economic justice at the center of everyday citizenship. The ideas espoused by the workers and the organizers in this book were not a radical solution to the inequality that permeates U.S. society. Many echoed the ideas attached to "just growth" theory, which is defined by C. Benner and M. Pastor as "a process—a sustained conversation about the future of the region in which the twin objectives of growth and equity become embedded in the region's norms and practices."[4] Just growth involves an ideological conversion that reframes what development means and how success is measured.[5] The principles of just growth are reflected in partnerships that include community benefits agreements, workforce development collaboratives, and community college investments.

This reframing of economic development requires a new approach and new leadership. Social justice organizations that were interviewed for this book felt isolated from the halls of policy and power. They also felt that policy makers and regional boosters were more focused on a politics of denial than on engaging in meaningful conversations about how to deal with economic and social disparities. For example, the halls of power quickly deployed their hounds to denigrate anyone who dared to suggest that dominant development strategies were not working for everyone. Such denigration isn't necessary. Those who want to remap the American Dream are not out to destroy the economic engine of regional growth. In fact, there is strong evidence that reducing economic hardship for the poor creates more sustainable growth in the long term.[6]

For social movements to be successful, they need to invest more heavily in the social infrastructure and human capital that will be necessary to transform inland Southern California into a more just and humane landscape. Money, grassroots leadership, and human capital were among the main obstacles during the WWU campaign. National union leaders in Washington set the parameters for the campaign. There were some benefits from this centralized organizing model. One included access to significant union resources. Another brought a regional and industry-wide approach that attempted to organize on a scale that was commensurate with global commodity chains. Nonetheless, there was a disconnect between some of the local staff and the national leadership. Local staff tried to build long-term grassroots leadership capacity but had to overcome top-down organizing metrics that were not always aligned with a long-term regional strategy. The region needs progressive local leadership, especially because changing demographics will provide new opportunities to build and hold power.

COUNTERING WHITE POLITICAL SPACE

I want to debunk a prevalent notion that inland Southern California's changing demographics will alter its political destiny. Changing demographics may provide fertile ground for change, but the work of cultivating and nourishing the seeds of change will require more. The types of changes I have outlined here require an intentional political strategy, not simply a transition from one racial political regime to another. To understand how and why, we need to take a quick trek through the region's political history. Inland California functioned as an electoral refuge for the state's shrinking Republican Party during the 1990s and 2000s. The share of registered Republicans living in the Inland Empire nearly doubled, from 7 percent of all California voters in 1978 to 13 percent in 2012.[7] A similar pattern occurred in the Central Valley and pockets of southern Orange County. Republicans maintained a strong political presence in inland counties even as conservatives lost control of many coastal jurisdictions. As a result, California's political geography was split into a liberal coastal block and a much more conservative inland zone.

The conservative political climate extended to the region's civil society. While unions and community-based organizations capitalized on the state's shifting demographics to push for progressive policies in Los Angeles County, the same did not happen in inland regions. Instead, inland Southern California's political terrain developed into fertile soil for the type of conservative and anti-immigrant sentiment and activists that dominated the state's election ballots in the mid-1990s, especially during Governor Pete Wilson's support of the anti-immigrant Proposition 187 ballot initiative. If Los Angeles and the rest of coastal California were able to move beyond the fractured and racialized political fights attached to immigration, bilingual education, and mandatory prison sentences, inland Southern California stood as a reminder of an entrenched racial politics that lingered in the institutions and relationships of white settler colonialism and reactionary nativist movements.

White political power and Republican Party building continued to dominate Inland Empire politics into the 2000s. According to the Public Policy

Institute of California, white residents represented 47 percent of Inland Empire adults in 2005, but they made up 62 percent of all registered voters.[8] Perhaps this accounts for the fact that while Latinxs, African Americans, and Asian Americans were elected to an increasing array of political offices in Southern California's coastal counties, that occurred at a much slower pace in the Inland Empire. The coastal political transition included much more than simply changing the racial makeup of elected representatives; it also meant a move away from conservative politics. Many of the newly elected coastal county politicians embraced more progressive political platforms that championed collective bargaining rights, community oversight, and economic polices like living wage ordinances. This was no coincidence, especially because prominent LA progressives who rose to political power, such as Karen Bass, Hilda Solis, Gilbert Cedillo, and Antonio Villaraigosa, all emerged from organizing backgrounds in labor, community, and immigrant rights struggles.

The story was different in the Inland Empire, where white politicians held onto political power, including the powerful county board of supervisors. Of the ten supervisors who govern the two counties, all but one were white and Republican as of 2010. There were, however, signs that the influx of Latinxs and liberal coastal transplants would whittle away at the established political order. Democrats gained a numerical majority among registered voters on the eve of the November 2008 elections in San Bernardino County. Riverside County is an entirely different story. Republicans managed to hold onto their numerical edge in Riverside County even when Barack Obama's presidential campaign motivated more Democratic Party–leaning Black and Latinx voters to register for the 2008 cycle.[9]

The combination of racial and conservative politics made immigrant advocates feel like political outsiders. Activists believed that the region's political climate was so overwhelmingly conservative that even Democrats, some of them Latinx, shied away from taking pro-immigrant and progressive stances because they were afraid of alienating the region's large share of independent and conservative voters.[10] Meanwhile, anti-immigrant activists forged close relationships with conservative Republican leaders. San Bernardino's Joseph Turner is one example. Turner founded the anti-immigrant group Save Our State and served as the western region representative for the Federation for American Immigration Reform (FAIR). Both of these groups opposed immigration and pressured local political leaders to adopt strict border enforcement and deportation policies. Turner gained national attention in 2006 when, as a member of the San Bernardino City Council, he championed a local ordinance to bar landlords from renting to people who could not prove their legal immigration status. This tactic, which relied on local jurisdictions to implement national immigration policies, became a key strategy for anti-immigrant activists across the country. Turner was ultimately unsuccessful and relinquished his seat on the council. His career as an elected official was relatively short, but Turner managed to embed himself into the region's political establishment by taking a senior staff position with a Republican San Bernardino County supervisor and as an adviser for a local police union.

Other anti-immigrant groups, like the Minutemen and various branches of the neo-Nazi movement, were also active in the Inland Empire's political scene. The Minutemen tried to frame themselves as a legitimate and nonracist border enforcement group. They were active throughout the Inland Empire but were especially concentrated in Rancho Cucamonga, Ontario, Riverside, San Bernardino, and Claremont, where they became vocal participants in local politics. José Calderon, an activist with the Latinx Roundtable, described the anti-immigrant political ecosystem as follows: "We've had an increase and rise of the Minutemen groups. Then we have the rise of the Nazis, who have had demonstrations in San Bernardino against immigrants and day laborers." Calderon explained that local politicians were also anti-immigrant leaders. "We have another congressman from Chino who has introduced a bill to not allow children of undocumented to be citizens. So you have politicians trying to tap the sincere sentiment of workers that they are out of jobs, that they're losing their housing, tapping that to blame immigrants."[11] Political candidates mastered the art of tapping into racial anxiety and economic despair by linking the region's economic crisis to immigration.

When the mayor of Rancho Cucamonga joined the race for an assembly seat in 2010, he ran on a platform that included banning the U.S.-born children of undocumented immigrants from becoming American citizens. It was another indicator of how conservative politics took on an anti-immigrant fervor and forged tighter alliances between elected officials and immigration activists. This was the case when the Mexican consulate in San Bernardino created a mobile unit to extend constituent services, such as consular identification cards or *matriculas*, to immigrants across the Inland Empire. *Matriculas* were state-sanctioned documents that gave immigrants access to services. Several key agencies, including the Riverside and San Bernardino county sheriff's departments, recognize *matriculas* as valid forms of identification. Immigrants could also use them to open bank accounts. The Minutemen and the Fire Coalition protested and demanded that the consulate stop all off-site mobile unit activities.[12] These protests inspired Corona-based congressman Ken Calvert to sponsor a bill that would bar federal agencies and banks from recognizing *matriculas* as valid forms of identification.

Inland California's mix of entrenched conservative leadership, vocal anti-immigrant sentiment, and a racialized electorate resulted in a distinct regional politics that stood in sharp opposition to the rest of Southern California. Evidence of this rift between inland Southern California and the rest of the state can be found in the different ways that political leaders supported or condemned Arizona's anti-immigrant SB 1070 law, also known as the "show me your papers" bill. While Los Angeles, San Francisco, and numerous other municipalities chose to boycott Arizona after it passed SB 1070, Inland Empire cities like Hemet, Lake Elsinore, and Highland passed resolutions in support of the legislation. Support for anti-immigrant laws wasn't purely symbolic. Several inland cities enacted ordinances that specifically targeted the immigrant community.[13] In fact, five Inland Empire cities passed laws requiring all local businesses to check the legal status of new employees via the federal government's E-Verify system.[14] Anti-immigration activists and Republican operatives had plans to implement a similar policy across all of Riverside County.

Not all Inland Empire cities embraced an anti-immigrant stance, particularly in jurisdictions with a more diverse political leadership. Ontario, the only large city with a Latino mayor during this period, refused to endorse or condemn Arizona's SB 1070. Local Minutemen and other activists crowded city council meetings and were angry when Ontario's elected officers refused to take an official position. In San Bernardino, the region's second largest city, a multiracial political coalition of African American, Latinx, and white liberal and centrist leaders took control of the city council in 2006 and provided a counterbalance to the more conservative inland jurisdictions. Led by Mayor Pat Morris, a self-identified Democrat, this new council majority opposed Joseph Turner's anti-immigrant ordinance. A number of interviewees claimed that while the new council majority was more open to immigrant issues, Mayor Morris wasn't willing to publicly support pro-immigrant campaigns. If conservative policy makers mobilized the local state apparatus to fight against immigration, more liberal politicians did not readily use their office to advocate for a pro-immigrant stance. As one activist noted, "He has said that it's not something local government can fix—it's up to the federal government."[15] San Bernardino's shifting political landscape was much different from the city of Riverside, where an almost all-white conservative political establishment maintained power. All but one of Riverside's eight city council members were white in 2010, a surprising situation in a city where whites made up only 35 percent of the population.

Inland Empire politicians used their conservative political base to establish themselves as key anti-immigrant voices in state and national legislative fights. For example, San Bernardino Republican state assemblyman Tim Donnelly, from District 59 in the northwestern part of the county, introduced a bill modeled after Arizona's SB 1070. Donnelly also pushed for ending in-state tuition for immigrant students. His efforts failed to gain traction in the Democratic-controlled state legislature. Democrats responded to calls for reform by successfully passing legislation that gave undocumented immigrant students access to private and public financial aid. This rift between Donnelly and California Democrats pointed to a major paradox within the Republican Party. Some California Republicans supported comprehensive immigration reform as a political survival strategy. They argued that if Republicans continued to support anti-immigrant measures, they would alienate the state's growing Latinx electorate. California Republicans from inland agricultural areas took very different positions from those in the Inland Empire. While inland farmers pressed for immigration reform as a strategy to secure larger pools of cheap immigrant labor, business leaders in exurban residential communities didn't take the same public position. For example, while Central Valley Republicans like Jeff Denham and David Valadao joined with Democrats to support comprehensive immigration reform, Inland Empire representatives like Ken Calvert and Paul Cook supported staunch enforcement-only policies. One notable exception was Jim Brulte, a former California State Senate Republican leader and San Bernardino assemblyman, who told a group of influential business and political leaders at a 2010 Inland Action meeting that the Republican Party would become irrelevant if it kept attacking Latinxs and immigrants.

Let me conclude by pointing out something that probably seems obvious at this point; Donald Trump's election in 2016 raised many of the same political issues that I have discussed in this book. The feeling of displacement and blue-collar decline that Tom Metzger and other racists tried to capitalize on in inland Southern California during the 1980s and 1990s was alive and well in the industrial suburban and rural districts that handed Donald Trump the presidency in 2016. What comes next, and what can abandoned spaces like inland Southern California teach us about the future?

NOTES

INTRODUCTION

1. For an explanation of how capital has continually reproduced itself through space, see Lefebvre (1991, 21). As Lefebvre argues, "Capitalism has found itself able to attenuate (if not resolve) its internal contradictions for a century, and consequently, in the hundred years since the writing of Capital, it has succeeded in achieving 'growth'. We cannot calculate at what price, but we do know the means: by occupying space, by producing a space."

2. For more on commodity chains see Bair and Gereffi (2001); Ramaswamy and Gereffi (2000).

3. Nicosia and Mayer (2007).

4. I use the descriptor "Latinx" to disrupt the heteronormative and patriarchal practice of describing people of all genders with the male pronoun Latino. The term is problematic to those who reject the term Latin as a proxy for a Eurocentric ethnic identity. That debate is for another book to resolve. In the meantime, unlike nationalist-based identifiers such as Mexican or Guatemalan, the continental reference to Latin America in the term Latinx helps recognize the multilayered histories and places that have shaped the people of Las Americas.

5. See McDowell (2008) for an explanation of hegemonic identities.

6. Hall (1986, 3) was referring to Gramsci's methodological approach.

7. Cox (2004).

8. Gilmore (2007, 187).

9. Leitner and Miller (2007, 117).

10. Harrison (2007, 322).

SCENE I

1. Mydans (1994).

2. The monotony of work life was broken up by supervised weekly excursions to the beach or market. Yet most of their time in Fontana revolved around the Kaiser

mill and the makeshift labor camp at a nearby hotel. See Associated Press (1993); Gorman (1993).

3. Gorman (1993).

CHAPTER I

1. Robinson (1983, 24).
2. Escobar (2008, 1).
3. Coe et al. (2004).
4. Cox (1997); Hall (1997).
5. Brenner and Theodore (2002).
6. Brenner (2000, 371).
7. For more on representations of space, see Lefebvre (1991).
8. For an explanation of how cultural geography moved away from material landscapes to go beyond the constraints of environmentally or economic determinist studies, see Mitchell (1996).
9. Stuart Hall makes this point to challenge Foucault's focus on discursive power (Grossberg 1986).
10. Butler and Athanasiou (2013).
11. See Mitchell (1996).
12. Mitchell (1996, 5).
13. For more on the relationship between material and discursive spaces, see Keith and Pile (1993).
14. For more on how regions are produced as territorial units, see Harrison (2007, 322).
15. Jonas and Ward (2007, 169). Jonas and Ward review the extensive literature that has covered changes in global political economy.
16. For more on how scholars framed urbanization in the age of globalization, see Brenner (2000).
17. Harrison (2007, 322).
18. Boudreau (2007, 2596).
19. Quoted in Boudreau (2007, 2596). See Woods (2000). His work on the Mississippi Delta showed how Black and white spatial imaginaries were deployed to produce the region's racial and class orders. Woods was able to trace how various collective interests used discursive and material tactics to define and maintain regional space.
20. Stuart Hall noted this connection between cognitive and material force when he defined ideology as "the concepts and the languages of practical thought which stabilize a particular form of power and domination" (1996, 27).
21. For a discussion of the relationship among military Keynesianism, race, and class, see Gilmore (2007). See Hise (1997) and Nicolaides (2002) for examples of industrial suburbs.
22. For more on postwar urbanization in the West, see Findlay (1992).

23. See Ethington (2000) for a longer analysis of Los Angeles's history of segregation.

24. See Williams (1973) for a discussion of landscape and class erasure in English pastoral paintings and literature.

25. I use "Black" and "Brown" because I agree with Kimberle Crenshaw (1988, 1332) when she writes, "when using 'Black,' I shall use an upper-case 'B' to reflect my view that Blacks, like Asians, Latinos, and other 'minorities,' constitute a specific cultural group and, as such, require denotation as a proper noun." Likewise, Cheryl Harris (1993, 1710) points out that writing racial identities with lower- and uppercase letters is a political act. According to Harris: "Although 'white' and 'Black' have been defined oppositionally, they are not functional opposites. 'White' has incorporated Black subordination; 'Black' is not based on domination." For a history of segregation in Los Angeles, see Ethington, Frey, and Myers (2001); Kurashige (2008); Sánchez (1993); Sides (2003); and Widener (2010).

26. Anzaldua (1987); Fregoso (2003); Saldivar-Hull (2000); Brady (2000); Saldívar (1997).

27. Garcia (2001); Sánchez (1993); Villa (2000).

28. See Crenshaw (1991) and Collins (1990). Geographers have pointed out this move toward spatial concepts and cultural identity, not always in a positive light. Smith and Katz (1993) provide a review of this discussion.

29. For more on space, mobility, and race, see Kruse (2007); McKittrick and Woods (2007); and Jaffe (2012).

30. Cheng's (2013) work on Asian and Latinx identity formation in the San Gabriel Valley is a good example.

31. Kun and Pulido (2014). See Kelley (2003) for a definition of *polyculturalism*.

32. Chakravartty and Da Silva (2012, 370).

33. Lefebvre (1991, 370).

34. Several scholars have used the phrase "premature death." My use follows Gilmore's (2002) theoretical interventions on race, space, and power.

35. For more on the need to study specific spatial processes, see Herod and Wright (2001).

36. The literature on this topic is extensive. See Cox (1997) and Hall (1997) for an overview of some of the major arguments/approaches.

37. Smith's ideas about uneven development spurred important conversations among those interested in speculative capital, urban space, and difference. He claimed that "economic expansion today no longer takes place purely via absolute geographical expansion but rather involves internal differentiation of already developed spaces. At the urban scale, this is the importance of gentrification vis-à-vis suburbanization. The production of space in general and gentrification in particular are examples of this kind of uneven development endemic to capitalist societies" (2004, xvi).

38. See Massey (1995) for an explanation of this argument.

39. This argument is partly rooted in Gramsci's (2000) idea of the dynamic social production of class that is always in process. It is also indebted to Raymond Williams's (1977) ideas on structures of feeling.

40. Mitchell (1997, 104).

41. King (1997, 29).

42. Tilly (2012).

43. Gupta and Ferguson (1992, 8).

44. Gupta and Ferguson (1992, 8).

45. Canclini (2001, 3) argues that globalization is a "process of fragmentation and recomposition" and not a process of global homogenization. According to him, "globalization reorders differences and inequalities without eliminating them."

46. Graham (2002, 1).

47. Bluestone and Harrison (1982).

48. Davis (1990).

49. Walker (2004, 435).

50. For more on the relationship between capitalism and creative destruction, see Schumpeter (1962). Arrighi (2004) writes more extensively about spatial-temporal relationships and capitalism.

51. Harvey (1981).

52. See Associated Press (1993). Even though the mill had been shuttered, some lawmakers protested the sale and claimed that it would hurt the U.S. economy by helping to build China's industrial capacity. Yet company officials tried to reassure doubters by saying that the Chinese were buying "old and used equipment" that was not used in "state-of-the-art steelmaking" (*Wall Street Journal* 1983).

53. Nolan (2002) claims that the plan to use Kaiser's salvaged parts at a new plant in Qilu, China, was overturned in 1995 by the government. Nonetheless, the story exemplifies the deep connections that existed between China's industrialization and Southern California's new economic development path.

54. Associated Press (1992).

55. Arrighi (2004, 532).

56. Industrial Development Organization (2013).

57. Industrial Development Organization (2013).

58. Allen and Turner (1997).

59. Pastor (2013) provides an excellent demographic overview of Southeast LA and discusses the varied suburban experiences that Latinos face in Los Angeles County.

60. See García Bedolla (2005) and Valle and Torres (2000) for an analysis of this transition.

61. Pastor (2013).

62. Coe et al. (2004); Cox (2004); Eisinger (1988); Jonas and Ward (2007); Storper (1997).

63. Tavasszy, Ruijgrok, and Thissen (2003).

64. McCartin (2011).

65. Harvey (2005).

66. Cowie (2001).

67. Boyer (2006).

68. Camarillo (2007, 15).

69. For more on deindustrialization and race, see Massey and Denton (2003); Wilson (1987); and Byrne (2015).

70. Omi and Winant (1994).

71. Gilmore (2008, 35).

72. Spatial segregation made working-class and poor neighborhoods more vulnerable to capital flight. For more on this see Massey and Denton (2003). See also Byrne (2015).

73. Interview with author, February 10, 2010, Maywood, CA.

74. Quoted in Davis (2000, 377). Postwar Southeast LA provided new terrain for manufacturers and white workers to construct idyllic lives where "workers may live close to their work in inexpensive homes of individuality, where flowers and gardens may be grown the year around." It was marketed as the place where "White help prevails."

75. Interview with author, February 10, 2010, Maywood, CA.

76. Interview with author, February 10, 2010, Maywood, CA.

77. Hall (1996, 27) argues that "the problem of ideology, therefore, concerns the ways in which ideas of different kinds grip the minds of the masses, and thereby become a 'material force'."

CHAPTER 2

1. See Foley (1986) and Marx (1867) for a more extensive discussion of commodity fetishism and the social division of labor. Tucker (2007) provides excellent case studies that link consumption and political ecology.

2. Becker (2008).

3. Trevor Barnes and Eric Sheppard (1992) argue that rational choice theory depends on its abstraction of social actors, as individuals, from the geographical and historical contexts that, in part, determine their very identity. For more on a critique of rational choice models, see Buck-Morss (1995, 446); Patel (2009); and Polanyi (2001).

4. Taken from Marx (1867).

5. Urry (2003, x).

6. See Lefebvre (1991) for more on the relationship between abstract space and capitalism.

7. See Zukin and Maguire (2004) for more on the relationship between consumption and urban space. For more on the retail revolution, see Appelbaum and Lichtenstein (2006); and Lichtenstein (2009).

8. Geographers and urban scholars adopted the term "glocalization" to signify the dynamic local and global forces responsible for producing globalization's new spatial scales. See Brenner and Theodore (2002).

9. Soja (1989, 62).

10. Matsuoka et al. (2011).

11. Smith (2004).

12. Marx (1867).

13. Marx (1867).

14. See Marx (1867) for a more precise reading of the relationship between production and consumption. He argues that consumption "creates the need for new production."

15. For more on the lack of academic research into logistics and urbanization, see Aoyama, Ratick, and Schwarz (2006) and Hesse (2004). See Castells (1996) and Hudson (2004) for more on the shift to global flows.

16. For more on the shipping container and logistics, see Bonacich and Wilson (2008); Herod (1998); and Levinson (2008).

17. Coe et al. (2010); Hesse and Rodrigue (2006).

18. Hall (2007); Notteboom and Rodrigue (2005).

19. Herod (2000); Saxenian (1994); Scott and Storper (2007).

20. Peter Dicken (2007) elaborates on this point.

21. See Harvey (1990) for a more detailed review of this theme.

22. Florida (2012); Sassen (1992).

23. Castells (1996).

24. Saskia Sassen (1992) provides an example of how London and New York entrenched themselves as control centers that helped to finance and manage the expanding global economic network.

25. See Martin (1999) for a critique of approaches that stress individual desire and consumer subjectivity. Francesco Nicosia and Robert Mayer (2007) showed that most consumer research focuses on the decision-making process of the individual. Other academics challenge the notion that consumption structures social classes in a postmodern consumer society (Holt 2007). This more contemporary approach does not completely dismiss Pierre Bourdieu's earlier work (1986), in which he argued that taste and lifestyle are firmly rooted in class.

26. Bourdieu (1986).

27. Martin (1999).

28. Based on the author's analysis of data from the Federal Reserve. The numbers represent nonseasonally adjusted monthly flows of revolving consumer credit.

29. Cline (2013) and Martin (1999).

30. See Conca, Princen, and Maniates (2001, 6). They also state that "the simple, linear notion of a chain is a useful approximation that directs attention both upstream and downstream from what is otherwise the conventional emphasis on individual choices of atomized consumers." See Judd (2006) for more on using commodity chains as a research method.

31. Conca, Princen, and Maniates (2001) point out some spatial implications of commodity chains. According to them, distance and social fragmentation remove social relations that can provide ecological and social feedback. Actors located along the commodity chain nodes are isolated and do not comprehend the entire chain.

32. Industrial Development Organization (2013).

33. Data from the United Nations Conference on Trade and Development, http://unctadstat.unctad.org.

34. Author's analysis of data from the U.S. Department of Commerce and the U.S. International Trade Commission, https://www.usitc.gov/research_and_analysis.htm.

35. Husing (2004, 27).

36. Erie (2004).

37. Data taken from the U.S. Department of Transportation Maritime Administration (2008).

38. The TEU corresponds to shipping containers that measured twenty feet, even though most modern shipping containers now measure forty feet.

39. Logistics-related economic data are difficult to track. For example, it's not entirely clear how container traffic impacts the local economy. SCAG estimates that 50 to 70 percent of waterborne container traffic that enters through the ports is scheduled for delivery outside of Southern California (Li 2007). These figures are estimates and may contradict other findings. Other estimates claim that approximately 37 percent of the containers that enter through the San Pedro Bay are loaded onto trains and shipped to eastern markets (Leachman 2007). The remaining 63 percent of containers are processed locally for distribution to regional markets.

40. Kaneko and Nojiri (2008, 156).

41. For an example of earlier pull systems see Fields (2004).

42. See Dicken (1987); and Herod (2000).

43. Fields (2004).

44. Lynn (2005, 102).

45. See Sanderson and Uzumeri (1995) for more on how Sony developed market-specific products.

46. Zukin and Maguire (2004).

47. Burnson (2009b); Lichtenstein (2009); Moreton (2009).

48. See Lowe and Wrigley (1996).

49. Lowe and Wrigley (1996, 22). They also point out that not all retail is focused on leisure. Some spaces have been produced as women-centered in order to tackle domestic shopping. Given this context, shopping functions as domestic labor.

50. Sorkin (1992).

51. Holt (1998); Veblen (1899).

52. Herod (2000, 1781).

CHAPTER 3

1. Jonas and Ward (2007, 169) review the extensive literature that has covered changes in global political economy. Scott and Storper (2007) discuss new regionalism.

2. Jonas and Ward (2007, 170).

3. From Mitchell (1996).

4. Lefebvre (1991).

5. See Harvey (1987) for a more extensive discussion of these four points.

6. More of this discussion on how cities turned to tourism and consumption can be found in Sorkin (1992); Urry (2002); and Zukin (1995).

7. Crisis has often been used to implement radical capitalist reforms. See Klein (2008).

8. Quoted in Pesick (2008).

9. Kyser (n.d.).

10. Raine (2008).

11. Southern California Association of Governments (2005b, 22).

12. See Southern California Association of Governments (2005b). For example, a proposed grade separation at the Colton Crossing would allow volumes to increase from 135 per peak day in 2005 to 255 crossings by 2025 (Wilbur Smith Associates 2008).

13. Larry Keller, Executive Director, Port of Los Angeles, in *The Alameda Corridor Project* (2001).

14. Data from Sargent (1989).

15. Logan and Molotch (1987, 12).

16. Southern California Association of Governments (2005a).

17. Buck-Morss (1995).

18. See Storper and Walker (1989) for more on the relationship between the structural relations of accumulation and human agency. This idea is closely tied to Marx's argument that individual capitalists may not understand the complexities of the market as a whole, but their desire for profit and the logic of their individual interests help to propel capitalism.

19. As Robinson notes, there is a constant tension between rational economistic thinking and the often messy social realities of political currents: "A primary consequence of the conflict between those two social tendencies was that capitalists, as the architects of this system, never achieved the coherence of structure and organisation which had been the promise of capitalism as an objective system" (1983, 145). Lefebvre refers to similar challenges when he discusses abstract space, or the rational planning needed to achieve efficient capitalist social relations. Both of these scholars point out some of the tensions between capitalism as an ideology and the production of space within capitalist social relations that are not completely defined by rationalist economistic thinking. This is exactly why things like race and gender cannot be relegated to economistic explanations: they do not yield to the imaginaries needed by abstract space.

20. The San Pedro Bay port complex is composed of two separate but neighboring ports that are located in the cities of Los Angeles and Long Beach. Each port is governed by an independent and semiautonomous harbor commission, which is appointed by the mayor of each city.

21. Each municipality maintains a list of procedural rules that allow the mayor, city council, and city manager (in the case of Long Beach) to affect port decisions. Municipal charter reform campaigns during the late 1990s were supposed to create greater transparency and public accountability by government agencies. According to Steven P. Erie (2004), while these reforms gave elected officials new oversight powers, they led to greater day-to-day port autonomy that gave the port of Long Beach a competitive advantage over Los Angeles.

22. For an example of these documents see Husing (2004, 2006b); Southern California Association of Governments (2005b); and Wilbur Smith Associates (2008).

23. See Erie (2004) for additional details on infrastructure spending during the 1980s.

24. Birch (1999); Gramsci (2000).

25. Jeffrey Brown, CA State Office of Research, in *The Alameda Corridor Project* (2001).

26. *Alameda Corridor Project* (2001).

27. *Alameda Corridor Project* (2001).

28. *Alameda Corridor Project* (2001).

29. Gill Hicks, in *Alameda Corridor Project* (2001).

30. Gill Hicks, in *Alameda Corridor Project* (2001).

31. Los Angeles Economic Development Corporation (2003, 7).

32. Cowen (2014).

33. Gill Hicks, in *Alameda Corridor Project* (2001).

34. Larry Keller, in *Alameda Corridor Project* (2001).

35. See Harvey (1978) for a longer explanation of how the state manages and shapes the market.

36. Jeff Holt, Goldman Sachs, in *Alameda Corridor Project* (2001).

37. James Hankla, CEO ACTA, in *Alameda Corridor Project* (2001).

38. www.fhwa.dot.gov/ipd/tifia/.

39. Other members included the cities of Long Beach and Los Angeles, the California Air Resources Board, the Federal Fish and Wildlife Service, the Southern California Association of Governments, and the South Coast Air Quality Management District.

40. Southern California Association of Governments (2007).

41. Percentage from Leachman (2007).

42. See Grubbs (2004) for more details on these strategies.

43. Ward (2009).

44. Panama Canal Authority (2011).

45. Burnson (2009a).

46. Marroquin (2009).

47. The plan was entitled A Program for Establishing Public-Private Partnerships for Infrastructure Financing and The Improvement of Harbor Drayage Trucks In the State of California (Dot et al. 2008).

48. Raine (2008).

49. The biggest threat posed by other ports comes from competition for discretionary cargo, freight that is scheduled to be shipped to midwestern and eastern markets. At this time, Canadian and other West Coast ports pose the most serious competition.

50. Bluestone and Harrison (1982); Bronfenbrenner (2000).

51. *Alameda Corridor Project* (2001).

52. Figures from State of California (2008).

53. Pelisek (2005).

54. Quoted in Larrubia (2008).

55. See Matsuoka (2008) for further elaboration on this point.

56. White (2008).

57. Pastor, Benner, and Matsuoka (2009).

58. Port of Los Angeles and Port of Long Beach (2006).

59. Private-sector workers face a litany of legal and illegal barriers to unionization under existing processes of the National Labor Relations Act. See Bronfenbrenner (1994).

60. Quoted in Larrubia (2008).

61. Vara-Orta (2009).

62. Vara-Orta (2009).

63. White (2009).

64. This is something that happened during an earlier period of port growth, when places like Commerce, the City of Industry, and the South Bay were part of the initial outward growth from the ports.

65. Inland distribution functions are becoming more important factors in port competitiveness. See Notteboom and Rodrigue (2005) for a more thorough review of this theory.

66. In Southern California, local port authorities function as public-private entities that embrace the entrepreneurial business ethic.

67. Wilbur Smith Associates (2008).

68. Author's notes on Empire Symposium, Cal Poly Pomona, November 7, 2007.

69. SCAQMD (2008).

70. Li (2007).

71. Hricko (2008).

72. SCAQMD (2008).

73. *Fontana Herald News* (2008).

74. Data from Wilbur Smith Associates (2008).

75. Author's notes from Moving Forward: A Conference on Healthy Solutions for Communities Impacted by Trade, Ports and Goods Movement, Los Angeles, CA, December 1, 2007.

76. Quoted in Macduff (2007).

77. Integrated logistics centers are a relatively new phenomenon in the United States. The first ILC was built in Fort Worth, Texas, and opened in 1994. Most of the existing ILCs were built after 2002 (HDR|HLB Decision Economics 2006). Several industrial developers became key players in the inland port industry. For example, Hillwood, a leading developer of Inland Empire logistics centers, was the main contractor for the Alliance Texas Logistics Park. The Alliance Park is fifteen miles from the Dallas-Fort Worth market. It is served by BNSF, which recently moved its Dallas hub to the new Hillwood logistics park (Tioga Group 2008). Hillwood is also the lead developer for the Alliance California logistics hub, which is located on the former Norton Air Force Base in San Bernardino; plans called for BNSF to play a key role in developing an intermodal facility for the Norton logistics base.

78. Tioga Group (2008).

79. Mentioned by a company spokesperson during a panel discussion. Author's notes, Faster Freight Cleaner Air Conference, Long Beach, CA, March 23, 2009.

80. Data from the U.S. Census Bureau, Economic Indicators Division (Harrison 2007, 322).

81. Schrack (2009).

82. Public testimony, Long Beach City Council Meeting, May 12, 2009.

83. Baye Larsen, analyst, Moody's Investor Service, quoted in Ward (2009).

84. Author's analysis of annual budgets for ports of Long Beach and Los Angeles.

85. See Hanson (2008) for more details on port expenditures.

86. Public testimony, Long Beach City Council Meeting, May 12, 2009.

87. See Mongelluzzo (2009b).

88. Data from Mongelluzzo (2009a). Long Beach also considered a $20 to $40 per container incentive for nonlocal cargo. Both of the ports have acknowledged that the adoption of rail incentives is an economic maneuver to lure shippers who need to distribute nonlocal containers and have the option of using various West Coast ports (Lloyd's List 2009).

SCENE 2

1. The description of this scene is taken from the author's field notes, 2009.

CHAPTER 4

1. See, for example, Wilding and Delgado (2004); and Brea-Solís, Casadesus-Masanell, and Grifell-Tatjé (2015).

2. Cowen (2014) provides an excellent review of how logistics became part of the total systems analysis business model.

3. Moreton (2009).

4. See Bonacich and Wilson (2008) and Lichtenstein (2009) for a more detailed account of how Walmart revolutionized the retail industry through its use of POS.

5. Walton (1993).

6. Wolf, Burritt, and Boyle (2010).

7. Bonacich and Wilson (2008).

8. Interview with author July 14, 2010.

9. Kulwiec (2004).

10. Braverman (1974).

11. Maier (1970, 27).

12. Interview with author June 30, 2010.

13. Napolitano (2008); Saxena (2007).

14. Kaneko and Nojiri (2008).

15. Bartholdi and Gue (2004).

16. Bartholdi and Gue (2004).

17. For example, the average value of Asian imports that flowed through West Coast ports was $22.66 per cubic foot. East Coast ports processed Asian imports with an average value of $18.57 per cubic foot (Leachman 2007).

18. Ray (2010).

19. Napolitano (2008).

20. Barnard (2008).

21. The separation between physical and virtual logistics services has led some to argue that the informational space of logistics is as important as the physical space of commodity transport. See Schwarz (2006) for more on this debate.

22. Plant (2002).

23. McGowan (2005).

24. Aoyama, Ratick, and Schwarz (2006).

25. *Creating Tomorrow's Surface Transportation Systems* (1994, 43).

CHAPTER 5

1. Klein (1997, 5).

2. This idea of method and hegemony is discussed by Sonia Saldivar-Hull (2000).

3. Butler and Athanasiou (2013).

4. Williams (2016).

5. Giri (1992).

6. See Grossberg (1986) for more on regimes of truth and the power and politics of discourse.

7. Doreen Massey (1995) cites Stuart Hall to challenge the structural determinist idea of pre-given common interests.

8. Boudreau argues that actors can open up new political spaces by using particular spatial practices: "Spatial practices are behavioural elements of everyday life, the aggregation of which form the spatial fabric of one's routine and sense of political allegiance"(2007, 2595).

9. Garcia (2001, 9). Garcia (1996) also discusses how this point applies to Chicanx labor historiography.

10. Author's field notes, April 9, 2013.

11. Wright continues, "No matter how repressive was the American environment, the Negro never lost faith in or doubted his deeply endemic capacity to live. All blues are a lusty, lyrical realism charged with taught sensibility" (quoted in Woods 2000, 19).

12. Lefebvre (1991, 162).

13. Author's notes, April 9, 2009.

14. Interview with author, February 12, 2010.

15. Approximately 371,000 people fled the U.S.-backed civil war in El Salvador and migrated to the United States between 1980 and 1990 (Terrazas 2010).

16. Interview with author, July 14, 2010.

17. The California Budget Project and the Economic Policy Institute have developed basic family wage indexes that can be applied to the Inland Empire. These living wage indexes measure what workers must earn to pay for basic family expenses.

18. Butler and Athanasiou (2013) were referring to "a style of masculinism that effaces sexual difference and enacts mastery over the domain of life."

19. Interview with author, June 30, 2013.

20. Interview with author, June 30, 2013.

21. Interview with author, June 30, 2013.

22. Interview with author, June 30, 2013.

23. For an explanation about apparel and global trade, see Collins (2003).

24. Interview with author, June 30, 2013.

25. Jamieson (2012).

26. Interview with author, July 14, 2010.

27. Interview with author, July 14, 2010.

28. Interview with author, July 14, 2010.

29. Interview with author, July 14, 2010.

30. Interview with author, July 14, 2010.

31. Interview with author, July 14, 2010.

32. Interview with author, July 14, 2010.

33. Interview with author, June 30, 2010.

34. Interview with author, June 30, 2010.

35. Interview with author, June 30, 2010.

36. Interview with author, July 14, 2010.

CHAPTER 6

1. Leitner, Sheppard, and Sziarto (2008, 169).

2. See Pastor et al. (2000) for a discussion of how regions are created and defined.

3. Union leaders were concerned that shipping containers would push distribution work into inland warehouse facilities and erode the ILWU's membership base by winnowing away jobs from the docks. ILWU leaders claimed that the actual work of deconsolidating less-than-full container shipments at container freight station (CFS) facilities was replacing traditional break-bulk work that its members once performed on the docks (Herod 1998).

4. Herod (1998, 187).

5. Interview with author, 2008.

6. Author's notes, union leadership meeting, December 4, 2008.

7. Author's notes, union leadership meeting, December 9, 2008.

8. Herod (1994); Lipietz (1997).

9. Author's field notes, December 7, 2009.

10. Lerner (2007).

11. Bronfenbrenner et al. (1998); Bronfenbrenner and Hickey (2004).

12. Aguiar and Ryan (2009).

13. Quoted in Bronfenbrenner (2005, 19).

14. Quoted in Bronfenbrenner (2005, 19).

15. See Herod (1994) for a more thorough discussion of this.

16. For more on the history of labor movement reform see Fantasia and Voss (2004).

17. Paraphrased from author's field notes, August 13, 2010.

18. Remarks made at Getting the Goods Conference, University of California, Riverside, author's notes, November 13, 2008.

19. Carl Wood, former member of the California Public Utilities Commission and an officer in the Utility Workers of America, ran as a reform candidate and vowed to turn the CLC into a relevant political institution. According to Mike Hartigan, head of the Local CWA and a Wood supporter, "Organizing has come to a standstill. Political influence has become nil. There's a litany of problems we see. This is a working blue-collar area that doesn't have a viable central labor council. We believed it was time to bring some positive change" (Granelli 2004).

20. These campaigns created new class narratives and organizing strategies that were different from local strategies. To be successful, the new models would require institutional changes to the local labor movement. Organizers believed that these changes were necessary because the old way of doing things had failed. They claimed that local unions that continued to deploy old strategies could not effectively keep up with new economic strategies. As a result, unions would be unable to expand their membership base as shifts in regional accumulation strategies created new employment sectors.

21. PWF and CLUE are national organizations that function as policy and community links on community and labor issues. IVLAN is a multi-campus-based network of faculty and students who are interested in labor issues. Unions also reached out and formed a working relationship with an active San Bernardino–based ACORN chapter. Participating unions and PWF's national leadership struggled for more than a year to find a person who understood and could navigate the region's complex political, social, and economic geography. PWF's protracted search for an executive director and the decision by organized labor to build its own grassroots infrastructure demonstrate how the political geography of a place like the Inland Empire can shape the ways that unions organize and contest the social production of space.

22. Author's field notes, October 30, 2008.

23. Author's notes, WWU strategy meeting, November 24, 2008.

24. See Friedman (1997) and Herman (2001).

25. Author interview with CTW staff member, December 4, 2008.

26. Interview with author, December 4, 2008.

27. Author's field notes, December 9, 2008.

28. This image of the Lost Boys was a common topic of discussion. My description is based on in-person observations and formal interviews with union staff.

29. Interview with author, February 19, 2013.

30. Husing (2004). This is an impressive figure, especially when compared to other blue-collar sectors like construction ($40,439) and manufacturing ($43,871). Based on 2003 wages for the SCAG region.

31. Husing (2004, 27).

32. Paul Granillo and John Husing, interview with author, May 26, 2011.

33. See Agamben (2009) for a more elaborate definition of an apparatus.

34. Wholesale trade (NAICS 42), Truck transportation (NAICS 484), Support activities for transportation (NAICS 488), General Warehouse & Storage (NAICS 493), Non-Local Couriers (NAICS 492110), Air Transportation (NAICS 481), Rail transportation (NAICS 482), and Water transportation (NAICS 483).

35. The Council of Supply Chain Management defines logistics thus: "Supply chain management encompasses the planning and management of all activities involved in sourcing and procurement, conversion, and all logistics management activities. Importantly, it also includes coordination and collaboration with channel partners, which can be suppliers, intermediaries, third party service providers, and customers. In essence, supply chain management integrates supply and demand management within and across companies" (https://cscmp.org/supply-chain -management-definitions, 2016).

36. Based on the California Employment Development Department's list of thirty occupations in logistics (http://www.labormarketinfo.edd.ca.gov).

37. These occupations include the following categories: Laborers and Freight, Stock, and Material Movers, Hand; Stock Clerks and Order Fillers; Truck Drivers, Heavy and Tractor-Trailer; Customer Service Representatives; Packers and Packagers (based on data from the May 2007 Occupational Employment Statistics survey at https://www.bls.gov/oes/). For example, one way to account for the difference between a white-collar logistician and a blue-collar warehouse worker is to measure incomes by occupational status. Data from the OES survey measure mean and median wages by geographic designation and job categories. The report is produced by the Bureau of Labor Statistics using data compiled from a semiannual mail survey that collects responses from nonfarm business establishments. The California Employment Development Department (CA EDD) has listed thirty-one of these OES occupations as logistics-related employment opportunities. Using these data to construct a more accurate and differentiated wage scale for warehouse workers, one can show that the average warehouse worker earns a mean annual wage of $26,081, based on an average of the five largest target occupational categories. I excluded administrative, management, and highly skilled occupations (like pilots and rail engineers). Other occupations with job descriptions that did not match my target constituency (e.g., sales representatives) were also excluded. I then cross-checked the remaining occupations with OES data to verify that logistics industries were the major employers of these occupations. Other industries may be

included in the employee pool. These occupational categories do include temporary workers.

38. Based on author's analysis of data from the Bureau of Labor Statistics at https://www.bls.gov/oes/.

39. Author's analysis of data from the 2007–2011 American Community Survey at https://www.census.gov/programs-surveys/acs/technical-documentation/table-and-geography-changes/2011/5-year.html.

40. Jamieson (2011).

41. See Massey and Denton (2003) for a discussion of the duality of labor and capital; they tie immigration to a permanent demand for cheap labor, especially in segmented labor markets. They use Piore to argue that the difference between fixed and variable capital leads to a segmented labor force. The capital-intensive primary sector employs longer term, permanent workers, who receive higher wages because of their skilled relationship with fixed capital. This seems to match what happens with clerical and tech-based logistics workers.

42. For more on the temporary industry see Theodore and Peck (2002). They were able to show that temp agency expansion outpaced aggregate employment growth in emerging labor markets. They used location quotients to document how temporary staffing industry (TSI) expansion outpaced general employment during economic restructuring. Penetration rates were at parity in the 1980s and showed strong divergence at the end of the 1990s.

43. Author calculations from the Bureau of Labor Statistics' Quarterly Census of Employment & Wages, 2000–2010 (https://www.bls.gov/cew/).

44. Based on location quotients calculated by the author. Location quotients allow us to see how concentrated a particular industry is in relation to a reference area. The location quotient for the Inland Empire's temporary employment industry increased from 0.61 in 1990 to 1.48 in 2007. Any location quotient above 1 signifies a higher concentration of temporary employment than the rest of California.

45. Pare (2011).

46. Based on real estate market data from CoStar Group, 2009 (www.costar.com).

47. Most of the literature on temporary employment has focused on white-collar and clerical labor (Kallerberg, Reskin, and Hudson 2000; Smith 1997, 1998).

48. From interview with author, December 22, 2008. Instant verification refers to the federal government's E-Verify computer system, which allows employers to instantaneously determine a job applicant's legal work status.

49. Kallerberg, Reskin, and Hudson (2000) dispute the idea that all workers prefer the flexible work schedules offered by contingent work.

50. Interview with author, June 22, 2010.

51. Interview with author, March 30, 2011.

52. Author's field notes, March 30, 2011.

53. Author's field notes, March 30, 2011.

54. Author's field notes, March 30, 2011.

55. Interview with author, July 14, 2010.

56. Interview with author, July 14, 2010.

SCENE 3

1. Hansen and Boster (2016); CNN (2013).
2. *NBC News* (2014).
3. See Calavita (1996) for more on California's contentious immigration politics.
4. See USC Dornsife/Los Angeles Times Poll (2013).

CHAPTER 7

1. Anicic (2006).
2. Didion (1968, 3).
3. Esquivel (2013).
4. Davis (1990) makes this argument.
5. For a variation of this argument see Kotkin and Frey (2007).
6. Horsman (1981); Molina (2013).
7. Didion (1968, 4).
8. Alamillo (2006); Garcia (2001); Gonzalez (1994); Zierer (1934).
9. Population estimates are based on author's calculations from the 1980, 1990, and 2010 U.S. Censuses and from the California Department of Finance.
10. Frey (2010).
11. Singer and Wilson (2010) show a decline in the Inland Empire's foreign-born population, from a total of 911,982 in 2007 to 883,150 in 2009; this represents a 3.2 percent decline.
12. Bronfenbrenner et al. (1998).
13. Fontana Steel (1948).
14. Big Steel was the common name given to the United States Steel Corporation, which was founded, in part, by J. P. Morgan. See Warren (2001).
15. See Davis (1990).
16. Holifield (1947).
17. Fontana Steel (1948).
18. Fontana Steel (1948).
19. Cohen (2004).
20. Foster (1989).
21. Interview with author, 2013.
22. Interview with author, 2013.
23. Foster (1989).
24. Foster (1989).
25. *Los Angeles Tribune* (1946).
26. See Camarillo (2007) for a more general description of how economic restructuring affected racial formation in California's inner-ring suburbs.
27. Huntington (2004).

28. Cleaver (1980a).

29. Christmas (1980).

30. Quoted in Cleaver (1980b).

31. Quoted in Christmas (1980).

32. Berry (1993).

33. Christmas (1980); Cleaver (1980a).

34. Quoted in Dulaney (2010).

35. Peterson (1997).

36. Hudson (2004). See Williams (1977) for a more thorough discussion on the relationship between place and feeling.

37. I borrow this notion from Gupta and Ferguson, who claim, "Homeland in this way remains one of the most powerful unifying symbols for mobile and displaced peoples" (1992, 11).

38. Gilroy (2005).

39. Quoted in Peterson (1997).

40. This confluence provides us with an opportunity to link the literature on the production of space to the literature on racial formation. See Cheng (2013) for an excellent review of regional racial formation.

41. Durian (2009).

42. Sahagun (1988a).

43. Metzger wasn't acting alone. Other groups participated in local racist activities, including the White Mafia, Aryan Youth Movement, and a KKK Imperial Wizard named James Ferrands who travelled from Connecticut. Quoted in Associated Press (1988).

44. Quoted in Green (1988).

45. A reporter who talked to Metzger wrote that the KKK reached 100 members in Fontana during the 1980s, when the Kaiser mill shut down (Peterson 1997).

46. Taken from Peterson (1997).

47. Anderson (1997).

48. Quoted in Peterson (1997).

49. One obvious question that is beyond the scope of this project is how race was shaped by imported histories of racialized social relations and how it was shaped by the local historical context.

50. The all-white Hells Angels Motorcycle Club—which was founded in Fontana, San Bernardino, and Bloomington—epitomizes this link between Fontucky as a racial geography and the development of a particular white working-class regional aesthetic. While not explicitly racist in purpose, the Hells Angels are an example of how working-class white identity enabled cognitive mappings of Fontana and the Inland Empire as a conservative racialized landscape.

51. Quoted in *Chicago Sun-Times* (1988).

52. Quoted in Sahagun (1988b).

53. Pulido (1996) cites Paul Gilroy to make this point.

54. Pulido (1996).

55. Interview with author, 2012.

CHAPTER 8

1. Personal observation by author, January 8, 2009.

2. Lee (2008a).

3. Personal observation by author, January 8, 2009.

4. For more on what the right to the city means, see Merrifield (2011) and Mitchell (2003).

5. Based on author's calculations of 1990 and 2010 U.S. Census data.

6. The African American population went from 13 to 18 percent, while the Asian and Pacific Islander population registered a slight increase, from 6.7 to 7.6 percent.

7. The distribution center was scheduled to be built south of the 60 freeway, between Redlands Boulevard and Theodore Street. Highland Fairview agreed to complete the distribution center by January 2009 or incur a fine. According to the contract, Highland Fairview would have to pay Skechers up to $2.2 million to cover the cost of temporary facilities.

8. Benzeevi, PowerPoint presentation, January 8, 2009, author's field notes.

9. Lee (2008a).

10. Lee (2008e).

11. Brenner and Theodore (2002, 375).

12. Benzeevi contributed nearly $125,000 to local city council elections in 2004. Of the top ten campaign donors in local politics, seven were developers, and Highland Fairview gave the most (Lee 2005).

13. Anonymous (2007).

14. Unemployment figures calculated by author using 2009 data from the California Department of Finance (http://www.dof.ca.gov). Mayor Batey quoted in Lee (2008e).

15. Lee (2008d).

16. Lee (2009).

17. Author's field notes, January 8, 2009.

18. Author's field notes, January 2009.

19. Author's field notes, January 2009.

20. Interview with author, February 22, 2010.

21. Benzeevi denied initial job projections during his presentations before the planning commission and would not commit to an actual number (author's notes, planning commission meeting January 8, 2009). This estimate on the number of jobs for warehouse projects is from The Tioga Group (2008).

22. Author's field notes, January 8, 2009.

23. Lee (2008b).

24. Author's field notes, January 8, 2009.

25. Author's field notes, January 8, 2009.

26. Author's field notes, January 2009.

27. Author's field notes, January 2009.

28. Barraclough (2011, 121).

29. Barraclough (2011, 118).

30. Williams makes this argument by looking at English poetry: "Poets have always lent their tongues to princes, who were in a position to reply. What has been lent to the shepherds is more doubtful" (1968, 279).

31. See Hall (1980) for further elaboration on the relationship between culture, hegemony, and power. For example, Hall uses Williams to argue that "no 'whole way of life' is without its dimension of struggle and confrontation between opposed ways of life-and attempts to rethink the key issues of determination and domination via Gramsci's concept of 'hegemony'" (Hall 1980, 61).

32. Author's field notes, January 8, 2009.

33. Author's field notes, January 8, 2009.

34. For example, speakers claimed that the city's existing general plan was supposed to protect their pastoral lifestyle by limiting the size of industrial development projects to fifty thousand square feet. To approve the project, the city council would have to make an exception to a general plan rule that held all industrial property developments to that size or smaller.

35. Harvey (2003); Attoh (2011).

36. Price and Young (1959).

37. Wolch, Pastor, and Dreier (2004).

38. Author calculations based on data from the California Department of Conservation, http://www.conservation.ca.gov.

39. The preserve was established in 1967.

40. Data from the Milk Producers Council at www.milkproducerscouncil.org/.

41. The Planning Center (2003).

42. Quoted in Sanchez (2002). Devereaux was an influential figure who would go on to serve as San Bernardino County's chief financial officer.

43. http://www.ranchobelago.com.

44. Phoebe S. Kropp (2008) provides excellent examples of how boosters deployed the Spanish fantasy aesthetic to produce distinct commodified, gendered, and racialized landscapes.

45. Gutierrez (1993, 524).

46. Rosa Linda Fregoso describes the "fantasy heritage as the process of historical recovery that glosses over contradictions, struggles, and conflicts" (2003, 108).

47. Patricia Nelson Limerick (1987) provides a more detailed account of how land titles and property rights shaped the American West.

48. Pullen (1973).

49. http://www.ranchobelago.com.

50. Neil Smith (2004) discusses how the surveyor's gaze was the precursor to the subsequent mapping that pointed the way for empire.

51. http://www.ranchobelago.com.

52. Urry's (2002) work on signs and tourism is helpful here. He claims that signs represent a link between the physical landscape and the tourist gaze: "The gaze is constructed through signs, and tourism involves the collection of signs. When tourists see two people kissing in Paris what they capture in the gaze is 'timeless

romantic Paris'." Tourists then go out in search of these signs to collect the true experience of place. Urry seems to distinguish between gaze and landscape by tying gaze to the subjective cognitive mapping/fantasy of the tourist and defining landscape as the physical world (place) that is the object of the gaze. This differs from the use of "landscape" here.

53. The city eventually approved installation of 115 signs with modifications that would avoid litigation from Beverly Hills (Lucas 2010).

54. Mitchell (1996, 4).

55. Mary Pat Brady (2000, 20) makes a more explicit connection between cognitive mappings and racial geographies by using popular literature and racial discourse.

56. Husing (2006a).

57. LiUNA' estimates that the top five national builders developed about 50 percent of all new homes in the Inland Empire. Figures from an internal union document.

58. Wrye (2008).

59. See Hesse (2004) for a discussion of real estate speculation and land markets.

60. Heschmeyer (2007). Riverside and San Bernardino Counties had the highest industrial real estate net absorption rate in the country as of July 2007. Absorption rates measure how much real estate space was put into actual or intended use during a specific period.

61. Husing (2008).

62. This is calculated as floor area ratio, which is .50 for mega-distribution centers. Figures from The Tioga Group (2008).

63. "Inland Empire Top Leasing Firms" (2007).

64. This approval period could be very contentious, especially when groups challenged the environmental impact of a specific project through the terms established by the California Environmental Quality Act of 1970.

65. Troianovski (2009).

66. ProLogis is the Inland Empire's self-proclaimed leader in industrial warehouse space; it led the march inland by purchasing and developing large tracts of land in the eastern Inland Empire. ProLogis expanded its Inland Empire holdings by acquiring existing property and actively constructing new projects. The company was making new warehouse acquisitions as late as April 2007. For example, it purchased and immediately leased two Ontario properties that provided a total of 855,000 square feet. More recent developments include the Kaiser Commerce Center, 5.9 million square feet of industrial space that reached full capacity in January 2009. ProLogis has also worked closely with BNSF as part of a strategy to expand services near the railroad company's Transload Logistics Center. It purchased thirty-nine acres from BNSF in Fontana during October 2004. Company officials planned on building approximately 849,000 square feet of distribution space on the Fontana property.

67. Hirsh (2008).

68. Troianovski (2009).

69. Moreno Valley planning commissioners, including George Riechers, Maria Marzoeki, Douglas Merkt, and Rick De Jong, all cited traffic and pollution concerns as reasons for their rejection of the project. Despite these concerns, the city council voted unanimously to approve the project on February 10, 2009.

70. Author's notes on public testimony, city planning commission meeting, January 8, 2009.

71. Lucas (2010).

CHAPTER 9

1. Johnson, Reed, and Hayes (2008).

2. Cited in Gorman and Connell (2009).

3. Kotkin and Frey (2007).

4. Jim Spect, Republican congressional spokesperson, interview with author, March 19, 2010.

5. Interview with author, March 15, 2010.

6. Interview with author, March 15, 2010.

7. Interview with author, March 15, 2010.

8. Interview with author, March 15, 2010.

9. Gonzales (2014).

10. For more on the 287(g) program, see ww.ice.gov. ICE claimed that the 287(g) program led to the identification of "402,079 potentially removable aliens" between 2006 and 2015.

11. Wong (2012).

12. Gonzales (2014).

13. Interview with author, February 22, 2010.

14. Jim Spect, U.S. representative, interview with author, March 19, 2010.

15. Both Riverside and San Bernardino Counties signed 287(g) agreements with ICE. Spect, interview with author, March 19, 2010.

16. See, for example, Hancock (2004).

17. Schmidt Camacho (2008).

18. Gorman and Connell (2009).

19. John Husing, interview with author, May 26, 2011.

20. Husing cited the 2010 U.S. Census in reference to this figure.

21. Author calculations based on data from the 2010 U.S. Census.

22. From author's calculations based on California Department of Education 2009 data (www.cde.ca.gov).

23. Based on author's calculations using data from the American Community Survey, 1990 and 2010 (https://www.census.gov/programs-surveys/acs/data.html).

24. Frey (2010).

25. Interview with author, May 26, 2011.

26. From author's calculations based on 2010 data from the California Department of Education (www.cde.ca.gov).

27. Klampe (2011).

28. Author calculations based on data from www.ed-data.k12.ca.us.

29. Three school board members, interviews with the author, March 15 and 26, 2010.

30. Victoria Baca, interview with author, March 15, 2010.

31. Chiang (1996).

32. Based on author calculations of data from www.cde.ca.gov.

33. Interview with author.

34. Interview with author, March 15, 2010.

35. (Wall 2009)

36. Members of the JIC filed a Freedom of Information Act request demanding to see documents from the local border patrol office in order to document what they claimed was a growing connection between immigration and local police enforcement.

37. Young (2009).

38. Interview with author, February 19, 2010.

39. Olson (2012).

40. Interview with author, February 19, 2010.

41. Interview with author, March 16, 2010.

42. McKinnon and Burge (2008).

43. Local police agencies received funding for checkpoints from the California Office of Traffic Safety. The state increased checkpoint grants from $5 million in 2009 to $8 million in 2010 (McKinnon 2010).

44. McKinnon (2010).

45. Interview with author, April 30, 2010.

46. This information about Bishop Barnes and his impact on the church was gathered during interviews with several diocese staff and members of the JIC in March 2010.

47. From an interview the author conducted on March, 31, 2010, with the head priest of the Riverside parish in question.

48. In addition, the diocese worked with the U.S. Department of Labor and the Mexican consulate to support a program called Empleo, which served as a hotline for workers (including immigrant workers) to report mistreatment in the workplace. More than one million assistance calls had been processed at the time of our interview (February 17, 2010).

49. Interview with author, March 16, 2010.

50. Border patrol officials announced that they would close the facility in 2012 to focus on areas closer to the U.S.-Mexico border. The Riverside office was finally shut down in 2014.

51. Interview with author, February 19, 2010.

1. Gilmore (2007, 17).

2. Herod notes, "Discursive practices, how a dispute, process or situation is represented to a broader audience—can thus be important elements in the institutional reproduction of labor markets and, consequently, of workers themselves" (1998, 178).

3. For more on hegemony and development, see Evans (2000).

4. Benner and Pastor (2012, 15).

5. Benner and Pastor call this ideological conversion an "epistemic community." Community benefits agreements are an example of a just growth practice that reframes development by including equity and broader participation. These agreements help to develop an epistemic community and are "important for the understanding they promote as the benefits they deliver" (2012, 15).

6. Lopez and Serven (2009); Ostry and Berg (2011).

7. Data from the Field Poll (2009) and author's analysis of voter registration statistics from the California Secretary of State, 2008 (http://www.sos.ca.gov /elections/voter-registration/).

8. Johnson, Reed, and Hayes (2008).

9. Data from California Secretary of State, 2008 (http://www.sos.ca.gov /elections/voter-registration/).

10. Ramakrishnan (2007).

11. Interview with author, April 30, 2010.

12. Olson (2008). Klan members showed up during a Minutemen protest in Rancho Cucamonga in March 2007 (Johnson 2007).

13. Kohout (2009).

14. Lovett (2011).

15. Interview with author, February 22, 2010.

REFERENCES

Agamben, Giorgio. 2009. *What Is an Apparatus? And Other Essays.* Edited by Werner Hamacher. Stanford, CA: Stanford University Press.

Aguiar, Luis L. M., and Shaun Ryan. 2009. "The Geographies of the Justice for Janitors." *Geoforum* 40 (6): 949–58. doi:10.1016/j.geoforum.2009.09.012.

The Alameda Corridor Project: Its Successes and Challenges. 2001. Washington, DC: U.S. Government Printing Office. www.house.gov/reform.

Alamillo, José M. 2006. *Making Lemonade out of Lemons: Mexican American Labor and Leisure in a California Town, 1880–1960.* Urbana: University of Illinois Press.

Allen, James P., and Eugene Turner. 1997. *The Ethnic Quilt: Population Diversity in Southern California.* Northridge: The Center for Geographical Studies, California State University.

Anderson, Dianne. 1997. "Parents Protest School Racism in Fontana." *Precinct Reporter*, February, sec. A.

Anicic, John Charles. 2006. *Kaiser Steel Fontana.* Images of America. San Francisco, CA: Arcadia Publishing.

Anonymous. 2007. "SKECHERS Footwear Enters into a Lease Agreement for a 1.8 Million Square Foot Distribution Facility." *Business Wire*, October. www.businesswire.com.

Anzaldua, Gloria. 1987. *Borderlands: The New Mestiza = La Frontera.* San Francisco: Spinsters/Aunt Lute.

Aoyama, Yuko, Samuel Ratick, and Guido Schwarz. 2006. "Organizational Dynamics of the U.S. Logistics Industry: An Economic Geography Perspective." *Professional Geographer* 58 (3): 327–40. doi:10.1111/j.1467-9272.2006.00571.x.

Appelbaum, Richard, and Nelson Lichtenstein. 2006. "A New World of Retail Supremacy: Supply Chains and Workers' Chains in the Age of Wal-Mart." *International Labor and Working-Class History*, no. 70: 106–25.

Arrighi, Giovanni. 2004. "Spatial and Other 'Fixes' of Historical Capitalism." *Journal of World-Systems Research* 10 (2): 527–39.

Associated Press. 1988. "KKK Held at Bay, Yet Two Arrested at King Holiday Event." *Los Angeles Sentinel*, January 21, sec. A.

————. 1992. "China to Buy Used Mill: A New Approach to Exporting Steel." *New York Times*, November 4, late ed., sec. D.

————. 1993. "Chinese Dismantle U.S. Plant: 22-Story Steel Facility Headed for Homeland." *Cincinnati Post*, October 9, C9.

Attoh, Kafui A. 2011. "What Kind of Right Is the Right to the City?" *Progress in Human Geography* 35 (5): 669–85.

Bair, Jennifer, and Gary Gereffi. 2001. "Local Clusters in Global Chains: The Causes and Consequences of Export Dynamism in Torreon's Blue Jeans Industry." *World Development* 29 (11): 1885–1903,

Barnard, Patrick. 2008. "The New Big Thing: Super-Size DCs." *Multichannel Merchant*, November: 51–53.

Barnes, Trevor J., and Eric Sheppard. 1992. "Is There a Place for the Rational Actor? A Geographical Critique of the Rational Choice Paradigm." *Economic Geography* 68 (1): 1–21.

Barraclough, Laura R. 2011. *Making the San Fernando Valley Rural Landscapes, Urban Development, and White Privilege*. Athens: University of Georgia Press. http://site.ebrary.com/id/10426595.

Bartholdi, John J., and Kevin R. Gue. 2004. "The Best Shape for a Crossdock." *Transportation Science* 38 (2): 235–44.

Becker, Gary Stanley. 2008. *The Economic Approach to Human Behavior*. Chicago: University of Chicago Press.

Benner, C., and M. Pastor. 2012. *Just Growth: Inclusion and Prosperity in America's Metropolitan Regions*. Regions and Cities. London: Routledge. https://books.google.com/books?id=WKxOpwAACAAJ.

Berry, W.K. 1993. "Getting Away with Murder: Hate Crimes." *Precinct Reporter*, July 15, sec. A.

Birch, Vicki. 1999. "Contesting the Hegemony of Market Ideology: Gramsci's 'Good Sense' and Polanyi's 'Double Movement.'" *Review of International Political Economy*, 6 (1): 27–54.

Bluestone, Barry, and Bennett Harrison. 1982. *The Deindustrialization of America: Plant Closings, Community Abandonment, and the Dismantling of Basic Industry*. New York: Basic Books.

Bonacich, Edna, and Jake B. Wilson. 2008. *Getting the Goods: Ports, Labor, and the Logistics Revolution*. Ithaca, NY: Cornell University Press.

Boudreau, Julie-Anne. 2007. "Making New Political Spaces: Mobilizing Spatial Imaginaries, Instrumentalizing Spatial Practices, and Strategically Using Spatial Tools." *Environment and Planning A* 39 (11): 2593–2611.

Bourdieu, Pierre. 1986. *Distinction: A Social Critique of the Judgement of Taste*. London: Routledge & Kegan Paul.

Boyer, Kate. 2006. "Reform and Resistance: A Consideration of Space, Scale and Strategy in Legal Challenges to Welfare Reform." *Antipode* 38 (1): 22–40. https://doi.org/10.1111/j.0066-4812.2006.00563.x.

Brady, Mary Pat. 2000. "The Fungibility of Borders." *Nepantla: Views from the South* 1 (1): 171–90.

Braverman, Harry. (1974) 1998. *Labor and Monopoly Capital: The Degradation of Work in the Twentieth Century*. Edited by Paul M. Sweezy. New York: Monthly Review Press.

Brea-Solís, Humberto, Ramon Casadesus-Masanell, and Emili Grifell-Tatjé. 2015. "Business Model Evaluation: Quantifying Walmart's Sources of Advantage." *Strategic Entrepreneurship Journal* 9 (1): 12–33. doi:10.1002/sej.1190.

Brenner, Neil. 2000. "The Urban Question as a Scale Question: Reflections on Henri Lefebvre, Urban Theory and the Politics of Scale." *International Journal of Urban and Regional Research* 24 (2): 361–78.

Brenner, Neil, and Nik Theodore. 2002. "Cities and the Geographies of 'Actually Existing Neoliberalism.'" *Antipode* 34 (3): 349–79.

Bronfenbrenner, Kate. 1994. "Unions and the Contingent Workforce." In *The Labor Law Rights of Contingent Workers: Organization and Representation Issues*, edited by G.J. Gall, 2–14. University Park: Department of Labor Studies and Industrial Relations of the Pennsylvania State University. http://digitalcommons.ilr.cornell.edu/articles/20.

———. 2000. "Raw Power: Plant-Closing Threats and the Threat to Union Organizing." *Multinational Monitor* 21 (12): 24–29.

———. 2005. "What Is Labor's True Purpose? The Implications of SEIU's Unite to Win Proposals for Organizing." *New Labor Forum* 14 (2): 19–26. doi:10.1080/1095760590934670.

Bronfenbrenner, Kate, Sheldon Friedman, Richard W. Hurd, Rudolph A. Oswald, and Ronald L Seeber, eds. 1998. *Organizing to Win: New Research on Union Strategies*. Ithaca, NY: ILR Press.

Bronfenbrenner, Kate, and Robert Hickey. 2004. "Changing to Organize: A National Assessment of Union Organizing Strategies." In *Rebuilding Labor: Organizing and Organizers in the New Union Movement*, edited by R. Milkman and K. Voss, 17–60. Ithaca, NY: Cornell University Press/ILR Press. http://digitalcommons.ilr.cornell.edu/articles/54.

Buck-Morss, Susan. 1995. "Envisioning Capital: Political Economy on Display." *Critical Inquiry* 21 (2): 434. doi:10.1086/448759.

Burnson, Patrick. 2009a. "Florida Shippers Poised to Take Advantage of Regional Marketing Alliance." *Logistics Management*, May 26. www.logisticsmgmt.com.

———. 2009b. "Global Supply Chain Management: Wal-Mart Tells Retailers to Embrace 'Change.'" *Logistics Management*, January 13. www.logisticsmgmt.com.

Butler, Judith, and Athena Athanasiou. 2013. *Dispossession: The Performative in the Political*. Digital ed. Malden, MA: Polity.

Byrne, David. 2015. "Deindustrialisation and Dispossession: An Examination of Social Division in the Industrial City." *Sociology* 39 (1): 95+.

Calavita, Kitty. 1996. "The New Politics of Immigration: 'Balanced-Budget Conservatism' and the Symbolism of Proposition 187." *Social Problems* 43 (3): 284–305.

Camarillo, Albert M. 2007. "Cities of Color: The New Racial Frontier in California's Minority-Majority Cities." *Pacific Historical Review* 76 (1): 1–28.

Canclini, Nestor Garcia. 2001. *Consumers and Citizens: Globalization and Multicultural Conflicts.* Minneapolis: University of Minnesota Press.

Castells, Manuel. 1996. *The Rise of the Network Society.* 2nd ed. Chichester, West Sussex; Malden, MA: Wiley-Blackwell.

Chakravartty, Paula, and Denise Ferreira Da Silva. 2012. "Accumulation, Dispossession, and Debt: The Racial Logic of Global Capitalism—An Introduction." *American Quarterly* 64 (3): 361–85.

Cheng, Wendy. 2013. *The Changs Next Door to the Díazes: Remapping Race in Suburban California.* Minneapolis: University of Minnesota Press.

Chiang, Sharline. 1996. "Pupils Protest, Claiming Race Bias at School." *Press-Enterprise*, May 10, sec. Local.

Chicago Sun-Times. 1988. "Extremists Heckle Calif. King March." January 18, "News," 4.

Christmas, Faith. 1980. "Blacks Protest Klan Terrorism." *Los Angeles Sentinel*, July 31, A1.

Cleaver, James H. 1980a. "KKK Blamed in Murder Try: Reputed Klansman Shoots Fontana Man." *Los Angeles Sentinel*, July 10, A1.

———. 1980b. "Fontana Anti-Klan Rally Draws Hundreds: Cops Contain Klansmen in Clash." *Los Angeles Sentinel*, August 14, sec. A.

Cline, Elizabeth L. 2013. *Overdressed: The Shockingly High Cost of Cheap Fashion.* New York: Penguin Group.

CNN. 2013. "Showdown: California Town Turns Away Buses of Detained Immigrants." July 3., www.cnn.com/2014/07/02/us/california-immigrant-transfers/index.html.

Coe, Neil M., Peter Dicken, Martin Hess, and Henry Wai-Cheung Yeung. 2010. "Making Connections: Global Production Networks and World City Networks." *Global Networks* 10 (1): 138–49. doi:10.1111/j.1471-0374.2010.00278.x.

Coe, Neil M., Martin Hess, Henry Wai-chung Yeung, Peter Dicken, and Jeffrey Henderson. 2004. "'Globalizing' Regional Development: A Global Production Networks Perspective." *Transactions Insitute of British Geographers* 29: 468–84.

Cohen, Lizabeth. 2004. *A Consumers' Republic: The Politics of Mass Consumption in Postwar America.* New York: Vintage Books.

Collins, Jane L. 2003. *Threads: Gender, Labor, and Power in the Global Apparel Industry.* Vol. 15. Chicago: University of Chicago Press.

Collins, Patricia Hill. 1990. *Black Feminist Thought: Knowledge, Consciousness, and the Politics of Empowerment.* Boston: Unwin Hyman.

Conca, Ken, Thomas Princen, and Michael F. Maniates. 2001. "Confronting Consumption." *Global Environmental Politics* (August): 1–10.

Cowen, Deborah. 2014. *The Deadly Life of Logistics: Mapping Violence in Global Trade.* Minneapolis: University of Minnesota Press.

Cowie, Jefferson R. 2001. *Capital Moves: RCA's 70-Year Quest for Cheap Labor.* New York: New Press.

Cox, Kevin R., ed. 1997. *Spaces of Globalization: Reasserting the Power of the Local*. Perspectives on Economic Change. New York and London: Guilford Press.

Cox, Kevin R. 2004. "Globalization and The Politics of Local and Regional Development: The Question of Convergence." *Transactions Institute of British Geographers* 29: 179–94.

Creating Tomorrow's Surface Transportation Systems. 1994. *Hearing before the Subcommittee on Technology, Environment, and Aviation of the Committee on Science, Space, and Technology, House of Representatives*. 103rd Cong., 2nd sess. (May 12, 1994). (Statement of Chia Shih, Associate Administrator for Research, Technology, and Analysis, U.S. Department of Transportation).

Crenshaw, Kimberle. 1991. "Mapping the Margins: Intersectionality, Identity Politics, and Violence against Women of Color." *Stanford Law Review* 43 (6): 1241. doi:10.2307/1229039.

Crenshaw, Kimberle Williams. 1988. "Race, Reform, and Retrenchment: Transformation and Legitimation in Antidiscrimination Law." *Harvard Law Review* 101 (7): 1331. doi:10.2307/1341398.

Davis, Mike. (1990) 1992. *City of Quartz: Excavating the Future in Los Angeles*. London: Verso.

———. 2000. "Sunshine and the Open Shop: Ford and Darwin in 1920s Los Angeles." *Antipode* 29 (4): 356–82.

Dicken, Peter. 1987. "Japanese Penetration of the European Automobile Industry: The Arrival of Nissan in the United Kingdom." *Society* 78 (2): 94–107.

———. 2007. *Global Shift: Mapping the Changing Contours of the World Economy*. New York: Guilford Press.

Didion, Joan. (1968) 2008. *Slouching Towards Bethlehem*. New York: Farrar, Straus and Giroux.

Dot, Maine, Anne Kappel, World Shipping Council, Sean O'Dell, and Transport Canada. 2008. *Testimony before American Association of State Highway and Transportation Officials (AASHTO), National Freight Transportation Agenda Hearing*. February 27.

Dulaney, Josh. 2010. "Blacks Reflect on Legacy of Fontana." *San Bernardino Sun*, February 15, sec. News.

Durian, Hal. 2009. "Hal Durian's Riverside Recollections." *Press-Enterprise*, April 25. www.pe.com.

Eisinger, Peter K. 1988. *The Rise of the Entrepreneurial State: State and Local Economic Development Policy in the United States*. La Follette Public Policy Series. Madison: University of Wisconsin Press.

Erie, Steven P. 2004. *Globalizing L.A.: Trade, Infrastructure, and Regional Development*. Stanford, CA: Stanford University Press.

Escobar, Arturo. 2008. *Territories of Difference: Place, Movements, Life, Redes*. Durham, NC: Duke University Press.

Esquivel, Paloma. 2013. "In Huntington Beach, a New Wave of Resentment Revives '909er' Stereotype." *Los Angeles Times*, September 21, www.latimes.com.

Ethington, P.J. 2000. "Segregated Diversity: Race-Ethnicity, Space, and Political Fragmentation in Los Angeles County, 1940–1994." In *Final Report to the John Randolph Haynes and Dora Haynes Foundation*. www.usc.edu/dept/LAS /history/historylab/Haynes_FR/index.html.

Ethington, Philip J., William H. Frey, and Dowell Myers. 2001. "The Racial Resegregation of Los Angeles County, 1940–2000." Race Contours 2000 Study. Los Angeles: University of Southern California and University of Michigan.

Evans, Peter. 2000. "Fighting Marginalization with Transnational Networks: Counter-Hegemonic Globalization." *Contemporary Sociology* 29 (1): 230–41.

Fantasia, Rick, and Kim Voss. 2004. *Hard Work: Remaking the American Labor Movement*. Berkeley: University of California Press.

Field Poll. 2009. "The Changing California Electorate." California Opinion Index. Field Research Corporation. www.field.com.

Fields, Gary. 2004. *Territories of Profit: Communications, Capitalist Development, and the Innovative Enterprises of G. F. Swift and Dell Computer*. Stanford, CA: Stanford University Press.

Findlay, John. 1992. *Magic Lands: Western Cityscapes and American Culture after 1940*. Berkeley: University of California Press.

Florida, Richard L. 2012. *The Rise of the Creative Class, Revisited*. New York: Basic Books.

Foley, Duncan K. 1986. *Understanding Capital: Marx's Economic Theory*. Cambridge, MA: Harvard University Press.

Fontana Herald News. 2008. "Cancer Risk Is Higher in Local Area Because of Air Pollution." January 9. www.fontanaheraldnews.com/news/cancer-risk-is-higher -in-local-area-because-of-air/article_29e7dd5f-9662-5238-a0c5-7768cf7e7370.html.

Fontana Steel, Committee on Banking and Currency. 1948. Washington, DC.

Foster, Mark S. 1989. *Henry J. Kaiser: Builder in the Modern American West*. Austin: University of Texas Press.

Fregoso, Rosa Linda. 2003. *MeXicana Encounters: The Making of Social Identities on the Borderlands*. American Crossroads, no. 12. Berkeley; Los Angeles: University of California Press.

Frey, William H. 2010. "Race and Ethnicity." In *State of Metropolitan America: On the Front Lines of Demographic Transformation*, 50–63. Washington, DC: The Brookings Institution Metropolitan Policy Program.

Friedman, Sheldon. 1997. "We'll Take the High Road: Unions and Economic Development." *WorkingUSA* 1 (4): 58–67. doi:10.1111/j.1743-4580.1997.tb00051.x.

Garcia, Maria Cristina. 2006. *Seeking Refuge: Central American Migration to Mexico, the United States, and Canada*. Berkeley: University of California Press.

Garcia, Matt. 1996. "Chicana/O and Latina/O Workers in a Changing Discipline." *Humbolt Journal of Social Relations* 22 (1): 83–95.

———. 2001. *A World of Its Own: Race, Labor, and Citrus in the Making of Greater Los Angeles, 1900–1970*. Studies in Rural Culture. Chapel Hill; London: University of North Carolina Press.

García Bedolla, Lisa. 2005. *Fluid Borders: Latino Power, Identity, and Politics in Los Angeles*. Berkeley: University of California Press.

Gilmore, Ruth Wilson. 2002. "Fatal Couplings of Power and Difference: Notes on Racism and Geography." *Professional Geographer* 54 (1): 15–24.

———. 2007. *Golden Gulag: Prisons, Surplus, Crisis, and Opposition in Globalizing California*. Berkeley: University of California Press. www.loc.gov/catdir /enhancements/fy0642/2006011674-d.html.

———. 2008. "Forgotten Places and the Seeds of Grassroots Planning." In *Engaging Contradictions: Theory, Politics, and Methods of Activist Scholarship*, edited by Charles R. Hale, 31–61. The Global, Area, and International Archive. Berkeley: University of California Press.

Gilroy, Paul. 2005. *Postcolonial Melancholia*. New York: Columbia University Press.

Giri, Ananta. 1992. "Understanding Contemporary Social Movements." *Dialectical Anthropology* 17 (1): 35–49. doi:10.1007/BF00244454.

Gonzales, Alfonso. 2014. *Reform Without Justice: Latino Migrant Politics and the Homeland Security State*. New York: Oxford University Press.

Gonzalez, Gilbert G. 1994. *Labor and Community: Mexican Citrus Worker Villages in a Southern California County, 1900–1950*. Urbana: University of Illinois Press.

Gorman, Anna, and Rich Connell. 2009. "Latinos Who Flocked to the Once-Burgeoning Inland Empire Are Hard-Hit in Economic Downturn." *Los Angeles Times*, August 2. http://articles.latimes.com/2009/aug/02/local/me-immig2.

Gorman, Tom. 1993. "Union Dismayed Workers Who Helped Construct and Operate Kaiser Steel Plant Say They, and Not Foreign Nationals, Should Have Jobs Taking It Apart for Reassembly in China." *Los Angeles Times*, February 14, sec. A.

Graham, Stephen. 2002. "FlowCity: Networked Mobilities and the Contemporary Metropolis." *Journal of Urban Technology* 9 (1): 1–20.

Gramsci, Antonio. 2000. *The Gramsci Reader: Selected Writings, 1916–1935*. Edited by David Forgacs. New York: New York University Press.

Granelli, James S. 2004. "A PUC Consumer Champ Draws Ire." *Los Angeles Times*, September 20, 2004, home ed., sec. C.

Green, William. 1988. "King March Celebrates 'Light-Years' of Progress." *Fontana Herald News*, January. www.fontanaheraldnews.com.

Grossberg, Lawrence. 1986. "On Postmodernism and Articulation: An Interview with Stuart Hall." *Journal of Communication Inquiry* 10 (2): 45–60.

Grubbs, Michele. 2004. "Issues Facing Los Angeles/Long Beach Maritime Industry." PowerPoint presentation to Pacific Merchant Shipping Association, December.

Gupta, Akhil, and James Ferguson. 1992. "Beyond Culture: Space, Identity and the Politics of Difference." *Cultural Anthropology* 7 (1): 6–23.

Gutierrez, David G. 1993. "Significant for Whom? Mexican Americans and the History of the American West." *Western Historical Quarterly* 24 (4): 519–39.

Hall, Peter V. 2007. "Seaports, Urban Sustainability, and Paradigm Shift." *Journal of Urban Technology* 14 (2): 87–101. doi:10.1080/10630730701531757.

Hall, Stuart. 1980. "Race, Articulation, and Societies Structured in Dominance." In *Sociological Theories: Race and Colonialism*, 16–60. Paris: UNESCO.

———. 1986. "Gramsci's Relevance for the Race and Ethnicity Study." *Journal of Communication Inquiry* 10 (5): 5–27.

———. 1996. "The Problem of Ideology: Marxism Without Guarantees." In *Stuart Hall: Critical Dialogues in Cultural Studies*, edited by David Morley and Kuan-Hsing Chen, 28–44. New York; London: Routledge.

———. 1997. "The Local and the Global—Globalization and Ethnicity." In *Culture, Globalization, and the World-System: Contemporary Conditions for the Representation of Identity*, edited by Anthony D. King, 19–41. Minneapolis: University of Minnesota Press.

Hancock, Ange-Marie. 2004. *The Politics of Disgust: The Public Identity of the Welfare Queen*. New York: New York University Press.

Hansen, Matt, and Mark Boster. 2016. "Protesters in Murrieta Block Detainees' Buses in Tense Standoff." *Los Angeles Times*, July 1. www.latimes.com/local/lanow/la-me-ln-immigrants-murrieta-20140701-story.html.

Hanson, Kristopher. 2008. "Middle Harbor Overhaul Plan Progresses." *Press-Telegram*, August 17. www.presstelegram.com/?s=Middle+Harbor+Overhaul+Plan+Progresses&orderby=date&order=desc.

Harris, Cheryl I. 1993. "Whiteness as Property." *Harvard Law Review* 106 (8): 1707–91.

Harrison, J. 2007. "From Competitive Regions to Competitive City-Regions: A New Orthodoxy, but Some Old Mistakes." *Journal of Economic Geography* 7 (3): 311–32. doi:10.1093/jeg/lbm005.

Harvey, David. 1978. "The Marxian Theory of the State." *Antipode* 8 (2): 80–89.

———. 1981. "The Spatial Fix: Hegel, Von Thunen and Marx." *Antipode* 13 (12): 1–12.

———. 1987. "Flexible Accumulation through Urbanization: Reflections on 'Post-Modernism' in the American City." *Antipode* 19 (3): 260–86.

———. 1990. *The Condition of Postmodernity*. Cambridge, MA; Oxford: Blackwell.

———. 2003. "The Right to the City." *International Journal of Urban and Regional Research* 27 (4): 939–41.

———. 2005. *A Brief History of Neoliberalism*. Oxford: Oxford University Press. www.loc.gov/catdir/toc/ecip0516/2005019349.html.

HDR|HLB Decision Economics Inc. 2006. "CSX Real Property Inc.: Development of an Integrated Logistics Center in Winter Haven, Florida." Silver Spring, MD: HDR|HLB Decision Economics Inc.

Herman, Bruce. 2001. "How High-Road Partnerships Work." *Social Policy* 31 (3): 11.

Herod, Andrew. 1994. "Further Reflections on Organized Labor and Deindustrialization in the United States." *Antipode* 26 (1): 77–95. doi:10.1111/j.1467-8330.1994.tb00232.x.

———. 1998. "Discourse on the Docks: Containerization and Inter-Union Work Disputes in US Ports, 1955–85." *Transactions of the Institute of British Geographers*, 23 (2): 177–91.

———. 2000. "Workers and Workplaces in a Neoliberal Global Economy." *Environment and Planning A* 32: 1781–90.

Herod, Andrew, and Melissa W. Wright. 2001. "Theorizing Space and Time." *Environment and Planning A* 33 (12): 2089–93. doi:10.1068/a34183.

Heschmeyer, Mark. 2007. "Office, Industrial Markets Shake Off First Quarter Doldrums." CoStar Group, July 11. www.costar.com.

Hesse, Markus. 2004. "Land for Logistics. Locational Dynamics, Real Estate Markets and Political Regulation of Regional Distribution Complexes." *Tijdschrift Voor Economische En Sociale Geografie* 95 (2): 162–73.

Hesse, Markus, and Jean-Paul Rodrigue. 2006. "Global Production Networks and the Role of Logistics and Transportation." *Growth and Change* 37 (4): 499–509.

Hirsh, Lou. 2008. "Home Depot to Open Distribution Center in Redlands." *Press-Enterprise*, October 10. www.pe.com.

Hise, Greg. (1997) 1999. *Magnetic Los Angeles: Planning the Twentieth Century Metropolis*. Baltimore, MD; London: Johns Hopkins University Press.

Holifield, Chet. 1947. *Discriminatory Action of Interstate Commerce Commission Against Pacific Coast Steel Plant*. Washington, DC: Congressional Record Service.

Holt, Douglas B. 1998. "Does Cultural Capital Structure American Consumption?" *Journal of Consumer Research* 25 (1): 1–25.

———. 2007. "Consumption?" *Structure* 25 (1): 1–25.

Horsman, Reginald. 1981. *Race and Manifest Destiny: The Origins of American Racial Anglo-Saxonism*. Cambridge, MA: Harvard University Press.

Hricko, Andrea. 2008. "Global Trade Comes Home: Community Impacts of Goods Movement." *Environmental Health Perspectives* 116 (2): A78–A81.

Hudson, Ray. 2004. "Conceptualizing Economies and Their Geographies: Spaces, Flows and Circuits." *Progress in Human Geography* 28 (4): 447–71. doi:10.1191/0309132504ph497oa.

Huntington, Samuel P. 2004. *Who Are We? The Challenges to America's National Identity*. New York: Simon & Schuster. www.loc.gov/catdir/bios/simon052 /2004042902.html.

Husing, John. 2004. "Logistics & Distribution: An Answer to Regional Upward Social Mobility." Report for the Southern California Association of Governments.

———. 2006a. "Inland Empire 2006: Powerful Economic Growth Continues." *Inland Empire Quarterly Economic Report* (July). http://www.johnhusing.com /QER_articles.htm.

———. 2006b. "Logistics: A 1,000,000 Job Economic Development Strategy for Southern California." PowerPoint presentation, Los Angeles.

———. 2008. "International Trade and the Inland Empire." *Inland Empire Quarterly Economic Report* 20 (4): 1–3.

Industrial Development Organization, ed. 2013. *Sustaining Employment Growth: The Role of Manufacturing and Structural Change*. Industrial Development Report 2013. Vienna: UNIDO.

"Inland Empire Top Leasing Firms." 2007. CoStar Group. http://www.costar.com
/PowerBrokers/2007/Inland_Empire.htm.

Jaffe, Rivke. 2012. "Talkin' 'Bout the Ghetto: Popular Culture and Urban Imaginaries of Immobility." *International Journal of Urban and Regional Research* 36 (4):
674–88. doi:10.1111/j.1468-2427.2012.01121.x.

Jamieson, Dave. 2011. "The New Blue Collar: Temporary Work, Lasting Poverty and
the American Warehouse." *Huffington Post*, December 21.www.huffingtonpost
.com/2011/12/20/new-blue-collar-temp-warehouses_n_1158490.html.

———. 2012. "Walmart Outsourcing Depresses Wages in U.S. Warehouses:
Report." *Huffington Post*, June 6. www.huffingtonpost.com/2012/06/06/walmart
-outsourcing-depresses-wages_n_1573885.html.

Johnson, Hans P., Deborah Reed, and Joseph M. Hayes. 2008. "The Inland Empire
in 2015." Public Policy Institute of California.

Johnson, Jannise. 2007. "Klan's Presence in I. E. Dates to the 1920s." *Inland
Valley Daily Bulletin*, April 1. www-lexisnexis-com.libproxy.usc.edu/lnacui2api
/delivery/Print...827%3A412656394%2Fformatted_doc&fromCartFullDoc=false
&fileSize=5000.

Jonas, Andrew E.G., and Kevin Ward. 2007. "Introduction to a Debate on City-
Regions: New Geographies of Governance, Democracy and Social Reproduction." *International Journal of Urban and Regional Research* 31 (1): 169–78.

Judd, Dennis R. 2006. "Tracing the Commodity Chain of Global Tourism." *Tourism Geographies* 8 (4): 323–36.

Kallerberg, Arne L., Barbara F. Reskin, and Ken Hudson. 2000. "Bad Jobs in
America: Standard and Nonstandard Employment Relations and Job Quality in
the United States." *American Sociological Review* 65 (2): 256–78.

Kaneko, Jun, and Wataru Nojiri. 2008. "The Logistics of Just-in-Time between Parts
Suppliers and Car Assemblers in Japan." *Journal of Transport Geography* 16 (3):
155–73. doi:10.1016/j.jtrangeo.2007.06.001.

Keith, Michael, and Steve Pile. 1993. *Place and the Politics of Identity*. London; New
York: Routledge.

Kelley, Robin D.G. 2003. "People in ME." *ColorLines*, July 5. www.colorlines
.com.

King, Anthony D. 1997. *Culture, Globalization and the World-System: Contemporary Conditions for the Representation of Identity*. Minneapolis: University of
Minnesota Press.

Klampe, Michelle. 2011. "Districts, Schools Fail to Meet Federal Goals." *Press-
Enterprise*. September 1, A1.

Klein, Kerwin Lee. 1997. *Frontiers of Historical Imagination: Narrating the European Conquest of Native America, 1890–1990*. Berkeley: University of California
Press.

Klein, Naomi. 2008. *The Shock Doctrine: The Rise of Disaster Capitalism*. New York:
Picador.

Kohout, Michal. 2009. "Immigration Politics in California's Inland Empire." *Year-
book of the Association of Pacific Coast Geographers* 71: 120–43.

Kotkin, Joel, and William H. Frey. 2007. "The Third California: The Golden State's New Frontier." Research brief, The Brookings Institution.

Kropp, Phoebe S. 2008. *California Vieja: Culture and Memory in a Modern American Place*. Berkeley: University of California Press.

Kruse, Kevin Michael. 2007. *White Flight: Atlanta and the Making of Modern Conservatism*. Princeton, NJ:; Woodstock: Princeton University Press.

Kulwiec, Ray. 2004. "Crossdocking as a Supply Chain Strategy." *Target* 20 (3): 28–35.

Kun, Josh, and Laura Pulido, eds. 2014. *Black and Brown in Los Angeles: Beyond Conflict and Coalition*. Berkeley and Los Angeles: University of California Press.

Kurashige, Scott. 2008. *The Shifting Grounds of Race: Black and Japanese Americans in the Making of Multiethnic Los Angeles*. Princeton, NJ: Princeton University Press.

Kyser, Jack. n.d. "Goods Movement in Southern California: How Can We Solve Problems and Generate New State Sales and Income Tax Revenues?" Unpublished manuscript.

Larrubia, Evelyn. 2008. "Project Brings Unusual Merger of Union Bosses and Environmentalists." *Los Angeles Times*, November, 27. www.latimes.com/news/local/la-me-green27-2008nov27,0,3444566.story.

Leachman, Rob. 2007. "Progress Report: Port and Modal Elasticity Study—Phase II." January 17. Unpublished manuscript.

Lee, Dan. 2005. "Campaign Funds Revealed." *Press-Enterprise*, April 10, B01.

———. 2008a. "Video Provides Look at Proposed Skechers Distribution Center in Moreno Valley." *Press-Enterprise*, December 12, C01.

———. 2008b. "Growth Plans Threaten Rancho Belago Image." *Press-Enterprise*, January 12, B01.

———. 2008c. "Official Says Name Is Divisive." January 31, B01.

———. 2008d. "More Distribution Centers Proposed for Moreno Valley's Eastern Side." *Press-Enterprise*, August 21, C01.

———. 2008e. "Debate Flares over Time Allotted for Public to Review Documents Tied to Moreno Valley Distribution Center Proposal." *Press-Enterprise*, December 5, C01.

———. 2009. "Activist Raising Latinos' Influence in Moreno Valley." *Press-Enterprise*, July 11, C01.

Lefebvre, Henri. 1991. *The Production of Space*. Translated by Donald Nicholson-Smith. Oxford: Blackwell Publishing Limited.

Leitner, Helga, and Byron Miller. 2007. "Scale and the Limitations of Ontological Debate: A Commentary on Marston, Jones and Woodward." *Transactions of the Institute of British Geographers*, no. 419: 116–25.

Leitner, Helga, Eric Sheppard, and Kristin M. Sziarto. 2008. "The Spatialities of Contentious Politics." *Transactions of the Institute of British Geographers* 33 (2): 157–72.

Lerner, Stephen. 2007. "Global Unions: A Solution to Labor's Worldwide Decline." *New Labor Forum* 16 (1): 22–37.

Levinson, Marc. 2008. *The Box: How the Shipping Container Made the World Smaller and the World Economy Bigger*. Princeton, NJ; Woodstock: Princeton University Press.

Li, Rong-gong Lin. 2007. "County Offers Inland Port Plan." *Los Angeles Times*, July 12. http://articles.latimes.com/2007/jul/12/local/me-inlandport12.

Lichtenstein, Nelson. 2009. *The Retail Revolution: How Wal-Mart Created a Brave New World of Business*. New York: Metropolitan Books.

Limerick, Patricia Nelson. 1987. *The Legacy of Conquest: The Unbroken Past of the American West*. W. W. Norton. www.amazon.com/gp/product/0393304973%3ft ag=webservices-20%26link_code=xm2%26camp=2025%26dev-t=D35ON75 JZNYXMM.

Lipietz, Alain. 1997. "The Post-Fordist World: Labour Relations, International Hierarchy and Global Ecology." *Review of International Political Economy* 4 (1): 1–41.

Lloyd's List. 2009. "LA and Long Beach Turn to Trains to Save Container Volumes." *Lloyd's List*, February 23.

Logan, John R., and Harvey L. Molotch. 1987. *Urban Fortunes: The Political Economy of Place*. Berkeley and Los Angeles: University of California Press.

Lopez, H., and L. Serven. 2009. *Too Poor to Grow*. Policy Research Working Papers. World Bank. https://books.google.com/books?id=OP-ikgEACAAJ.

Los Angeles Economic Development Corporation. 2003. "National Economic Significance of Rail Capacity and Homeland Security on the Alameda Corridor East." Final Study: OnTrac Trade Impact Study. Los Angeles: Orange North-American Trade Rail Access Corridor (OnTrac) Joint Powers Authority.

Los Angeles Tribune. 1946. "FBI Considers Facts in Fontana Tragedy." January 19, 1.

Lovett, Ian. 2011. "Patch of California Cracks Down on Illegal Immigration." *New York Times*, January 4, U.S. sec.

Lowe, Michelle, and Neil Wrigley. 1996. "Towards the New Retail Geography." In *Retailing, Consumption and Capital: Towards the New Retail Geography*, edited by Neil Wrigley and Michelle Lowe, 3–30. Essex, UK: Longman Group Limited.

Lucas, Laurie. 2010. "Skechers Project Builder Seeks Concessions Regarding Dirt Trails." *Press-Enterprise*, May 13, A6.

Lynn, Barry C. 2005. *End of the Line: The Rise and Coming Fall of the Global Corporation*. New York: Currency/Doubleday.

Macduff, Cassie. 2007. "Pollution Problems." *Press-Enterprise*, July 10, B01.

Maier, C. S. 1970. "Between Taylorism and Technocracy: European Ideologies and the Vision of Industrial Productivity in the 1920s." *Journal of Contemporary History* 5 (2): 27–61. doi:10.1177/002200947000500202.

Marroquin, Art. 2009. "U.S. and Canadian Ports Gear up for Trade War." *Daily Breeze*, October 23, 1A. infoweb.newsbank.com/resources/doc/nb/news/12BA94 AB0D15EA20?p=AWNB.

Martin, John Levi. 1999. "The Myth of the Consumption-Oriented Economy and the Rise of the Desiring Subject." *Theory and Society* 28 (3): 425–53.

Marx, Karl. (1867) 1990. *Capital: A Critique of Political Economy*. London: Penguin Classics.

Massey, Doreen. 1995. *Spatial Divisions of Labor: Social Structures and the Geography of Production*. New York: Routledge.

Massey, Douglas S., and Nancy A. Denton. 2003. *American Apartheid: Segregation and the Making of the Underclass*. Cambridge, MA: Harvard University Press.

Matsuoka, Martha. 2008. "Clean and Safe Ports: Building a Movement Region by Region." *Race, Poverty, & the Environment* (Fall): 26–28.

Matsuoka, Martha, Andrea Hricko, Robert Gottlieb, and Juan D. De Lara. 2011. "Global Trade Impacts: Addressing the Health, Social and Environmental Consequences of Moving International Freight through Our Communities." Working paper, Occidental College and University of Southern California, Los Angeles.

McCartin, Joseph Anthony. 2011. *Collision Course: Ronald Reagan, the Air Traffic Controllers, and the Strike That Changed America*. New York: Oxford University Press.

McDowell, L. 2008. "Thinking Through Work: Complex Inequalities, Constructions of Difference and Trans-National Migrants." *Progress in Human Geography* 32 (4): 491–507. doi:10.1177/0309132507088116.

McGowan, Michael. 2005. "The Impact of Shifting Container Cargo Flows on Regional Demand for U.S. Warehouse Space." *Journal of Real Estate Portfolio Management* 11 (2): 167–85.

McKinnon, Julissa. 2010. "Immigrant Advocates Say Crackdown on Unlicensed Drivers Unfair." *Press-Enterprise*, May 15, A10.

McKinnon, Julissa, and Sarah Burge. 2008. "Good Luck Is Just Losing Car." *Press-Enterprise*, July 3, sec. A.

McKittrick, Katherine, and Clyde Adrian Woods, eds. 2007. *Black Geographies and the Politics of Place*. Toronto: Cambridge, MA: Between the Lines; South End Press.

Menjivar, Cecilia, and Nestor Rodriguez, eds. 2005. *When States Kill Latin America, the U.S., and Technologies of Terror*. Austin: University of Texas Press.

Merrifield, Andy. 2011. "The Right to the City and Beyond." *City* 15 (3–4): 473–81. doi:10.1080/13604813.2011.595116.

Meyer, David S. 2003. "How Social Movements Matter." *Contexts* 2 (4): 30.

Mitchell, Don. 1996. *The Lie of the Land: Migrant Workers and the California Landscape*. Minneapolis: University of Minnesota Press.

———. 2003. *The Right to the City: Social Justice and the Fight for Public Space*. New York: Guilford Press.

Mitchell, Katharyne. 1997. "Transnational Discourse: Bringing Geography Back In." *Antipode* 29 (2): 101–14.

Molina, Natalia. 2013. *How Race Is Made in America: Immigration, Citizenship, and the Historical Power of Racial Scripts*. Berkeley: University of California Press.

Mongelluzzo, Bill. 2009a. "LA, Long Beach Push Incentive Programs." *Journal of Commerce Online*, February 19. LexisNexis Academic.

———. 2009b. "LA-LB Programs Drive Shippers to Other Ports." *Journal of Commerce Online*, April 22. LexisNexis Academic.

Moreton, Bethany. 2009. *To Serve God and Wal-Mart: The Making of Christian Free Enterprise*. Cambridge, MA: Harvard University Press.

Mydans, Seth. 1994. "Steel Mill Is Shadow of What It Once Was." *New York Times*, September 6, late ed., sec. A.

Napolitano, Maida. 2008. "Warehousing and Distribution Center Management: The Cross-Dock Revolution, Are You in or Out?" *Logistics Management* (April 1).

NBC News. 2014. "Murrieta Protesters and Supporters Clash, with No Buses in Sight." July 4. www.nbcnews.com/storyline/immigration-border-crisis/murrieta-protesters-supporters-clash-no-buses-sight-n148481.

Nicolaides, Becky M. 2002. *My Blue Heaven: Life and Politics in the Working-Class Suburbs of Los Angeles, 1920–1965*. Chicago: University of Chicago Press.

Nicosia, Francesco M., and Robert N. Mayer. 2007. "Toward a Sociology of Consumption." *Sociology: The Journal of the British Sociological Association* 3 (2): 65–75.

Nolan, Peter. 2002. "China and the Global Business Revolution." *Cambridge Journal of Economics* 26: 119–37.

Notteboom, Theo E., and Jean-Paul Rodrigue. 2005. "Port Regionalization: Towards a New Phase in Port Development." *Maritime Policy & Management* 32 (3): 297–313.

Olson, David. 2008. "Minutemen Press on against Mexican ID Cards, Mobile Consulates." *Press-Enterprise*, May 8, B01.

———. 2012. "Joint Work with Police Stirs Fresh Debates." *Press-Enterprise*, December 14, B01.

Omi, Michael, and Howard Winant. 1994. *Racial Formation in the United States: From the 1960s to the 1990s*. New York: Routledge.

Ostry, J. D., and A. Berg. 2011. "Inequality and Unsustainable Growth: Two Sides of the Same Coin?" IMF Staff Discussion Notes Series. International Monetary Fund. https://books.google.com/books?id=T3Z4ngEACAAJ.

Panama Canal Authority. 2011. "Panama Canal and the Port of New Orleans Renew Strategic Alliance." http://portno.com/CMS/Resources/press%20releases/prsrel080811.pdf.

Pare, Mike. 2011. "3,000 Temps Among 4,500 Amazon Is Hiring." *Times Free Press*, October 19. www.timesfreepress.com/news/business/aroundregion/story/2011/oct/19/3000-temps-among-4500-amazon-is-hiring/61775/.

Pastor, Manuel. 2013. "Maywood, Not Mayberry: Latinos and Suburbia in Los Angeles County." In *Social Justice in Diverse Suburbs: History, Politics, and Prospects*, edited by Christopher Niedt, 129–54. Philadelphia: Temple University Press.

Pastor, Manuel, Chris Benner, and Martha Matsuoka. 2009. *This Could Be the Start of Something Big: How Social Movements for Regional Equity Are Reshaping Metropolitan America*. Ithaca, NY: Cornell University Press.

Pastor, Manuel, Peter Dreier, Eugene Grigsby, and Marta Lopez-Garza. 2000. *Regions That Work: How Cities and Suburbs Can Grow Together*. Minneapolis: University of Minnesota Press.

Patel, Raj. 2009. *The Value of Nothing: How to Reshape Market Society and Redefine Democracy*. New York: Picador.

Pelisek, Christine. 2005. "Smog Sick." *LA Weekly*, September 23. www.laweekly
.com/ink/printme.php?eid=68133.

Pesick, Jason. 2008. "Sen. Boxer Calls for Federal Action at Inland Empire Event."
Inland Valley Daily Bulletin. http://www.dailybulletin.com/ci_11124798.

Peterson, Anne M. 1997. "Fontana Confronts KKK Stigma." *Press-Enterprise*,
April 13, B01.

The Planning Center. 2003. "The Preserve Specific Plan." City of Chino, CA.

Plant, Jeremy F. 2002. "Railroad Policy and Intermodalism: Policy Choices After
Deregulation." *Review of Policy Research* 19 (2): 13–32.

Polanyi, Karl. 2001. *The Great Transformation: The Political and Economic Origins
of Our Time*. Boston: Beacon Press.

Port of Los Angeles and Port of Long Beach. 2006. "San Pedro Bay Ports Clean Air
Action Plan." Los Angeles; Long Beach: Port of Los Angeles and the Port of Long
Beach. www.cleanairactionplan.org.

Price, Edward T., and Robert N. Young. 1959. "The Future of California's Southland." *Annals of the Association of American Geographers* 49 (3): 101–17.

Pulido, Laura. 1996. "A Critical Review of the Methodology of Environmental
Racism Research." *Antipode* 28 (2): 142–59.

Pullen, William Augustus. 1973. "The Ramona Pageant: A Historical and Analytical Study." PhD diss., University of Southern California.

Raine, George. 2008. "Ship Cargo Volume Slumping at West Coast Ports." *San
Francisco Chronicle*, November 30. www.sfgate.com/business/article/Ship-cargo
-volume-slumping-at-West-Coast-ports-3183010.php.

Ramakrishnan, Karthick. 2007. "Survey of Political and Civic Engagement in the
Inland Empire." University of California Riverside. www.politicalscience.ucr.edu.

Ramaswamy, K. V., and Gary Gereffi. 2000. "India's Apparel Exports: The Challenge of Global Markets." *Developing Economies* 2 (June): 186–210.

Ray, Rajesh. 2010. *Supply Chain Management for Retailing*. New Delhi: Tata
McGraw-Hill Education.

Robinson, Cedric J. 1983. *Black Marxism: The Making of the Black Radical Tradition*. London; Totowa, NJ: Zed; Biblio Distribution Center.

Sahagun, Luis. 1988a. "Concern for His Safety Cited King's Son Won't Be in Fontana Parade." *Los Angeles Times*, January 6. http://articles.latimes.com/1988-01
-06/news/mn-22786_1_fontana-parade.

———. 1988b. "Marchers in Fontana Fete King, Draw Klan Taunts." *Los Angeles
Times*, January 18, sec. A.

Saldívar, José David. 1997. *Border Matters: Remapping American Cultural Studies*.
American Crossroads, no. 1. Berkeley: University of California Press.

Saldivar-Hull, Sonia. 2000. *Feminism on the Border: Chicana Gender Politics and
Literature*. Berkeley and Los Angeles: University of California Press.

Sánchez, George J. 1993. *Becoming Mexican-American: Ethnicity, Culture, and Identity in Chicano Los Angeles, 1900–1945*. New York: Oxford University Press.

Sanchez, Jesus. 2002. "Builders Turn to Upscale Projects in Inland Empire." *Los
Angeles Times*, December 26, C1.

Sanderson, Susan, and Mustafa Uzumeri. 1995. "Managing Product Families: The Case of the Sony Walkman." *Research Policy* 24: 761–82.

Sargent, Francis E. 1989. "Los Angeles–Long Beach Harbor Complex 2020 Plan Harbor Resonance Analysis: Numerical Model Investigation." Vicksburg, MI: Coastal Engineering Research Center, Department of the Army, Corps of Engineers.

Sassen, Saskia. 1992. *The Global City*. Princeton, NJ: Princeton University Press.

Saxena, Rajiv. 2007. "Cross-Docking Demystified." *Industrial Engineer*, July 24, 24.

Saxenian, AnnaLee. 1994. *Regional Advantage: Culture and Competition in Silicon Valley and Route 128*. Cambridge, MA; London: Harvard University Press.

SCAQMD. 2008. *Multiple Air Toxics Exposure Study in the South Coast Air Basin— MATES III*. South Coast Air Quality Management District.

Schmidt Camacho, Alicia R. 2008. *Migrant Imaginaries: Latino Cultural Politics in the U.S.-Mexico Borderlands*. New York: New York University Press.

Schrack, Don. 2009. "Outlook for Ocean Shipments Remains Rough." *The Packer*, February 3.

Schumpeter, Joseph A. 1962. *Capitalism, Socialism, and Democracy*. HarperPerennial.

Schwarz, Guido. 2006. "Enabling Global Trade above the Clouds: Restructuring Processes and Information Technology in the Transatlantic Air-Cargo Industry." *Environment and Planning A* 38: 1463–85.

Scott, Allen J., and Michael Storper. 2007. "Regions, Globalization, Development." *Regional Studies* 41 (supp. 1): S191–205. doi:10.1080/0034340032000108697.

Sides, Josh. 2003. *L.A. City Limits: African American Los Angeles from the Great Depression to the Present*. Berkeley: University of California Press.

Singer, Audrey, and Jill H. Wilson. 2010. "The Impact of the Great Recession on Metropolitan Immigration Trends." Metropolitan Policy Program, Brookings Institution.

Smith, Adam. (1902) 2014. *The Wealth of Nations*. New York: Collier.

Smith, Neil. 2004. *American Empire: Roosevelt's Geographer and the Prelude to Globalization*. Berkeley: University of California Press.

Smith, Neil, and Cindi Katz. 1993. "Grounding Metaphor: Towards a Spatialized Politics." In *Place and the Politics of Identity*, edited by Steve Pile and Michael Keith, 66–81. London; New York: Routledge.

Smith, Vicki. 1997. "New Forms of Work Organization." *Annual Review of Sociology* 23: 315–39.

———. 1998. "The Fractured World of the Temporary Worker: Power, Participation, and Fragmentation in the Contemporary Workplace." *Social Problems* 45 (4): 411–30.

Soja, Edward. 1989. *Postmodern Geographies: The Reassertion of Space in Critical Social Theory*. London; New York: Verso.

Sorkin, Michael, ed. 1992. *Variations on a Theme Park: The New American City and the End of Public Space*. New York: Hill and Wang.

Southern California Association of Governments. 2005a. "Goods Movement in

Southern California: The Challenge, the Opportunity, and the Solution." Southern California Association of Governments.

———. 2005b. "Southern California Regional Strategy for Goods Movement: A Plan for Action." Los Angeles. www.scag.ca.gov/goodsmove/reportsmove.htm.

———. 2007. "Southern California National Freight Gateway Cooperation Agreement." Los Angeles. www.portoflosangeles.org/Board/2007/October/100307 _item4_trans1.pdf.

State of California, Air Resources Board. 2008. "Methodology for Estimating Premature Deaths Associated with Long-Term Exposure to Fine Airborne Particulate Matter in California." www.arb.ca.gov/research/health/pm-mort /pm-mortdraft.pdf.

Storper, Michael. 1997. *The Regional World: Territorial Development in a Global Economy*. Perspectives on Economic Change. New York; London: Guilford Press.

Storper, Michael, and Richard Walker. 1989. *The Capitalist Imperative: Territory, Technology, and Industrial Growth*. Oxford; New York: Basil Blackwell.

Tavasszy, L. A., C. J. Ruijgrok, and M. J. P. M. Thissen. 2003. "Emerging Global Logistics Networks: Implications for Transport Systems and Policies." *Growth and Change* 34 (4): 456–72. doi:10.1046/j.0017-4815.2003.00230.x.

Terrazas, Aaron. 2010. "Salvadoran Immigrants in the United States." Migration Policy Institute. www.migrationpolicy.org/article/salvadoran-immigrants-united -states.

Theodore, Nik, and Jamie Peck. 2002. "The Temporary Staffing Industry: Growth Imperatives and Limits to Contingency." *Economic Geography* 78 (4): 463–93.

Tilly, Charles. 2012. "Social Movements as Historically Specific Clusters of Political Performances." *Berkeley Journal of Sociology* 38: 1–30.

Tioga Group, The. 2008. "Inland Port Feasibility Study." Southern California Association of Governments. http://tiogagroup.com/docs/Tioga_Grp_SCAGInland PortReport.pdf.

Troianovski, Anton. 2009. "Its Go-Go Business Model Blown Up, ProLogis Scales Back." *Wall Street Journal*, February 11. www.wsj.com/articles/SB12343208380 2971465.

Tucker, Richard P. 2007. *Insatiable Appetite: The United States and the Ecological Degradation of the Tropical World*. Concise rev. ed. Exploring World History. Lanham, MD: Rowman and Littlefield Publishers.

Urry, John. 2002. *The Tourist Gaze*. London: Sage Publications. www.loc.gov /catdir/enhancements/fy0658/2003267715-d.html.

———. 2003. *Global Complexity*. Cambridge, UK: Polity Press.

U.S. Department of Transportation Maritime Administration. Office of Intermodal System Development. 2008. "Public Port Finance Survey for FY 2006." https://www.marad.dot.gov/ports/.

USC Dornsife/Los Angeles Times Poll. 2013. "March 2013 Poll." USC Dornsife/*Los Angeles Times*. http://dornsife.usc.edu/usc-dornsife-los-angeles-times-march -2013-poll.

Valle, Victor M., and Rodolfo D. Torres. 2000. *Latino Metropolis*. Minneapolis: University of Minnesota Press.

Vara-Orta, Francisco. 2009. "Clean Truck Plan On Rocky Road?" *Los Angeles Business Journal*, April 20. www.labusinessjournal.com/print.asp?aid=1624253.74758 33.1770821.588713.6194621.302&aID2=136208.

Veblen, Thorstein. (1899) 1994. *The Theory of the Leisure Class*. New York: Penguin Books.

Villa, Raul Homero. 2000. *Barrio-Logos: Space and Place in Urban Chicano Literature and Culture*. History, Culture, and Society Series. Austin: University of Texas Press.

Voss, Kim, and Michelle Williams. 2012. "The Local in the Global: Rethinking Social Movements in the New Millennium." *Democratization* 19 (2): 352–77. doi:10.1080/13510347.2011.605994.

Walker, Richard A. 2004. "The Spectre of Marxism: The Return of *The Limits to Capital*." *Antipode* 36 (3): 434–43.

Wall, Stephen. 2009. "Coalition Forms to Combat Immigration Raids." *The Sun*, July 3. https://www.sbsun.com/2009/07/03/coalition-forms-to-combat-immigration-raids/.

Wall Street Journal. 1983. "Kaiser Steel Corp. Gets New Suitor; Assets May Be Divided." November 14, sec. 1, 6.

Walton, Sam. 1993. *Made in America: My Story*. Sebastopol, CA: GarmentoSpeak.

Ward, Andrew. 2009. "West Coast Ports Face Rough Seas." *The Bond Buyer*, May 1. www.bondbuyer.com/printthis.html?id=20090430SC4K7ABM.

Warren, Kenneth. 2001. *Big Steel: The First Century of the United States Steel Corporation*. Pittsburgh, PA: University of Pittsburgh Press.

White, Ronald D. 2008. "West Coast Ports Face Struggle to Maintain Relevance." *Los Angeles Times*, November 28. www.latimes.com/business/la-fi-ports28 -2008nov28,0,1371553.story?track=rss.

———. 2009. "Judge Blocks Part of Ports' Clean-Truck Program." *Los Angeles Times*, April 30. www.latimes.com/business/la-fi-trucks30-2009apr30,0,5161153 .story.

Widener, Daniel. 2010. *Black Arts West: Culture and Struggle in Postwar Los Angeles*. Durham, NC: Duke University Press.

Wilbur Smith Associates. 2008. "Multi-County Goods Movement Action Plan." Los Angeles County Metropolitan Transportation Authority (Metro), Orange County Transportation Authority (OCTA), Riverside County Transportation Commission (RCTC), San Bernardino Associated Governments (SANBAG), San Diego Association of Governments (SANDAG), Ventura County Transportation Commission (VCTC), Southern California Association of Governments (SCAG), and the California Department of Transportation (Caltrans).

Wilding, Richard, and Tiago Delgado. 2004. "RFID Demystified." *Logistics & Transport Focus* 6 (5): 32–42.

Williams, Matthew S. 2016. "Strategic Innovation in US Anti-Sweatshop Movement." *Social Movement Studies* 15 (3): 277–89. doi:10.1080/14742837.2015.1082466.

Williams, Raymond. 1968. "Pastoral and Counter-Pastoral." *Critical Quarterly* 10 (3): 277–90.

———. 1973. *The Country and the City*. New York: Oxford University Press.

———. 1977. *Marxism and Literature*. Oxford: Oxford University Press.

Wilson, William Julius. (1987) 1990. *The Truly Disadvantaged: The Inner City, the Underclass, and Public Policy*. Chicago: University of Chicago Press.

Wolch, Jennifer, Manuel Pastor Jr., and Peter Dreier, eds. 2004. *Up Against the Sprawl: Public Policy and the Making of Southern California*. Minneapolis: University of Minnesota Press.

Wolf, Carol, Chris Burritt, and Matthew Boyle. 2010. "Why Wal-Mart Wants to Take the Driver's Seat." *Business Week*, May 27. www.bloomberg.com/news /articles/2010-05-27/why-wal-mart-wants-to-take-the-drivers-seat.

Wong, Tom K. 2012. "287(g) and the Politics of Interior Immigration Control in the United States: Explaining Local Cooperation with Federal Immigration Authorities." *Journal of Ethnic and Migration Studies* 38 (5): 737–56. doi:10.1080 /1369183X.2012.667983.

Woods, Clyde. 2000. *Development Arrested: The Blues and Plantation Power in the Mississippi Delta*. London: Verso.

Wrye, Matt. 2008. "The Pie Grows Larger." *San Bernardino County Sun*, July 27. infoweb.newsbank.com/resources/doc/nb/news/12236888D0035998?p=AWNB.

Young, Paul. 2009. "Group Calls for Federal Probe of Border Patrol Raid Tactics." *Desert Sun*, July 3. www.mydesert.com/apps/pbcs.dll/article?AID=/20090703 /NEWS08/907030305&template=printart.

Zierer, Clifford M. 1934. "The Citrus Fruit Industry of the Los Angeles Basin." *Economic Geography* 10 (1): 53–73.

Zukin, Sharon. 1995. *The Cultures of Cities*. Cambridge, MA: Blackwell.

Zukin, Sharon, and Jennifer Smith Maguire. 2004. "Consumers and Consumption." *Annual Review of Sociology* 30 (1): 173–97.

INDEX

Figures, tables, and maps are indicated by page numbers followed by *fig.*, *tab.*, and *map*, respectively. Notes are indicated by page numbers followed by n.

Benzeevi, Ido, 128–131, 135, 139, 145–46
Big Steel, 117
Black and Brown people: defining, 171n25; erasure and, 75; racial violence and, 121, 125; war economy and, 14. *See also* African Americans; Latinx Americans
Black body, 77
Black Marxism (Robinson), 1
Black space, 125
Black workers: wage differences, 101, 119; war economy and, 14. *See also* African Americans
blue-collar workers, 98–100, 104
blues epistemology, 76–77
body: Black, 77; counternarratives of, 76; factory worker, 75; immigrant, 76; warehouse workers, 79–80
border patrol. *See* U.S. Border Patrol
Boudreau, Julie-Ann, 13, 180n8
Boyce, Clayton, 54
BP Alert program, 154–55
Bradshaw, Victoria, 145
Brady, Mary Pat, 142
Breitkreuz, Margie, 134
Brenner, Neil, 12, 130
Brulte, Jim, 168
Buck-Morss, Susan, 41
Burke, Yvonne, 47
Burlington Northern Santa Fe (BNSF), 58
business models: global production, 66; high velocity, 70; labor control in, 66; logistics-driven, 65–66; market-driven, 34, 36, 102; supply-chain, 50
Buster, Bob, 151
Butler, Judith, 13, 75, 82

Calderon, José, 166
California Department of Transportation (CADOT), 47
Calvert, Ken, 167–68
Camarillo, Albert, 22
cancer, 52, 56–57, 57*tab.*
Canclini, Nestor Garcia, 172n45
capitalism: colonialism and, 15; commodities and, 27; disruptions in, 18; imperialism and, 15; local specificities of space and, 16–17; logic of, 16; logistics industry and, 3, 11; production of space

and, 169n1, 176n19; race and, 2, 4; spatial fixing in, 18; state support for, 46. *See also* global capitalism
cash card payroll, 105–6
Catholic Church, 157–58
Cedillo, Gilbert, 165
Center for the Study of Hate and Extremism, 123
central labor councils (CLC), 94–95
Chakravartty, Paula, 15
Change to Win (CTW), 54, 76, 94, 160
Chicanx identity: spatial tropes in, 15; students and, 153; *testimonios*, 74
China: foreign investment in, 30–31; imports from, 31; industrialization of, 20–21; purchase of Kaiser Steel Mill, 9, 14, 18, 125, 172n52, 172n53; steel manufacturing in, 18–20
Chinese workers: discrimination against, 125; Kaiser steel mill dismantling, 9, 10*fig.*, 14, 19*fig.*
Chino, 137
citrus industry, 115
Clean Trucks Program (CTP), 53–54
Clergy and Laity United for Economic Justice (CLUE), 95, 160, 182n21
Clinton, Bill, 45
CLUE. *See* Clergy and Laity United for Economic Justice (CLUE)
Coalition for Clean and Safe Ports (CCSP), 52–54
cognitive mapping analysis, 12–13, 142
collective identity, 76–77
colonialism: racial capitalism and, 2, 15–16; racial violence in, 139–140; white settler narratives of, 139–142
commodities, 27
commodity chains: consumer choice and, 25, 29; consumption and, 1, 27; distribution in, 29–30, 32; globalization and, 28; innovations in, 66; major retail control of, 85–86; politics of organizing, 76–77, 92; protests against, 74; value of imports in, 31*fig.*; warehouses in, 67; workers in, 65, 75
Communication Workers of America, 95
Community Action and Environmental Justice, 57

Illegal Immigration Reform and
Immigrant Responsibility Act
(IIRIRA), 149
ILWU. *See* International Longshore and
Warehouse Union (ILWU)
IMC. *See* intermodal marketing companies
(IMCs)
immigrant bodies, 76
immigrant rights, 157–58
immigrants: activists for, 154–160, 165, 167;
American Dream and, 78–79, 82–84,
97; deportation of, 150, 154–56;
devalued bodies, 76; economic justice
and, 160; education outcomes, 153;
erasure and, 3; as illegitimate citizens,
148–49, 151; industrial suburbs and,
22–23; Inland Empire, 2, 21, 115; labor
control, 103–5; *matriculas* and, 166–67;
migration narratives, 148; ordinances
targeting, 167; policing of, 149–150,
154–160; protests for/against, 111–12;
undocumented, 83–84, 97, 102–5, 108,
111, 156; warehouse work and, 69, 81–84,
90–92, 102–3
Immigration and Customs Enforcement
(ICE), 149–150, 155–56
imperialism, 15, 142
imported goods: from China, 20–21, 31;
commodity chain value of, 31*fig.*;
consumption and, 31–32; decline of, 59
industrial suburbs: blue-collar, 18, 21–22;
decline of, 22; deindustrialization of, 23,
38; logistics industry and, 23; Southeast
Los Angeles, 14, 17–18; white flight in,
21, 23
information systems, 73
inland distribution networks: organizing,
91–92, 94–98; regional support for, 98;
shipper preference for, 55; spatial
politics of, 102; transportation
infrastructure for, 43; wage models,
100–101. *See also* distribution;
warehouses
Inland Empire, 6*map*; African Americans
in, 116; agricultural industry, 136–37;
anti-immigrant narratives, 147, 164–67;
Asian and Pacific Islanders (API) in,
115–16; changing demographics of, 120,

128, 147, 150, 152, 164; citrus industry,
115; civil society in, 164; conservatism
in, 164–68; conversion of agricultural
land in, 141–43; diesel emissions, 55–57;
diesel-related cancer cases, 57*tab.*;
English Language Learners (ELLs) in,
153; environmental impact on, 57–58;
ethnic diversity in, 115–16; finance
capital in, 142–43; hate groups in,
123; homeownership in, 114–15, 149;
housing development in, 137, 142,
143*tab.*; immigrants in, 2, 21–22, 115;
labor unions and, 94–96; landscape
of, 113–15, 122, 124; Latinx Americans
in, 2, 57, 79, 115, 116*fig.*, 126, 147–49;
logistics industry and, 11–13; Los
Angeles and, 114; in migration
narratives, 148; migration to, 114–17;
multiscalar reading of, 3; political
leadership in, 162, 164–68; population
growth in, 115, 116*fig.*, 117, 147; post-
Fordist development strategies in,
18; pro-business growth in, 99;
racialized labor force in, 115; racial
violence in, 120–24, 124*fig.*, 125–26;
segregation in, 116; social and political
environment of, 95–96, 125; spatial
politics of, 11; temporary workers in,
102–3, 103*fig.*; urbanization and, 122;
U.S. Border Patrol raids in, 154–56;
warehousing and distribution in,
55–58; white populations in, 115–16,
121–23, 165; white supremacy in,
122–26, 166–67; white working-class
narrative of, 122–23; youth population
of, 152. *See also individual cities and
counties*
Inland Empire CLC, 95
Inland Empire Economic Partnership
(IEEP), 99
inland Southern California. *See* Inland
Empire
Inland Valley Labor Action Network
(IVLAN), 95
intermodal marketing companies (IMCs),
73
Intermodal Surface Transportation
Efficiency Act (ISTEA), 45

International Brotherhood of Teamsters (IBT), 54, 93, 95
International Longshore and Warehouse Union (ILWU), 59, 91–92, 181n3
inventory systems, 65–66, 71

Jackson, Helen Hunt, 140–41
Jacob, Michael, 50
Janis, Madeline, 52–53
Jonas, Andrew E. G.,, 37
just growth theory, 163
Justice for Immigrants Coalition (JIC), 157–160
Justice for Immigrants Coalition of Inland Southern California (JICISC), 154–55
Justice for Janitors union, 94
just-in-time (JIT) management systems: cross-dock facilities and, 67–68, 71; development of, 33–35; impact on manufacturing, 30; logistics and, 26; shippers and, 49; technologies of, 65, 79–80; temporary workers and, 107; Toyota and, 33, 70; Walmart and, 34, 66–67; workers and, 75, 102

Kaiser, Henry, 113, 117–19
Kaiser steel mill, 10*fig.*, 19*fig.*, 20*fig.*; Black workers at, 119; construction of, 113; consumer goods and, 118; expansion of the West and, 117; investment in, 19–20; job reductions at, 120; manufacturing economy and, 115; sale to Chinese, 9, 14, 18, 125, 172n52, 172n53; spatial fixing, 18; wartime work and, 117–18; white cultural narratives and, 118–19, 122–23, 126
Keller, Larry, 40–41, 51–52
Kelley, Robin, 76
Keynesianism: blue-collar lifestyles and, 21–22; monetarist policies and, 21; spatial order in, 14–15
King, Martin Luther, III, 123, 125
King, Martin Luther, Jr., 123
Klein, Naomi, 74
Knatz, Geraldine, 49, 53
Ku Klux Klan, 120–21, 121*fig.*, 122–26
Kyser, Jack, 40

labor management techniques: barcodes, 65–66; computer tracking software, 65–66; cross-dock facilities and, 67–68, 70–71; human bodies and, 68; just-in-time (JIT) management systems, 65–68; productivity quotas, 69–70; radio-frequency identification (RFID), 65; surveillance technologies, 68–69, 69*fig.*, 70; technologies of, 65–66, 69–71
labor rights, 54, 76–78, 90–91
labor unions: on cash cards, 106; central labor councils (CLC), 94–95; criticism of, 60; decline of, 93; disconnect in, 163–64; environmental issues and, 52–54; global commodity networks and, 92; immigrant-focused organizing, 160–61; immigrant rights and, 160; longshore, 59, 91–92; organizing, 91–96, 105–6, 163; organizing narrative, 96–98, 182n20; port-based development and, 50, 52–53, 59–60; progressive politics and, 53; protests by, 90; reforms to, 93–94; regional policy and, 54; service sector and, 92–93; shrinking territory of, 92; social justice and, 95–96; super locals, 94
landscape: commodification of, 141–42; defining, 38; everyday, 140; pastoral, 134–35, 140; power and, 136; spatial ideologies of, 38, 135
land use politics: contested space and, 130; local government support and, 130–32; public debate over, 127–132, 145–46; race and class in, 130–36; rural aesthetics in, 136–37; spatial ideologies of, 139; ways of life in, 135; white-collar development in, 139, 141–43
Latino Roundtable, 155
Latinx American identity, 2, 15
Latinx Americans, 169n4; anti-Mexican discourse and, 126; changing demographics of, 53, 94, 120, 128, 147, 150, 152, 164; education outcomes, 153; environmental impact on, 57; hostile institutions and, 149–150, 152–53; Inland Empire and, 2, 57, 79, 115, 116*fig.*, 128, 147; political coalitions, 131–33; in

Southern California, 21; steelworkers, 119; violence against, 120, 123; wage differences, 101; youth population, 152

Latinx Roundtable, 166

law enforcement: checkpoints, 155–58; community pressure on, 157; criminal-immigrant discourse in, 150–51; deportation and, 150, 154–56; immigration agents and, 149–150, 154–56, 158–59; immigration raids, 158–59; Latinx American targets of, 149–151, 156–57

Lefebvre, Henri, 12, 15, 17, 38, 77, 169n1, 176n19

Leitner, Helga, 4, 90

Lewis, Jerry, 148, 150

Leyden, Tom, 122

LiUNA, 160–61

Logan, John R., 41

logisticians, 66, 69

logistics: as an analytical lens, 26; globalization and, 26; labor regimes and, 26; politics of regional development and, 26; research in, 28–29; spatial imaginary of, 26; urbanization and, 28

"Logistics & Distribution" (Husing), 98

logistics-driven business models, 65–66

logistics industry: apparatus of, 99; blue-collar workers and, 98–100; commodity chains and, 25; consolidation of, 72; defining, 183n35; deindustrialization and, 30; devalued industrial suburbs and, 23; development of, 11–12; economic data on, 175n39; economic justice and, 162–63; green growth policies, 50–54; ideology and, 38, 48; job growth and, 31–32, 98, 162; private sector and, 49–50; public debate over, 127–136; public spending on, 39, 44; racial capitalism and, 1–2; racial difference in support of, 127–28, 131–34; spatial divisions of labor in, 17; spatial ideologies of, 23–24; spatial politics of, 39, 51; temporary workers in, 102–3; traffic flows and, 56; wages in, 98–102; warehouse workers in, 61, 63, 74–81, 90–102

logistics infrastructure: environmental concerns, 50–52, 162; global and regional distribution and, 27–28, 49; government support for, 40–41, 44, 49–50; investment in, 3, 39–41, 98; public spending on, 44–47, 98; regional planning cooperation in, 43–47, 50; spatial ideologies and, 38, 41; state competition for, 41, 48–49

logistics workers: everyday lives of, 65, 68–70; logisticians, 66, 69; low wages of, 81–82, 92, 100, 102; organizing, 91–92, 103; protests by, 61, 62fig., 63. See also warehouse workers; workers

Long Beach: infrastructure investment, 32; logistics industry and, 12, 23; port authorities of, 12. See also Port of Long Beach

longshore unions, 59, 91–92

Los Angeles: changing demographics of, 94; deindustrialization of, 21–22; industrial suburbs of, 21; infrastructure investment, 32; Inland Empire and, 114; Latinx population in, 2; logistics industry and, 12, 23; port authorities of, 12; transpacific trade in, 32. See also Southeast Los Angeles

Los Angeles Alliance for a New Economy (LAANE), 52

Los Angeles County Federation of Labor (LA Fed), 94

Los Angeles County Metropolitan Transportation Authority (LACMTA), 44

Los Angeles County Transportation Commission (LACTC), 44

Los Angeles Economic Development Corporation (LAEDC), 40, 45

Lost Boys, 97–98

Lowe, Michelle, 35

Maier, C. S., 69

manifest destiny, 15

manufacturing economy: decline of, 18, 21, 30–32, 38; market-driven, 33–34; postwar boom in, 14, 23, 113, 117–18; war-related, 113, 117

MAPA. *See* Mexican American Political Association (MAPA)

Marx, Karl, 27, 174n14

MATES III study, 55–56

matriculas, 166–67

Maywood, California: deindustrialization of, 22; immigrants in, 21; industrial suburbs of, 14, 120; Latinx population growth in, 21

MCGMAP. *See* Multi-County Goods Movement Action Plan (MCGMAP)

Metzger, Tom, 122–25, 168

Mexican American Political Association (MAPA), 123–24, 132

Middle Harbor Project, 59–60

migration narratives, 148

Millender-McDonald, Juanita, 51

Miller, Byron, 4

Mitchell, Don, 13, 38, 142

Mitchell, Katherine, 16

mobility: of capital, 22; economic, 160; globalization and, 28; job, 100; space and, 15, 28. *See also* upward mobility

Molina, Jesse, 131

Molotch, Harvey L., 41

monetarist policies, 21

moral spatial economy: good life in, 142–43; precarity in, 132, 136; race and class in, 134

Moreno Valley: African Americans in, 116; conversion of agricultural land in, 139; Latinx Americans in, 116; logistics industry and, 127–28; police checkpoints in, 155; racial profiling in, 156; racist hiring and discipline in, 153; Rancho Belago, 131, 133–34, 139–143; Skechers shoe warehouse, 72, 127–136, 145–46; upscale housing in, 128, 134, 139–141; white population, 128

Moreno Valley Parent Association (MVPA), 131–32

Moreno Valley Planning Commission, 127–130

Moreno Valley Recreational Trails Board, 134

Moreno Valley Taxpayers Association (MVTA), 131

Morris, Pat, 167

Multi-County Goods Movement Action Plan (MCGMAP), 41, 55

multicultural neighborhoods, 15

multimodal shipping, 72–73

Murrieta, California, 111–12, 116

Narog, Marcia, 127, 130, 134–36

National Association for the Advancement of Colored People (NAACP), 119, 121

National Day Laborers Organizing Network (NDLON), 160

National Freight Gateway Strategy Agreement, 47

National Highway System Designation Act (NHSDA), 45

national security, 45

Nation of Islam, 121

neoliberalism: deregulation and, 21–22; impact of, 9; local actors in, 12; manufacturing economy and, 21; suburban decline and, 22

Newman, Penny, 57

Nolan, Peter, 172n53

North American Industry Classification System (NAICS) codes, 99

Obama, Barack, 165

offshore labor, 71

Ontario, California: conversion of agricultural land in, 137–38; Latinx Americans in, 84, 116, 167; police checkpoints in, 155; political leadership in, 167; warehouses in, 189n66; white supremacy and, 166

Orange County CLC, 94

organizing narrative, 96–98

PAC. *See* Ports Advisory Committee (PAC)

Pacific Merchant Shipping Association, 40, 59

Palomares, Louise, 134

PAR. *See* People Against Racism (PAR)

Partnership for Working Families (PWF), 93, 95, 182n21

Pastor, Manuel, 21, 163

pastoral landscapes, 134–35, 140

People Against Racism (PAR), 125

over, 127–28, 130, 133–36; racial
difference in support of, 128, 131–32,
134–36; settler narrative in, 140–41;
working class support for, 132–33
Smith, Adam, 27
Sniff, Stanley, 155
sobriety checkpoints, 155–56
social justice, 78, 95–96, 163
social movement organizations (SMO):
capitalism and, 46; environmental
issues and, 50–54; influence of, 50, 55;
investment in, 163; labor unions and,
52–54; local actors in, 17; networks of,
95, 161; political influence of, 53; on
port-hinterland relationship, 57;
progressive politics and, 53–54; pro-
immigrant activism, 156–160; protests
by, 61, 62fig., 63; regional policy and, 54;
spatial strategies of, 17; tactics of, 90,
159; threats to, 50
social status, 35–36
Solis, Hilda, 165
Sony Corporation, 34
South Carolina State Ports Authority, 48
South Coast Air Quality Management
District (SCAQMD), 55–56
Southeast Los Angeles: deindustrialization
of, 22; environmental waste in, 22–23;
industrial suburbs of, 14, 17; pastoral
landscapes of, 173n74; post-Fordist
development strategies in, 18; spatial
order in, 23
Southern California: agricultural industry,
113, 115, 117; Asian Americans in, 21;
changing demographics of, 53; Chinese
imports to, 31; conversion of agricultural
land in, 141–43; deindustrialization of,
14, 30; demographics of, 164; distribution
in, 37; finance capital in, 142; good life
in, 15; infrastructure investment in,
39–49; interregional competition in,
38–39, 41; job loss in, 30; Latinx
Americans in, 21; logistics industry and,
11–12, 30, 38–39, 42–48; manufacturing
economy of, 14, 18, 21, 113; national and
international real estate investors in, 144;
racial difference in, 15; transpacific trade
in, 39. See also Inland Empire

Southern California Association of
Governments (SCAG), 31, 40–44, 47,
55, 57–58, 98–99, 134
Southern California Distribution
Management Association, 55
Southern California Institution to Execute
Infrastructure Construction (SCIEIC),
41
space: collective identity and, 77; contested,
130, 134–35; culture and, 15;
differentiated, 14–15; globalization and,
16; local specificities of, 16–17; mobility
and, 15; politics of, 130–32; production
of, 24; race and, 15; regions and, 13–14;
uneven development of, 171n37
spatial difference, 136
spatial economy, 41, 132, 134, 136
spatial fixing: capitalism and, 18;
globalization and, 26; in regional
development, 14–15
spatial ideologies: logistics development
and, 38, 41, 135; methodology of, 24;
regional development and, 23, 139
spatial imaginaries: of capital investment,
26; race and class in, 170n19; racialized
working-class, 122–23; regions and, 13;
stories/testimonios, 74, 77–78; white,
125
spatial mismatch theory, 22
spatial narratives, 12, 90
spatial ontologies, 13
spatial politics, 39, 51, 102
spatial practices, 38, 135, 180n8
speculative development, 145
Stalnaker, Laurie, 94–95
steel manufacturing plants: in China, 20;
dismantling by Chinese, 9, 10fig., 14,
18–19, 19fig.–20fig.; East Coast, 117;
government support for, 117–18;
investment in, 19; racial tension in, 119;
steelworker recruitment, 118–19. See also
Kaiser steel mill
steelworkers, 118–19
Steinke, Richard, 59
Stern, Andy, 93
Stewart, Richard, 146
Stone, Jeff, 150
stories/testimonios, 74–78, 82

suburbs: blue-collar, 18, 21; decline of, 22; deindustrialization and, 22; immigrants in, 22–23; inland, 113–14; Latinx Americans, 79, 150; logistics industry and, 23; middle class, 21–22, 114, 118; white populations in, 121–22, 135. *See also* industrial suburbs

supply chains. *See* commodity chains

surveillance technologies, 68–69, 69*fig.*, 70, 86

Sweeney, John, 93

Target, 34, 67

Taylorist time and motion studies, 68–69

Temecula, California, 116

temporary staffing agencies, 83, 97, 102–7, 184n42

temporary workers: cash card payroll, 105–6; dead-end work of, 104–5; erasure and, 92, 100; everyday lives of, 82–83; expendability of, 102, 104; growth in, 102–3, 103*fig.*; labor surplus and, 106–7; off the clock work, 107; organizing, 92, 96–97; productivity quotas, 87; shape-ups, 106; wage levels, 101, 101*fig.*; warehouses and, 83, 92, 96–97, 100, 101*fig.*, 102–7

territorial entitlement, 123

territorial forms, 37

testimonios. *See* stories/*testimonios*

Theodore, Nik, 130

third-party logistics (3PL) companies, 65, 71–72, 86–87

Tilly, Charles, 17

Toyota Motor Corp., 33, 70

traffic congestion, 40, 43–45, 56

trains: competitive advantage of, 49; inland distribution and, 58; multimodal shipping, 72–73; transportation systems and, 28, 43, 58–59; trucking partnerships, 73

transloading facilities, 91

transpacific trade: local investment in, 37; Southern California, 32, 39

transportation infrastructure: development discourses and, 24; distribution in, 28; government support for, 44; information systems in, 73; inland distribution, 43; investment in, 11, 32, 40; local actors in, 26; multimodal shipping, 72–73; national security and, 45; oversight of, 41; public spending on, 41, 44–45; regional development and, 39; traffic flows and, 43; trains and, 28, 43, 58–59

Transportation Infrastructure Finance and Innovation Act (TIFIA), 47

trucking industry: competitive advantage of, 49; computer tracking software, 71; cross-dock facilities and, 67–68, 71; emission standards for, 53–54; environmental impact of, 55–58, 162; inland distribution and, 58; labor rights, 54; traffic congestion and, 56–58; train partnerships, 73; transportation systems and, 28, 43; Walmart control of, 67

Trump, Donald, 168

TRUST Act, 155

Turner, Joseph, 165–67

undocumented immigrants, 83, 97, 102–5, 108, 111, 156

Union Pacific (UP), 58, 72–73

United Students Against Sweatshops, 75

upscale housing, 128, 134, 139–141

upward mobility, 51, 78, 98

urbanization: just-in-time, 33–36; Latinx, 2; logistics industry and, 28

urban political economy: race and culture in, 1; regional competition and, 38–39

Urry, John, 26, 188n52–89n52

U.S. Border Patrol, 111, 150, 154–56, 159

U.S. Department of Transportation (USDOT), 47, 73

U.S. Steel, 117–18

Vackar, Tracey, 130

Valadao, David, 168

Villaraigosa, Antonio, 53, 165

wage models, 100, 100*fig.*, 101, 101*fig.*

Walker, Richard, 18

Walmart: control of distribution operations, 85–88; cross-dock facilities, 68, 71; globalization and, 27; high and tight rule, 88–89; hot orders, 87–88;

labor issues and, 60; low-wage jobs and, 84–85; market-driven production and, 34; off the clock work, 107; purchasing power of, 66–67; quota systems, 84–88; supply chain innovations of, 66–67; temporary workers and, 102, 107; truck fleet, 67; worker organizing, 77; working conditions, 78, 84–86

Walton, Sam, 66

Ward, Kevin, 37

warehouses: aesthetics of, 129; computer tracking in, 72; consolidated, 72; development of, 143–44; as distribution hubs, 67, 71–72, 91; increased size of, 71–72; land needed for, 144; large industrial investors in, 144–45, 145*fig.*; third-party logistics (3PL) companies, 71–72, 86–87

warehouse workers: blue-collar, 98–100, 100*fig.*; bodies of, 75–76, 79–80; body-worn barcode scanners, 80*fig.*; cash card payroll, 105–6; direct-hire, 105; dispossession and, 75; erasure and, 75, 78, 90, 92, 102; everyday lives of, 65, 99; job insecurity, 81; Lost Boys, 97–98; low wages, 81–82, 92, 100–102; native-born, 97–98; organizing, 76–78, 91–92, 94–98, 103, 105–6; protests by, 61, 63, 74, 77, 90; quota systems, 84–87; race and, 101; racial wage gap, 91; risks to, 63; social justice and, 78; spatial imaginary of, 77–78; spatial narratives by, 90; stories/*testimonios*, 74–78, 82; surveillance technologies, 86; undocumented immigrants as, 83–84, 97, 102–5, 108; wage models, 100, 100*fig.*, 101, 101*fig.*; women, 107–9; working conditions, 78–87, 98. *See also* logistics workers; temporary workers

Warehouse Workers United (WWU), 76, 78, 82, 90–92, 94–97, 161, 163

West, Frank, 131

White, Charles, 131

white-collar development, 139, 141–43

white-collar workers, 100, 104, 118–19, 139

white displacement narrative, 122–23

white populations: appropriation of land and culture by, 139–142; flight from industrial suburbs, 21, 23; frontier narratives, 140–41, 143; Inland Empire, 115–16, 121–23, 128; spatial imaginaries, 139; territorial entitlement, 123

white settler colonialism: frontier narratives, 114, 139–140; migration narratives and, 148; normalizing of, 140; pastoral landscapes and, 139–140; spatial imaginary of, 139

white supremacy, 15, 122–25, 135, 140, 166–67

white working-class oppression narrative, 123

Williams, Raymond, 122

Wilson, Pete, 164

Wilson, Raul, 132, 135–36

women: gendered management practice and, 107–9; sexual harassment, 107, 109

Wood, Carl, 182n19

Woods, Clyde, 76–77, 170n19

worker bodies, 68, 75–76, 79–80

Worker Rights Consortium, 75

workers: Black, 101, 119; blue-collar, 98–100, 104; cash card payroll, 105–6; Chinese, 30; cross-dock facilities, 68, 70–71; direct-hire, 105; flexibility in, 36, 81; garment, 84–85; Latinx Americans, 101; logistics industry and, 26; marginalized, 97; Mexican, 119; offshoring, 71; productivity quotas, 69–70, 84–87; protests by, 61, 62*fig.*, 63; racialized, 23, 115; regional competition and, 38; regional policy and, 54; skilled white, 100, 104, 118–19, 139; surveillance of, 68–70; tracking technologies for, 70; war economy and, 14, 21; white-collar, 100, 104, 139. *See also* logistics workers; temporary workers; warehouse workers

Wright, Richard, 77

Wrigley, Neil, 35